Professional Issues in Information Technology

The British Computer Society

The British Computer Society is the leading professional body for the IT industry. With members in over 100 countries, the BCS is the professional and learned Society in the field of computers and information systems.

The BCS is responsible for setting standards for the IT profession. It is also leading the change in public perception and appreciation of the economic and social importance of professionally managed IT projects and programmes. In this capacity, the Society advises, informs and persuades industry and government on successful IT implementation.

IT is affecting every part of our lives and that is why the BCS is determined to promote IT as the profession of the 21st century.

Joining the BCS

BCS qualifications, products and services are designed with your career plans in mind. We not only provide essential recognition through professional qualifications but also offer many other useful benefits to our members at every level.

Membership of the BCS demonstrates your commitment to professional development. It helps to set you apart from other IT practitioners and provides industry recognition of your skills and experience. Employers and customers increasingly require proof of professional qualifications and competence. Professional membership confirms your competence and integrity and sets an independent standard that people can trust.
www.bcs.org/membership

Further Information

Further information about the British Computer Society can be obtained from: The British Computer Society, 1 Sanford Street, Swindon, Wiltshire, SN1 1HJ, UK.
Telephone: + 44 (0)1793 417 424
Email: bcs@hq.bcs.org.uk
Web: www.bcs.org

Professional Issues in Information Technology

Frank Bott

THE BRITISH COMPUTER SOCIETY

The British Computer Society,
1 Sanford Street,
Swindon,
Wiltshire SN1 1HJ,
UK
www.bcs.org

ISBN 1-902505-65-4

British Cataloguing in Publication Data.
A CIP catalogue record for this book is available at the British Library.

Typeset and printed by Arrowsmith, Bristol

Contents

List of Figures and Tables

Author

Frank Bott studied Mathematics at Trinity College Cambridge, where he was awarded the Yates Prize. He worked in the University's Computing Laboratory before joining SPL International, where he managed large projects in the ship-building industry and Health Service. Frank has previously lectured at the University of Missouri and been head of the University of Wales Computer Science Department. He now lectures part time, and is an active member of the British Computer Society, sitting on their Board of Examiners.

Acknowledgments

I would like to record my grateful thanks to my Aberystwyth colleagues, Allison Coleman, Jack Eaton and Professor Diane Rowland, who collaborated with me in teaching a course on professional issues over many years and in writing an earlier, and very successful, book on the subject. I learned a very great deal from working with them. I must also acknowledge my colleagues involved in BCS examination work over the years, from whom I have also learned much. Special thanks are due to Professor Mike Tedd, my friend and colleague for more years than either he or I would wish to admit to. He it was who, in 1986, first encouraged me to put together a lecture course on professional issues in software engineering; he has read the complete draft of this book and it is much the better for his wise advice and suggestions. The faults that remain are, of course, entirely my responsibility.

Finally I would like to thank my wife for her patience, forbearance, love and support, not only during the period that this book was being written, but throughout our years together.

Abbreviations

ACAS	Advisory, Conciliation and Arbitration Service
ACM	Association for Computing Machinery
APIG	All-Party Parliamentary Internet Group
BCS	British Computer Society
CEHR	Commission for Equality and Human Rights
CEI	Council of Engineering Institutions
CEng	Chartered Engineer
CEPIS	Council of European Professional Informatics Societies
CPD	Continuing professional development
DCF	Discounted cash flow
ECDL	European Computer Driving Licence®
EU	European Union
EUCIP	European Certification of IT Professionals
FEANI	Fédération Européene d'Associations Nationales d'Ingénieurs (European Federation of National Engineering Associations)
GATT	General Agreement on Tariffs and Trade
ICANN	Internet Corporation for Assigned Names and Numbers
ICRA	Internet Content Rating Association
IEE	Institution of Electrical Engineers
IEEE	Institute of Electrical and Electronic Engineers
IEEE-CS	IEEE Computer Society
IEng	Incorporated Engineers
IRR	Internal rate of return
ISEB	Information Systems Examination Board
ISM	Industry Structure Model
ISP	Internet service provider
IT	Information technology
IWF	Internet Watch Foundation
MBO	Management by objectives
MP	Member of Parliament
NCMP	Non-constituency MP
NMP	Nominated MP
NPV	Net present value
PICS	Platform for Internet Content Selection
PIDA	Public Interest Disclosure Act 1998
PTO	US Patent and Trade Mark Office
QA	Quality assurance
RAM	Random access memory

RCVS	Royal College of Veterinary Surgeons
RIBA	Royal Institute of British Architects
SFIA	Skills Framework for the Information Age
TUPE	Transfer of Undertakings (Protection of Employment)
UML	Unified Modeling Language
W3C	World Wide Web Consortium
WIPO	World Intellectual Property Organization

Useful Websites

The following are the URLs of the websites referred to in the text. In most cases, we have given the URLs of the home pages of the sites, because these are much less likely to change than are the URLs of individual pages. References in the main text may give the URLs of relevant pages. All the URLs were checked and found to be correct on 16 January 2005.

UK government and official bodies

Her Majesty's Stationery Office   The site will give you the text of all acts of the UK Parliament and all secondary legislation back to 1988: *www.hmso.gov.uk*

Equal Opportunities Commission: *www.eoc.org.uk*
Commission for Racial Equality: *www.cre.gov.uk*
Disability Rights Commission: *www.drc-gb.org*
These websites provide valuable guidance on the interpretation of anti-discrimination legislation and on best practice for implementing it. The Disability Rights Commission's site contains its report 'The Web: Access and Inclusion for Disabled People'.

UK Information Commissioner   The website contains useful information relating both to data protection and freedom of information: *www.informationcommissioner.gov.uk*

UK Companies House   The website gives information about registering new companies and filing of required documents: *www.companieshouse.gov.uk*

Business Link   A website of the UK Department of Trade and Industry that contains practical advice about setting up and running a business: *www.businesslink.gov.uk*

UK Law Commission   A body whose duty it is to conduct reviews of areas of the law and make recommendations for changes to the government. The website includes all its recent reports, including 'Defamation and the Internet': *www.lawcom.gov.uk*

UK Parliament   This site is specifically concerned with the UK Parliament: *www.parliament.uk*

All Party Parliamentary Internet Group   Among other things, it contains the text of the group's 2004 review of the Computer Misuse Act: *www.apig.org.uk*

Advisory Conciliation and Arbitration Service Website where you can access copies of ACAS advisory material such as 'Discipline and grievances at work' and 'Redundancy handling': *www.acas.org.uk*

UK Patent Office The website contains the report produced by the Patent Office in March 2001 giving the UK government's position on the patenting of software and business methods: *www.patent.gov.uk*

Government sites in other countries

The US Government's Official Web Portal This site gives access to everything to do with the federal government (but not the government of individual states) of the USA, from the federal constitution to how to apply for government grants. It includes the texts of all recent acts of Congress, as well as the more important older ones: *www.firstgov.gov*

Missouri General Assembly Website of the State of Missouri, USA, where you can find the Revised Statutes of the State of Missouri. Chapter 327 (Architects, Professional Engineers, Land Surveyors and Landscape Architects) of these statutes is a good example of American legislation concerning engineers: *www.moga.state.mo.us*

Government of Hong Kong: *www.info.gov.hk*

Directory of Indian Government Websites: *goidirectory.nic.in*

Government of Mauritius: *ncb.intnet.mu/govt*

Government of Sri Lanka: *www.gov.lk*

Government of Singapore: *www.gov.sg*

Professional bodies and international organizations

The British Computer Society: *www.bcs.org.uk*

The Institution of Electrical Engineers: *www.iee.org*

UK Engineering Council: *www.engc.org.uk*
UK Standard for Professional Engineering Competence:
www.uk-spec.org.uk
The first site contains a link to the second site, which is where the standards for Chartered Engineer, Incorporated Engineer and Engineering Technician are to be found.

The Association for Computing Machinery: *www.acm.org*

The IEEE Computer Society: *www.computer.org*

Australian Computer Society: *www.acs.org.au*

Hong Kong Computer Society: *www.hkcs.org.hk*

Indian Computer Society: *www.csitvm.org*

Mauritius Computer Society: *ncb.intnet.mu/mcs.htm*

Singapore Computer Society: *www.scs.org.sg*

Fédération Européenne d'Associations Nationales d'Ingénieurs (European Federation of National Engineering Associations): *www.feani.org*

Council of European Professional Informatics Societies: *www.cepis.org*

International Federation for Information Processing: *www.ifip.or.at*

Codes of conduct

It is not always as easy as it should be to find codes of conduct of professional bodies by starting from their home pages. Accordingly, we list here the URLs giving direct access to the pages concerned. It should be borne in mind that such URLs are much more likely to change than are the URLs of organizations' home pages.

The BCS Code of Conduct: *www.bcs.org/BCS/Join/WhyJoin/Conduct.htm*

Software Engineering Code of Ethics and Professional Practices The Code of Conduct jointly produced by the IEEE-CS and the ACM for software engineers: *www.computer.org/tab/seprof/code.htm*

Australia Computer Society:
www.acs.org.au/national/pospaper/acs131.htm
Hong Kong Computer Society: *www.hkcs.org.hk/ethics.htm*

Indian Computer Society: *www.csitvm.org/ethics.html*

Singapore Computer Society:
www.scs.org.sg/cgi-bin/cgiwrap/scsorg/scs/scs.cgi?aboutus&codeofconduct

Codes of conduct of other professional bodies:

Royal Institute of British Architects:
www.architecture.com/go/Architecture/Using/Conduct_346.html

Royal College of Veterinary Surgeons:
www.rcvs.org.uk (click on Veterinary Surgeons and then Guide to Professional Conduct)

Institute of Physics: *about.iop.org/Iop/member/conduct.html*

Institution of Mechanical Engineers:
www.imeche.org.uk/membership/pdf/Code%20of%20Conduct.pdf

Other sites

The London Ambulance Service Case Study Website providing information about the London Ambulance System disaster, including a copy of the official report: *www.cs.ucl.ac.uk/staff/A.Finkelstein/las.html*

Therac-25 report An updated version of the paper, 'An investigation of the

Therac-25 accidents', by Nancy Leveson and Clark S. Turner: *sunnyday.mit.edu/therac-25.html*

National Business Angels Network: *www.nban.co.uk*

European Business Angels Network: *www.eban.org*

Institutional Voting Information Service A code of best practice concerning the duties of directors: *www.ivis.co.uk/pages/gdsc6_1.html*

W3C 'Web Content Accessibility Guidelines' version 1.0: *www.w3.org/TR/WAI-WEBCONTENT*

Bitlaw A statement of the position on the patenting of software and business methods in the USA: *www.bitlaw.com/software-patent/index.html*

The World Intellectual Property Association A website from where you can download 'The management of internet names and addresses: Intellectual property issues' (1999) and 'The recognition of rights and the use of names in the internet domain system' (2001): *www.wipo2.wipo.int*

Communication, Cultural and Media Studies Database Information about the laws governing pornography on the Internet: *www.cultsock.ndirect.co.uk/MUHome/cshtml/index.html*

The Internet Watch Foundation: *www.iwf.org.uk*

The Internet Content Rating Association: *www.icra.org*

Skills Framework for the Information Age Foundation: *www.sfia.org.uk*

Preface

When employers of newly qualified information systems professionals are asked what it is they would most like them to know, the answer is very rarely technical. Much more commonly, the answer is an understanding of the business environment. For this reason, the Engineering Council and the British Computer Society (BCS) both insist that accredited courses contain a significant element of 'professional issues' and, in its own examinations, the BCS requires candidates to take a compulsory paper entitled 'Professional Issues in Information Technology'. This book has been written as a guide for students taking that paper and it covers the whole syllabus. It is hoped, however, that the book will also prove useful to others, both students on other courses and those who are already embarked on a career in the information systems industry.

It is important for candidates to realize that mere knowledge of the syllabus is not enough, by itself, to pass the paper. Candidates are expected to be able to apply that knowledge to simple scenarios. Failure to do this is one of the commonest reasons for failing the paper. We have included many such scenarios in this book, some of them taken from past examination papers.

Many of the candidates for the Society's examinations are from overseas. The BCS is the *British* Computer Society and it has to give priority to the situation of the information systems professional in the UK. For this reason, the syllabus refers to British Acts of Parliament and to the laws of England and Wales. However, it is expected that overseas candidates will be concerned with the position in their own countries and, where relevant, this book tries to illustrate how this varies from country to country. (Nowhere is this more evident than when discussing the legal status of professional engineers.) I would also hope that UK candidates might find it beneficial to learn about the position in other countries.

Despite the existence of some very large and well-known multinational companies, much of the information systems industry consists of small enterprises with less than six employees. Very many young entrants to the profession aim to set up such a business of their own. One of the purposes of the Professional Issues module in the Society's Diploma examination is therefore to give practical guidance in a range of legal, financial and organizational areas relevant to small information systems businesses. This is reflected in many aspects of the book.

A word of warning is needed here. This book tries to explain the central principles and issues in the areas covered, so that you will be aware of areas you need to think about and areas where you will need professional advice.

The book should give you enough knowledge to talk intelligently to professionals in the fields that it covers. But what the book covers is inevitably introductory and much is omitted. Just as you would not regard an accountant who had read a book on computing and learned to use a spreadsheet and a word processor as competent to design the software for a space shuttle, so you must not regard yourself as a competent lawyer, accountant or other professional on the strength of having studied this book.

Structure of the book

The book can be regarded as falling into four main parts. The first part (Chapters 1 to 4) is concerned with the general context in which professionals work – the law and how it is created, the professions, and the nature of commercial organizations.

The second part (Chapters 5 to 8) is concerned very specifically with financial matters – the financing of start-up companies, the nature of financial statements, costing, budgeting and cash flow, and the evaluation of investment proposals.

In the third part (Chapters 9, 10 and 11), we cover the human aspects of running a company, including organizational structures and human resource management.

More specific legal issues are covered in the fourth part, including software contracts and liability, intellectual property rights, and legislation that affects the way in which computers are used or misused. Many of these topics are matters of day-to-day concern for most computer users.

Finally, the appendices include the BCS Code of Conduct and examples of standard agreements, standard terms and conditions, and a contract of employment.

There are 'Further reading' sections at the end of each chapter (and consolidated at the end of the book). They are intended to:

- enable those who are teaching courses for the examination to deepen and broaden their knowledge so that they can respond to questions and initiate discussion in their classes;
- help students who feel they need to read more in order to get a better understanding of the material;
- provide guidance to readers who need or want to go more deeply into particular topics to satisfy their own professional needs.

The further reading suggested is *not* necessary for students who simply want to pass the examination.

The following table shows the correspondence between chapters of the book and the sections of the BCS syllabus:

BCS syllabus section	Corresponding chapters
1	2, 3
2	4, 9
3	5, 6
4	7, 8
5	11, 12, 14, 15, 16
6	13
7	16
8	3
9	10, 11

Complete sets of examination papers for the BCS Professional Examinations can be found on the Society's website, along with examiners' reports that give guidance on the answers expected. We have included some of these questions here, at the ends of the relevant chapters, in some cases with specimen answers. Because of the recent updates to the syllabus, there are some topics on which no questions are available.

Frank Bott
Aberystwyth
October 2004

1 Law and Government

After reading this chapter, you should:

- *understand the nature of the law and the difference between criminal law and civil law;*
- *understand what is meant by the terms* legislature, judiciary *and* executive *and appreciate the variety of ways in which these concepts are implemented in different countries;*
- *understand the ways in which law comes into existence.*

INTRODUCTION

The British Computer Society (BCS) syllabus for the Professional Issues module does not call directly for any general knowledge of legal concepts. However, much of the syllabus is concerned with specific legislation (that is, laws) and it is therefore helpful to understand something about the nature of the law and how it comes into being. This is what this chapter is about.

WHAT IS THE LAW?

There are many ways of defining the law. For the purpose of this book, we shall take a very straightforward definition. We shall define law as 'a set of rules that can be enforced in a court'. These rules are different in different countries. The best known examples of such differences are probably in the rules governing such things as divorce or the sale of alcohol. From the point of view of the information systems professional, however, differences in the rules governing data protection, the rights of access to information, and the misuse of computers are much more significant.

As well as having different laws, different countries have different legal systems, that is, different systems of courts, different rules for court procedure, different procedures for appealing against a court decision, and so on. The word *jurisdiction* is used to mean the area covered by a single legal system and set of laws.

Even within a single country, the law and the legal system may be different in different areas. This is most obviously the case in large countries with a federal system of government, where the country is divided into a number of states, each of which can make its own laws in certain areas. Obvious examples are India and the United States of America (USA).

In the United Kingdom (UK), for historical reasons, Scotland, Northern Ireland and the Isle of Man each have different legal systems and different laws. However, as far as the topics covered in this book are concerned, their laws are, in almost all cases, the same as those of England and Wales. When we refer to British law or UK law, we shall be referring to laws that apply across the UK. Sometimes we shall refer to the law of England and Wales, indicating that there are differences elsewhere in the UK.

CRIMINAL LAW AND CIVIL LAW

The popular image of the law sees it as the set of mechanisms that tries to punish wrongdoers, by fines or imprisonment. This aspect of the law is known as the *criminal law*. It can be considered to represent society's view of the minimum standard of acceptable behaviour. It defines what constitutes a crime, lays down the mechanisms for deciding whether a person accused of a crime is guilty or innocent, and specifies the range of punishments applicable to different categories of crime.

In general, the police are responsible for discovering who has carried out a specific criminal offence and for collecting evidence that will convince a court that the person in question really did commit the offence. The state, in the form of the Crown Prosecution Service in England and Wales, will then start proceedings by prosecuting the person concerned (who is known as the *accused* or the *defendant*) in a criminal court. The court will decide whether or not the case against the person has been proved and, if it finds the case proved, will sentence the offender to a suitable punishment.

We shall not be very concerned with the criminal law in this book. We shall be much more occupied with the *civil law*. The purpose of the civil law is to provide rules for settling disputes between people.

Notice that we have referred to disputes between people. Does this mean that the civil law doesn't apply if one or both sides in a dispute are companies or organizations of some other kind? It doesn't mean this, of course, but, in order to overcome the difficulty, we need the idea of a *legal person*. A legal person is an organization that has gone through a process, called *incorporation*, that gives it the same legal status, so far as the civil law is concerned, as a *natural person*, that is a human being. There are several different ways in which an organization can be incorporated. In Britain, an organization can be incorporated by an Act of Parliament, by registering as a company, or by the grant of a Royal Charter. We shall discuss this process in Chapters 2 and 4.

Court action under the civil law is known as litigation. It must be initiated by one of the *parties to the dispute*, that is, by the person, legal or natural, who feels they have been wronged. The person who initiates the court action is known as the *plaintiff*.

Two important differences between British civil law and criminal law relate to the *standard* of proof and the *burden* of proof.

For a person to be found guilty of a criminal offence, the prosecution must demonstrate that they are guilty beyond all reasonable doubt. For a plaintiff to win their case under civil law, they only have to show that their claim is correct on the balance of probabilities. In other words, the standard of proof required in criminal cases is higher than that required in civil cases.

In a criminal case, the burden of proof lies on the prosecution. This means that it is up to the prosecution to prove its case. The defendant does not need to prove their innocence. They are assumed to be innocent until proved guilty. In a civil case, on the other hand, both parties present their arguments and must convince the court of their correctness.

WHERE DOES THE LAW COME FROM?

The two main sources of law in England and Wales are the *common law* and *statute law*. The common law is essentially traditional law that is not written down, but which depends on the judgement of judges over the centuries. When deciding the rights and wrongs of a case, a court will look at the way in which similar cases have been decided in the past; such cases are known as *precedents*.

The common law tradition is shared by many other countries. Almost all the countries of the Commonwealth share the tradition; so, most importantly, does the USA. This means that a judgement made by a judge in the USA can be used as a precedent in, for example, a court in Singapore.

The tradition of common law is not found in the countries of continental Europe, such as France and Germany. Their law is based entirely on written codes, one for the criminal law and one for the civil law. Those parts of the world that were once colonized by such countries have generally kept such a system of written codes. Confusingly, this system of written codes is often also referred to as civil law. However, in this book, we shall always use the term civil law in the sense described in the previous section, that is, the law used for settling disputes between people.

Statute law is law laid down by Acts of Parliament. It is often referred to as *legislation*. Two hundred years ago, most cases that came to trial would have been tried under the common law. There was comparatively little statute law. Over the past two hundred years the position has changed a lot. On the one hand, technical developments and social changes make new laws urgently necessary. Laws to regulate child labour and laws to prevent the misuse of computers are just two examples of Parliament creating new laws for such reasons. On the other hand, in some areas the millions of common law judgements from the past make it increasingly difficult for courts to apply the common law and Parliament has passed legislation to bring together the common law in these areas into a single statute. A good example of this is the Theft Act 1968, which consolidated the common law provisions regarding crimes involving stealing.

THE LEGISLATIVE PROCESS IN THE UK

Like many other democratic countries, the UK has what is known as a *two-chamber* or *bicameral legislature*. This means that the law-making body (the legislature) is made up of two chambers or groups of people.

The British legislature is known as *Parliament*. One of the chambers is called the House of Commons; its members are elected and everyone over the age of 18 has a vote. The country is currently divided into 659 constituencies, each of which elects one Member of Parliament (MP), who is the person who gets the most votes in the election. This is known as the 'first past the post' system.

The other chamber in the UK Parliament is known as the House of Lords; most of its members are appointed, but a significant number are chosen from among the hereditary peers, although this situation may not last very much longer. (Reform of the House of Lords has been an active political issue in Britain for at least 100 years but, while most people agree that reform is needed, it has proved impossible to get general agreement on what form it should take.)

The British government is made up of members from both the House of Commons and the House of Lords. Members of the House of Lords are never more than a small proportion and the Prime Minister, the Chancellor of the Exchequer, the Foreign Secretary and the Home Secretary are now always members of the House of Commons.

Most new legislation is initiated by the government, although it is possible for individual Members of Parliament to initiate legislation in certain circumstances. It is introduced in the form of a *bill*; this is a set of proposals that parliament is invited to discuss, possibly modify and then approve. The bill is usually introduced first in the House of Commons. It will be discussed and possibly amended there, a process that includes a number of stages. If it is approved by the House of Commons, it is passed to the House of Lords. If the House of Lords approves the bill, it becomes an Act of Parliament. It is then passed to the Queen for her formal approval (the *royal assent*), after which it becomes law. (The Queen cannot refuse to give her approval when parliament has approved a bill.)

If the House of Lords rejects a bill or modifies it, the bill is returned to the House of Commons for further consideration. The House of Commons has the power to override any changes that may have been made by the House of Lords or even to insist that a bill rejected by the House of Lords should, nevertheless, be passed and proceed to receive the royal assent. The justification for this is that the House of Commons is democratically elected and so represents the will of the people in a way that the members of the House of Lords, not being elected, cannot do.

In many cases, the government may want to canvass opinion before asking Parliament to approve legislation. It may publish a *green paper*, which typically explains why the government wants to create new laws in a certain area, and discusses a number of possible approaches. The green paper will be discussed by Parliament and comments on it will be invited from the public and from bodies that have an interest in the area. Thus, the BCS, along with many other bodies, was specifically asked for its views when the question of legislation to address the problem of computer misuse was raised.

Once the government has decided on its general approach, it may publish a *white paper*, which describes the proposed legislation and will be used as the basis for discussing and possibly modifying the details of what is proposed. At the end of this process, the government will take into account these discussions and produce a bill.

Acts of Parliament constitute what is known as *primary legislation*. The complexity of modern society makes it impossible for all laws to be examined in detail by parliament. To overcome this difficulty, an Act of Parliament will often make provision for *secondary* legislation to be introduced. This means that detailed regulations can be introduced without full discussion in parliament. Instead, the proposed regulations are placed in the library of the House of Commons so that members of either house can look at them. If no objections are raised within a fixed time period, the regulations become law. An example of secondary legislation in the computer field are the regulations that were produced to apply the Copyright, Designs and Patents Act 1988 to protect the design of semi-conductor chips.

The UK is a member of the European Union (EU). This is a grouping of 25 European countries (15 until May 2004) that are working towards a high level of economic and social integration involving the harmonization of many of their laws. The EU has its own Parliament, elected by individual voters in all the member countries. The EU is run by a commission that has the power to issue directives that require member countries to modify their own legislation, if necessary, to meet a common standard. These directives must be discussed by the European Parliament and approved by the member states before they come into effect. Several of these directives relate to topics, such as data protection and the protection of software, that are particularly important for information systems engineers and we shall be referring to many of them later in the book.

In addition to the British national Parliament, there are separate elected assemblies in Wales and Northern Ireland, and a Scottish Parliament. These have certain limited powers, but they do not affect the topics covered in this book.

THE LEGISLATIVE PROCESS IN OTHER COUNTRIES

The BCS examination is concerned with the situation in Britain but the Society expects that candidates in other countries will want, as part of their professional development, to understand something about the law in their own countries and the way it is made. This section tries to describe very briefly the position in a few representative countries.

The USA

In the USA, the legislature is known as Congress. It consists of two houses, the Senate and the House of Representatives. Both houses are elected but on very different terms. Members of the House of Representatives (*congressmen*) are elected for a period of two years. Each congressman represents a district and each district contains (roughly) the same number of people. The Senate contains two members (*senators*) for each state; senators are elected for seven years.

Legislation must be approved by both the Senate and the House of Representatives before it can become law; neither chamber can override the other. Furthermore, the President must also give his assent before an Act of Congress becomes law. Unlike the Queen, who cannot withhold her assent to legislation passed by Parliament, the President is allowed to veto legislation passed by Congress and this regularly happens. As in other countries with a written constitution, there is also a Supreme Court, which can strike out legislation approved by Congress and the President, on the grounds that it is unconstitutional. As we shall see in Chapter 16, this has happened with legislation concerned with pornography on the internet.

The members of the government of the USA are not members of Congress. The President is, in practice though not in theory, directly elected by the people. The members of the government are individuals chosen by the President and their appointment must be approved by Congress. The founders of the USA believed that it was very important to separate the three following functions:

- the legislature, that is, Congress, which makes laws;
- the judiciary, that is, the judges and other legal officials, which applies and enforces these laws in particular cases; and
- the executive, that is, the President and the other members of the government, which carries on the actual business of government.

The separation of these functions is recognized in many other countries. Historically, they have not been separated in the UK, but reforms are currently being discussed which will move further in this direction.

The legislative situation in the USA is made more complicated by the fact that the country is a federation of 50 states. Each state has its own legislature, most of them modelled on the federal legislature, and its own government. On some topics each state can make its own laws, but in other areas the law is made at federal level. For example, as we shall see in Chapter 2, each state has its own laws regarding who can call themselves an engineer. The issue of 'states' rights', that is, the extent to which federal law can override laws made by individual states, has been a live political issue throughout the existence of the USA and remains so today. A similar pattern applies in other countries with a federal constitution, such as India or Australia.

Singapore

In contrast to the UK and the USA, Singapore has a *unicameral* legislature, that is, its parliament consists of only one chamber. In many other respects, however, it follows the British model. Most members of the government are MPs. The head of the government is the Prime Minister. The Head of State is a separate non-executive President; since 1993 Heads of State have been directly elected by the citizens. Their role is largely ceremonial, but they have more powers than the Queen. Their signature is required before a bill becomes law; they can veto government budgets and public appointments but they can only withhold their signature if they consider that a bill is unconstitutional.

Singapore is a multiracial society and the electoral system includes special features to ensure that minority races will always be represented in Parliament. As well as traditional constituencies that elect as MP the candidate who gets the most votes, there are 14 *group representation constituencies.* In these, each political party puts forward a small team of candidates, one of whom must belong to a minority race. This means that the parties must fight the election as multiracial parties and ensures that there will always be at least 14 MPs from the minority races.

The Singapore electorate has consistently voted for the People's Action Party, to such an extent that the government has felt it necessary to modify the constitution in order to ensure that there is adequate representation of opposition representatives in Parliament. It provides for the appointment of up to three Non-Constituency MPs (NCMPs) from the opposition political parties. A further constitutional provision for the appointment of up to nine Nominated MPs (NMPs) was made in 1990 to ensure a wider representation of views in Parliament. NMPs are appointed by the President of Singapore for a term of two years on the recommendation of a Special Select Committee of Parliament chaired by the Speaker

Singapore not only shares the common law with England and Wales but it also shares much of British statute law. The courts in Singapore had always been ready to apply British statutes in situations where there were no applicable Singaporean statutes. In 1993, the position was formalized when parliament passed the Application of English Law Act. This specified precisely which existing Acts of the British Parliament were to be applicable to Singapore and what procedure had to be followed to incorporate new Acts. This practice of adopting British statute law avoids the need to generate very large quantities of legislation, something that would be very onerous (and very expensive) for a small country like Singapore. Some legislation that is very important for the information systems professional has been incorporated into Singapore law in this way.

Sri Lanka

When Sri Lanka became independent in 1948, it did so under a bicameral constitution closely modelled on that of the UK. A revised constitution in

1970 introduced a unicameral legislature, but continued to follow the British model in which power lies with the Prime Minister rather than with the Head of State. In 1978, this was replaced by a constitution more like those of France or the USA. The Head of State is directly elected and serves for six years, appointing the Prime Minister and presiding over cabinet meetings. The legislature consists of a single body with 225 members. Of these, 196 are elected to represent individual multimember districts, using proportional representation, and the remaining 29 are apportioned to the parties in proportion to their share of the national vote. *Proportional representation* is a system in which political parties are allocated seats in proportion to the number of votes that they get. The Parliament is elected for a six-year period, although the President can dissolve it and call fresh elections before the end of the period.

Intercommunal strife between the Tamil and Sinhalese communities has, unfortunately, been a feature of Sri Lankan life for many years and has led to a lengthy and damaging civil war. At the time of writing, a ceasefire has been in place for two years. There has been little progress in peace negotiations, but any successful conclusion to the talks will almost certainly involve substantial changes to the existing constitution.

Sri Lankan law is derived from a number of sources, but the Civil Law Ordinance No. 5 of 1852 provides that English law shall be used in commercial matters except where there is a Sri Lankan statute with contrary effect. Other aspects of English law have been taken over both explicitly by statute and implicitly through decisions of the courts.

Mauritius

In Mauritius, the legislature consists of a single body, known as the National Assembly. It consists of 62 members directly elected by constituencies, plus a further eight of the 'best losers' from that election. The head of state is the President, who is elected by the National Assembly. The President appoints the Prime Minister, on the basis of the make-up of the Assembly, and other ministers on the recommendation of the Prime Minister.

The law in Mauritius is based on an unusual mixture of English common law and French civil law, although there is much modern statute law that resembles UK law.

SUMMARY

The law is generally divided into criminal law, which tries to ensure that individuals do not act in ways that are unacceptable to society as a whole, and civil law, which provides rules for settling disputes between people.

Different countries have different laws and different procedures for applying their laws. In England and Wales, the USA, and many other countries that were formerly ruled by Britain, a form of law known as common law exists; this is based on precedent, that is, on decisions made by judges in the past.

Increasingly, common law is being replaced by statute law, that is, law made by legislative bodies.

Some countries have bicameral legislatures and some have unicameral ones. There are a variety of ways in which the members of the legislature may be elected. In countries with a bicameral legislature, one chamber may be appointed rather than elected. In some countries, the government is made up of members of the legislature; in others it may be separate from the legislature. In countries with a federal constitution, there are legislatures at the level of the individual state.

In countries with a written constitution, there is usually a court with the power to strike out legislation that breaches the constitution.

FURTHER READING

Ten years ago, it was difficult to get information about the legislative process in countries other than the one in which you were living. It meant going to specialist libraries or to the embassies of the countries concerned. The development of the web has changed all this and it is now very easy to obtain this material from websites.

The following is a list of home pages for the government websites of the countries mentioned in this chapter.

UK: www.parliament.uk

USA: www.firstgov.gov

Sri Lanka: www.gov.lk

Mauritius: ncb.intnet.mu/govt

Singapore: www.gov.sg

Most of these websites contain pages explaining in more detail how the legislative process in the country works and, in most cases, copies of recent Acts of Parliament are available on the web. In the USA, most of the individual states have similar sites describing the legislative process in the state and, in many cases, most of the statutes of the state are available on the web.

2 The Nature of a Profession

After studying this chapter, you should understand:

- *the legal status of professional bodies;*
- *the ideas of reservation of title and reservation of function;*
- *the current status of the engineering profession in the UK, the USA and internationally;*
- *the arguments for and against the licensing of information systems engineers or software engineers.*

INTRODUCTION

Words like *profession* and *professional* are used in many different ways. A professional footballer is one who makes his living from the game. Professional employees are employees of a certain status, who are expected, within limits, to put the interests of the organization they work for above their own convenience. To describe someone as a 'real professional' implies that they can be relied on to carry out their work competently and conscientiously regardless of the circumstances. A professional piece of work means a piece of work that meets established standards of quality. However, the terms can also have negative overtones – a professional foul is one committed by deliberately by a professional footballer who calculates that, on the balance of probabilities, it will work out in his favour. The term *pro* is used as a colloquial shorthand for a professional and for a prostitute.

There is no single definition of a profession. The meaning of the word depends on who is using it and what the context is. However, if we look at a range of occupations that would commonly be described as professions – lawyers, doctors, dentists, accountants, veterinary surgeons, architects, and so on – we see that there are a number of characteristics that most of them have in common:

- substantial education and training are required in order to practise the profession;
- the members of the profession themselves decide the nature of this training and, more generally, control entry to the profession;
- the profession is organized into one or more professional bodies;
- the profession lays down standards of conduct with which its members must comply and, where necessary, enforces these through disciplinary procedures.

In Chapter 3, we shall be dealing with what professional bodies in computing do, but in this chapter we are more concerned with the legal status of professions.

PROFESSIONAL BODIES

As we have already stated, a profession is typically organized into one or more professional bodies. What is a professional body?

A professional body usually starts by a group of people coming together because of a shared interest in a particular type of activity. The BCS was set up in 1957 by a group of people working in the new and expanding field of computers, who wanted the opportunity to exchange ideas. The Institution of Electrical Engineers, the other main body in the UK that includes information systems engineers among its members, is older. It was set up in 1871 by people with an interest in the developing field of electrical engineering that could not be met by the existing engineering institutions. A professional body may also be started by people engaged in the same type of activity, who want to protect their business against others who may be trying to enter it without having the proper knowledge or who may be practising it dishonestly.

As the professional body matures, it is likely to develop a range of functions, of which the following are the most important:

- establishing a code of conduct to regulate the way members of the body behave in their professional lives and a disciplinary procedure to discipline members who breach this code;
- establishing mechanisms for disseminating knowledge of good practice and new developments to its members, typically through publications and conferences but increasingly also through the use of the worldwide web;
- setting standards of education and experience that must be met by people wishing to become members of the body;
- advising government and regulatory bodies about matters within its area of expertise.

In the UK, any organization that believes its main objectives are in the public interest can enter into discussions with the Privy Council with a view to being awarded a royal charter. A royal charter is a formal document, written in rather quaint language and signed by the Queen, which establishes the organization and lays down its purpose and rules of operation. As they grow into mature organizations, most professional bodies seek and obtain a royal charter. The BCS was awarded its Royal Charter in 1984.

RESERVATION OF TITLE AND FUNCTION

In certain cases, where it is considered to be in the public interest, Parliament may agree to grant the members of a professional body some sort of legal monopoly. There are two different ways in which this can be done. First, the use of the name of the profession may be restricted to those people who are appropriately qualified. A restriction of this sort is called *reservation of title*. In the UK, for example, the Architects Act 1997 makes it a criminal offence to call yourself an architect unless you are registered with the Architects Registration Board.

Secondly, the law may state that certain activities are restricted to people with appropriate qualifications. This is called *reservation of function*. For example, in England and Wales, only members of the Institute of Chartered Accountants and the Association of Certified Accountants are allowed to audit the accounts of public companies. Auditing accounts is an example of reservation of function where there is no corresponding reservation of title. Anyone can call themselves an accountant, provided this is not done for fraudulent purposes.

An example where both reservation of title and reservation of function apply is veterinary surgery. Under the Veterinary Surgeons Act 1966, you are not allowed to call yourself a veterinary surgeon unless you are registered with the Royal College of Veterinary Surgeons (RCVS); in order to be registered, you must have the proper qualifications. And, subject to certain limitations, it is a criminal offence to carry out surgical procedures on animals unless you are registered with the RCVS.

In the USA, title and function are usually reserved not to members of professional bodies, but to people whose names are on a register maintained by a state government. Recent developments have shown a tendency for the UK to move in the same direction. For example, until the passage of the Architects Act 1997, it was an offence to 'practise or carry on business under any name, style or title containing the word "architect"', unless you were a member of the Royal Institute of British Architects (RIBA). The 1997 Act established the Architects Registration Board, registration with which now replaces membership of the RIBA as the requirement for calling yourself an architect.

The reason for this change is that professional bodies are often seen as white collar trade unions, which use their monopoly power to limit competition and maintain high charges for their services, while doing little to enforce the codes of conduct that they publish.

SOFTWARE DEVELOPMENT AS ENGINEERING

The development of software and information systems in general is now usually regarded as a branch of engineering and the people who practise it are considered to be engineers.

Traditional engineers design and build a wide variety of objects – dams, bridges, aeroplanes, cars, radio and television transmitters and receivers, computers, plants to make fertiliser or plastics, and so on. There are two constraints that apply to all such activities and which can be regarded as characteristic of engineering:

- engineering involves designing and building things that must work properly, that is, must meet a set of predetermined requirements concerning their functionality, their performance, and their reliability;
- the process of designing and building the object must be completed within specified constraints of time and budget.

These characteristics are not shared by activities such as accounting, consultancy, marketing, or medicine; this is not to criticize such activities, simply to point out that they are of a different nature. On the other hand, most software development does share these characteristics. This is why the terms software engineering and information systems engineering have come into use and why the rest of this chapter will be concerned specifically with the status of engineering as a profession.

THE STATUS OF ENGINEERS

The legal status of the engineering profession varies a lot from one country to another. In the USA, the profession is very strictly controlled. Both the title of engineer and the function of engineering are reserved. Because the relevant legislation is state legislation rather than federal legislation, the details vary a little from state to state. Essentially, however, the position is that:

- it is illegal to call yourself an engineer in a given state unless you are registered with the State Engineers Registration Board;
- it is illegal for a company to use the word 'engineering' in its name unless it employs at least one registered engineer;
- academic programmes including the term engineering in their title must be taught mostly by registered engineers;
- it is illegal to carry out engineering work except under the supervision of a registered engineer.

In most states, this legislation was introduced in the first half of the 20th century, following a number of disasters in which members of the public were killed and much damage was done by the failure of engineering works, typically large civil engineering works.

In order to become a registered engineer in the USA, you must have an approved bachelor's degree in engineering, have four years' experience of working under a registered engineer, and have passed two eight-hour public examinations, one in the fundamentals of engineering and the other in the principles and practice of engineering. The public examination in the principles and practice of engineering is taken in the specific branch of engineering in which the candidate has worked. Fifteen such branches are recognized and some allow candidates to specialize in a sub-branch, giving a total of 27 areas, ranging from agricultural engineering to structural engineering.

The only one of the 27 areas that approaches information systems engineering or software engineering is the computer sub-branch of the electrical and computer engineering branch. Although a part of this is concerned with software, it is primarily aimed at hardware engineers. The formal position is therefore that the terms 'information systems engineer' and 'software engineer' should not be used in the USA.

In practice, this rule is enforced rather patchily. Companies like Sun Microsystems and Microsoft award titles such as 'certified systems engineer' and 'network engineer' to those who can demonstrate skills and knowledge in these area using the companies' products, with no action being taken. On the other hand, Tennessee prohibits the use of the term software engineering in business literature and advertising and the University of Texas has been prevented from offering degrees in software engineering.

There have been recent attempts to introduce a software engineering branch into the principles and practice examination. Unfortunately, these attempts have been unsuccessful because of the difficulty of agreeing on the material to be covered.

The situation in the USA represents an extreme form of regulation. While some professions (the law, veterinary medicine, for example) in the UK are regulated in very similar ways, engineering is not. Neither the title of engineer nor the function of engineering are in any way reserved. Anyone is free to call themselves an engineer and to carry out engineering work. Indeed the word 'engineer' is often used to mean no more than a maintenance technician.

Nevertheless, the engineering profession in the UK has a formal structure and meets the criteria for a profession identified at the beginning of this chapter. There are 35 engineering institutions covering the different branches of engineering. Most of these were established in the 19th century as the different branches of engineering developed. They were, and still are, independent bodies. It was not until the early 1960s that they began to see the value of co-operation and established the Council of Engineering Institutions. The low status of engineering in the UK was one of the major concerns that led to the setting up of the Council. However, despite much good work by the Council, the status of engineers continued to be a problem and, in 1977, the government set up a committee of enquiry into the engineering profession, chaired by Sir Monty Finniston, a distinguished engineer and industrialist.

One of the key recommendations of the committee was the setting up of a statutory body to maintain registers of qualified engineers. In the event, the government did not accept the recommendation in that form but, instead, agreed to set up a chartered body to be called the Engineering Council, which would deal with issues affecting the engineering profession as a whole. The Engineering Council has undergone several changes since then and its latest charter was approved in 2002.

The objectives of the Engineering Council are to advance education in, and to promote the science and practice of, engineering (including relevant technology) for the public benefit and thus to promote industry and commerce in the UK and elsewhere. In order to do this, it does the following:

- sets standards of education, experience and competence for initial registration as a qualified engineer and for continuing professional development (see Chapter 3);
- maintains registers of Chartered Engineers, Incorporated Engineers, and Engineering Technicians;
- licenses appropriate professional bodies ('licensed members') to admit their members to these registers;
- maintains registers of accredited or approved programmes of education;
- acts as the UK representative to relevant international bodies;
- receives and responds to requests for assistance and advice from the government.

In particular, it has a duty under its charter to maintain a register of engineers in three sections, one section for *chartered engineers*, one for *incorporated engineers*, and one for *professional engineering technicians*. Each of the 35 engineering institutions is licensed to nominate suitably qualified members to the appropriate section of the register.

The Engineering Council UK gives the following definition of the three sections of the register:

Chartered Engineers are characterized by their ability to develop appropriate solutions to engineering problems, using new or existing technologies, through innovation, creativity and change. They might develop and apply new technologies, promote advanced designs and design methods, introduce new and more efficient production techniques, marketing and construction concepts, pioneer new engineering services and management methods.

Incorporated Engineers (IEng) are characterized by their ability to act as exponents of today's technology through creativity and innovation. To this end, they maintain and manage applications of current and developing technology, and may undertake engineering design, development, manufacture and operation.

Professional Engineering Technicians are involved in applying proven techniques and procedures to the solution of practical engineering problems. They carry supervisory or technical responsibility, and are competent to exercise creative aptitudes and skills within defined fields of technology. Professional Engineering Technicians contribute to the design, development, manufacture, commissioning, operation or maintenance of products, equipment, processes or services. Professional Engineering Technicians are required to apply safe systems of work.

Registration as a Chartered Engineer requires a four-year programme of higher education at the level of a UK bachelor's degree with honours in Engineering or Technology followed by a master's degree, or equivalent. In addition, candidates must be able to demonstrate appropriate professional experience. The educational requirement for registration as an Incorporated Engineer is a UK bachelor's degree in Engineering or Technology or a Higher National Diploma with a year's further study, or equivalent. There is a similar requirement to demonstrate appropriate professional experience. For registration as a Professional Engineering Technician, a wider range of qualifications is available but essentially these amount to two years of relevant further education plus appropriate professional experience.

Through its licensed members, the Engineering Council UK operates a system of accreditation for educational qualifications. This means that specific qualifications from specific institutions are recognized as meeting the educational requirements for specific levels of registration. The qualifications of candidates for registration who do not have accredited qualifications have to be assessed individually; a time-consuming process. More details of the accreditation process are given in the next chapter.

INTERNATIONAL RECOGNITION OF ENGINEERING QUALIFICATIONS

Recognition within Europe

The EU has issued several *mobility directives*. They are intended to encourage the movement of qualified professionals between countries of the EU. The general principle is that, if you are qualified to practise your profession in one country of the EU, you will be treated as qualified to practise it in any country of the EU.

Registration as a Chartered Engineer in the UK generally allows an engineer to be recognized as qualified to practise elsewhere in Europe. This is done through FEANI (*Fédération Européene d'Associations Nationales d'Ingénieurs* (European Federation of National Engineering Associations)). FEANI was founded in 1951. One of its objectives is specifically 'to facilitate the freedom of engineers to move and practice within and outside Europe'. It maintains a register of European Engineers, that is, engineers who are qualified and registered at the level of Chartered Engineer in their own country and who have registered with FEANI. They are entitled to use the title EurIng.

Twenty-six countries belong to FEANI and the EurIng title indicates recognition of professional status by the professional bodies in all of them; legal recognition, however, applies only in the countries of the EU. In many of these countries, there is statutory protection of the title of engineer and in some it confers a licence to practise.

Washington Accord

In 1989, the engineering professions in Australia, Canada, Ireland, New Zealand, the UK and the USA agreed that the standards and procedures that they each used to accredit the academic component of an engineer's education and training were similar enough for each of them to recognize and accept such qualifications (essentially accredited degrees) gained in any of the other countries. The agreement is fairly limited: it commits the signatories only to the mutual recognition of undergraduate degrees accredited at the level of professional engineer. It does not imply any mutual recognition of professional qualifications such as registered or chartered engineer status.

This agreement is known as the Washington Accord. Since it was originally signed, Hong Kong and South Africa have also signed up to the agreement, and Germany, Malaysia, Japan and Singapore are currently signed up provisionally.

More recently, the Washington Accord has been supplemented by the Sydney Accord (2001) and the Dublin Accord (2002), which provide for similar mutual recognition for accredited academic qualifications leading to professional qualifications at the level of IEng and at the level of engineering technician, respectively. Not all the signatories to the Washington Accord are signatories to these later agreements.

International Register of Professional Engineers

The countries that are signatories to the Washington Accord have also established a body called the Engineers' Mobility Forum, which maintains the International Register of Engineers. The Register began operation in 2002 and is open to engineers qualified at the level of Chartered Engineer. The intention is to work towards mutual recognition of professional engineering qualifications (i.e. not just the academic component) but this is some way off.

COMPULSORY REGISTRATION OF SOFTWARE ENGINEERS

A number of disasters can be traced directly to lack of professional competence on the part of the software engineers who developed the systems. Therac-25 in the USA and the London Ambulance System in the UK are only two of many examples that show how the professional incompetence of software developers can lead to avoidable deaths. In both these examples, the developers lacked any professional qualifications in software engineering and were ignorant of such elementary topics as the risks of concurrent access to shared memory and the dangers of dynamic memory allocation, as well as many more advanced topics. While the immediate cause of the failure of these systems was programming error arising from ignorance of elementary topics, these errors occurred in a context that showed a much broader lack of professionalism.

Danger to the public arising from professional incompetence was one of the driving forces that led to American legislation reserving the engineering function to those who were properly registered and hence appropriately qualified. It is not surprising, therefore, that there have been calls for the compulsory registration of software engineers and for legislation to ensure that software engineering activities are carried out under the supervision of registered software engineers.

Despite the efforts to introduce such a regime in the state of Texas (see the article by Bagert (2002) listed in the 'Further reading' section below), there has been very little progress in this direction. Furthermore, the profession is very divided on the issue.

Some members of the profession have advocated a legal requirement that all software must be written by registered software engineers, or at least under their supervision. Such a regulation would be impossible to enforce. The number of people qualified to be registered as software engineers is vastly fewer than the number of people developing software. If such a regulation were introduced, the amount of new software that could be developed would be enormously reduced or, more likely, software development would go underground. Furthermore, there would be considerable opposition to the regulation. Many software developers would see it as an attempt to establish a monopoly by a small number of people with specific qualifications, with the intention of pushing up their own earnings. The public would share this view and see the move as unnecessary, because most software is not critical.

It would be more realistic and more defensible to require that the design and implementation of all 'critical' systems should be under the control of a registered software engineer (i.e. in the UK, a Chartered Engineer whose experience and qualifications are in software engineering). By a critical system, we mean a system whose failure to operate correctly could result in physical injury or loss of life, or catastrophic economic damage. Society is justified in demanding that such systems are designed and implemented by properly qualified and experienced engineers.

One difficulty is that the boundary between critical and non-critical systems is not always well defined. While it is clear that an air traffic control system should be considered critical, because a failure can result directly in loss of life, should we consider a medical records system to be critical, because the loss of information concerning, say, a patient's allergy to penicillin could in some circumstances lead to the death of the patient? A second difficulty is that many Chartered Engineers who are qualified in software engineering have not studied the rather specialized techniques needed for working on critical systems. Nor, for the jobs they are doing, is it necessary that they should.

In the UK context, compulsory reservation of function for software engineers, even for critical systems work, is unlikely to be realistic except as part of a move towards reservation of function for engineers more generally. There is little sign of this happening. If anything, it is indirect pressures from the Health and Safety Executive or from insurers providing professional indemnity insurance that is likely to increase the emphasis on registration as a Chartered Engineer.

EXAMINATION QUESTIONS

The examination questions below relate to the material covered in this chapter.

APRIL 2000 QUESTION 5(b)

Write short notes on FIVE of the following:

...

b) the structure of the engineering profession in the UK;

...

[5 marks]

The engineering profession in the UK has a two-tier structure. At the upper level is the Engineering Council. Its members are the professional engineering institutions. Individuals can only be members of the latter. The Engineering Council itself has responsibility for matters affecting the engineering profession as a whole. In particular, it lays down general criteria for entry to the profession and is responsible for maintaining registers of qualified engineers. It also has responsibility for promoting the public image of engineering.

The second level consists of the professional engineering institutions themselves. There are some 40 of these and they are specific to particular engineering disciplines. They interpret the Engineering Council regulations regarding registration in the context of their own discipline and nominate suitably qualified members for registration. They also promote education and continuing professional development in the discipline, and function as learned societies in encouraging and facilitating research.

APRIL 2001 QUESTION 2(a)

Describe the changes that have taken place in the structure of the UK engineering profession over the last 40 years and discuss briefly the factors that caused these changes.

[15 marks]

Fifty years ago, there was a large number of independent professional engineering institutions, who talked to each other very little. The technological revolution that began in the 1950s showed the need for interdisciplinary engineering and the status of engineering in the UK was felt to be low. These two factors led to the setting up of the Engineering Institutions Joint Council in 1962, which acquired a Royal Charter and became the Council of Engineering Institutions (CEI) in 1963.

The CEI set up the present three tiers of engineering qualifications and the registration system that supports it. It did not, however, succeed in making employers or the general public respect the qualifications.

In 1977, the Labour government set up a commission of enquiry into the engineering profession under Sir Monty Finniston. This recommended statutory registration of engineers, but not statutory licensing of engineers. It also recommended the introduction of BEng and MEng degrees. While the report was accepted, its recommendations were not acted upon in the original form. It led to the formation of the Engineering Council, but as a chartered body rather than a statutory body.

Although the Engineering Council introduced such things as the uniform system of accreditation of engineering courses, the profession has remained fragmented. This has led to further attempts to unify the profession, including grouping the individual professional bodies into 'colleges'.

APRIL 2003 QUESTION 1(a) AND (c)

a) Describe the origin of UK engineering bodies, the development of the current structure and how the BCS fits into the current structure.

[9 marks]

In the 1950s, there were many independent engineering institutions, but the status of engineering was low. This led to the setting up of the Engineering Institutions Joint Council in 1962, which changed its name to the Council of Engineering Institutions (CEI) in 1965 when it received the Royal Charter. Despite these changes the status remained low and so the government set up the Finniston enquiry in 1977. The enquiry recommended the statutory registration of engineers. Following the report of that enquiry, a chartered body, the Engineering Council, was formed to implement a uniform system of qualifications (CEng, IEng, EngTech) based on the accreditation of academic awards (BEng, MEng degrees and HNDs) and recognition of approved experience, and to maintain a register of qualified engineers. This was to be done through the member bodies, that is, the professional engineering institutions.

The BCS was formed in 1957. It received its Royal Charter in 1984 and shortly afterwards was recognized as a professional engineering institution, responsible for the registration of information systems/software engineers. It works within the Engineering Council's structures and guidelines.

c) Beynon-Davies is quoted in the September 1999 issue of *The Computer Bulletin* as saying that 'information systems is currently at best a semi-profession'.

Discuss this statement by comparing the information systems development profession with other professions such as medicine and law.

[10 marks]

To answer this question, you need to say what the characteristics of a profession are and then discuss how far information systems development shows these characteristics.

The introduction to this chapter lists four characteristics:

- substantial education and training are required in order to practise the profession;
- the members of the profession themselves decide the nature of this training and, more generally, control entry to the profession;

- the profession is organized into one or more professional bodies;
- the profession lays down standards of conduct with which its members must comply, and where necessary, enforces these through disciplinary procedures.

All of these characteristics apply to law and medicine. In both cases, to be registered as a member of the profession, you must pass a lengthy sequence of exams, either set by the professional bodies or set by institutions accredited by them. The professional bodies (the Law Society, the Bar Council, the General Medical Council, and the Royal Colleges) also lay down the level of practical experience required for registration and set and enforce codes of conduct.

None of these characteristics apply to information systems development in general. There are very large numbers of people who develop information systems who have no formal education or training in the field; they do not belong to any professional body and are subject to no code of conduct. It cannot therefore be said that information systems development is a profession. However, those information systems developers who belong to professional bodies such as the BCS or the IEE (Institution of Electrical Engineers) can be regarded as constituting a profession, in that membership of those bodies does demonstrate the characteristics identified above, although the 'experience only' route would be regarded by many as jeopardizing the claim to professional status.

OCTOBER 2003 QUESTION 1(a)

Briefly identify five roles that the Engineering Council plays within the engineering profession.

[5 marks]

See the list of six points in 'The status of engineers' (page 16).

FURTHER READING

The primary sources for the material in this chapter are the statutes governing the various professions in different countries or different states with federal countries, the charters, bye-laws and other documents produced by the professional institutions. Most of these are readily available on the web.

The following list gives the addresses of the websites of the most relevant bodies referred to in this chapter:

BCS: www.bcs.org.uk

FEANI: www.feani.org

Engineering Council: www.engc.org.uk

Institution of Electrical Engineers: www.iee.org

The websites of the BCS and the IEE include the full text of their royal charters, as well as much information about the organizations and the way they function.

A fairly typical example of the legislation governing the engineering profession in the USA can be found in Chapter 327 (Architects, Professional Engineers, Land Surveyors and Landscape Architects) of the Revised Statutes of the State of Missouri, available on the website www.moga.state.mo.us.

The definitions of Chartered Engineer and Incorporated Engineer quoted above are taken from the Engineering Council UK documents, 'Chartered Engineer and Incorporated Engineer Standard' and 'Engineering Technician standard', which can be found on the web as follows:

> www.ukspec.org.uk/files/CE_IE.pdf
>
> www.ukspec.org.uk/files/EngTech.pdf

The situation regarding the registration of software engineers in the USA is documented in various journal articles. The following article, by the first person to be registered as a software engineer in Texas and in the USA, gives a good picture of the current position in that country.

Bagert, Donald J. (2002) Texas licensing of software engineers: All's quiet, for now. *Communications of the ACM*, 45(11), 92–94.

The Washington Accord has an informative website at
www.washingtonaccord.org

All candidates for the Professional Issues module in the BCS Diploma examination should be familiar with a few examples of disasters caused by software. Two of the best documented and most instructive examples are those referred to above, namely the London Ambulance System and Therac-25. The authoritative description of the London Ambulance disaster will be found in:

Thames Regional Health Authority (1993) *Report of the Inquiry Into The London Ambulance Service.* Communications Directorate, South West Thames Regional Health Authority.

This report and some related material are available on the web through:
www.cs.ucl.ac.uk/staff/A.Finkelstein/las.html

The Therac-25 disaster is described in a number of books and articles. A readily available source is:

Leveson, Nancy, and Turner, Clark S. (1993) An investigation of the Therac-25 accidents. *IEEE Computer*, 25(7), 18–41.

An updated version of the paper is available from
sunnyday.mit.edu/therac-25.html

3 Professional Bodies in Computing

After reading this chapter, you should:

- *be aware of the most important professional bodies in computing across the world;*
- *understand the membership structure of the BCS;*
- *be familiar with the range of activities carried out by professional bodies in computing;*
- *understand the obligations that professional bodies in computing impose on their members and, specifically, be familiar with the BCS's Code of Conduct;*
- *be familiar with the services that professional bodies offer to their members in order to help them meet those obligations.*

INTRODUCTION

In the previous chapter we studied the role of professional bodies in establishing and maintaining the status of the professions. In this chapter, we shall look at some of the ways in which they serve their members and the public. The emphasis will be on the activities of the BCS, but we shall refer to the activities of other professional bodies where this is appropriate.

THE DEVELOPMENT OF PROFESSIONAL BODIES IN COMPUTING

The Institute of Electrical and Electronic Engineers (IEEE) is a professional engineering society based in the USA but with members and activities spread worldwide. It was under the aegis of the IEEE that the first professional society in the field of computing was founded in 1946. This was the IEEE Computer Society (IEEE-CS); today it has over 100,000 members. It was closely followed by the Association for Computing Machinery, universally known as the ACM. This was founded in 1947 and now has over 75,000 members. Like the IEEE-CS it is primarily an American organization, but it has members and activities in many countries.

The BCS was founded in 1957. Initially it saw itself as primarily a learned society and a British equivalent of the ACM. However, the way that the professions are organized and regulated in the UK led it to see itself increasingly as a professional, qualification-awarding body. This position was formalized in the mid-1960s. Also in the UK, the IEE has many members active in the field of computing. It was founded in 1871 and today has over 130,000 members worldwide. For many years, it restricted its activities in computing to hardware and to scientific and engineering software; in particular, it held itself aloof from work in information systems. Nowadays, however, it is active across the whole range of software and hardware.

The 1960s saw a great expansion in national computer societies. The Italian Association for Informatics and Automatic Computing was formed in 1961, societies in the individual states of Australia were formed in the next few years and joined together to form the Australian Computer Society in 1966. The Computer Society of India was founded in 1965, the Singapore Computer Society and the Irish Computer Society in 1967 and the German Informatics Society in 1969. The Computer Society of Sri Lanka followed in 1976 and that of Mauritius in 1998.

PROFESSIONAL CONDUCT

All professional bodies lay down a code of conduct that their members are required to obey. This, indeed, is one of the most important characteristics of a professional body. Sometimes the code is called a code of ethics. There is some confusion about terminology in this area. In this book, we shall regard codes of ethics and codes of conduct as meaning the same thing. A code of practice is different, however. A code of *conduct* sets out the standards of behaviour that members of the body are expected to follow in their professional life. It looks outwards, in the sense that it is concerned with the relationship between members and society as a whole. A code of *practice* lays down the best way to practise your profession. For example, it might contain a clause such as: 'Every statement in the code must be executed at least once during testing and testing must be carried out in such a way that it can be demonstrated that this requirement has been met.' The BCS produced a completely new Code of Practice just as this book was going to press.

The BCS's Code of Conduct is included in this book as Appendix A. It has been revised many times since it was first formulated. The result is a code that is easy for the ordinary member to understand.

The Code is divided into the following sections:

1. The Public Interest
2. Duty to the Relevant Authority
3. Duty to the Profession
4. Professional Competence and Integrity

The Public Interest

This section starts by saying that members should carry out their professional duties with 'due care and diligence', that is, with the proper care and attention. This is what society has the right to demand of any professional. It is also stated that if members find that their professional advice is being ignored, they must point out the likely consequences.

The section goes on to say that members are required to be aware of, and to comply with, relevant aspects of the law and other forms of regulation. More generally, they are required to safeguard public health, protect the environment, avoid discrimination and have regard for human rights. They are very specifically forbidden to accept bribes. Oddly, perhaps, there is no similar explicit statement forbidding members from offering bribes, although this would certainly contravene some of the more general clauses in the Code.

Duty to the Relevant Authority

The term relevant authority means the person or organization that has authority over what you are doing. If you are employed by an organization, this is likely to be your employer; if you are an independent consultant, it will be your client; and if you are a student, it will be your school, college or university. In some cases, there may be several relevant authorities; for example, if you are a part-time student who is also employed part time, then the relevant authority as far as your work as a student is concerned will be your school or college, but the relevant authority in your employment will be your employer.

Members of the BCS are expected to behave professionally towards the relevant authority and this means, in particular, the following:

- Avoid conflicts of interest. Suppose, for example, that your client has asked you to select the supplier for a new and expensive computer system and your husband or wife is the sales manager of one of the potential suppliers. In this situation, it may well be that your judgement would be compromised. You should tell your client about the conflict of interest and explain that it would be better if they found someone else to make the selection.

- Avoid misrepresentation, for example, claiming that a piece of software can do something that it can't, or that your company is competent in an area where it is not. In particular, don't take advantage of the fact that other people know less than you. This clause addresses a failing which is, sadly, only too common in the software industry.

- Don't pass on confidential information without permission. Confidential information may include technical information about a company's products, management information relating, say, to its financial position, sales leads, and so on. The law relating to confidential information is covered in Chapter 13.

Duty to the Profession

Like other professions, information systems professionals have not always had a good press. System development has been plagued by delays, budget overruns and complete failures, and these have been well publicized. Too often, the systems themselves do not meet the needs of their users. And information systems professionals have, on occasions, been perceived as behaving in an unprofessional manner. The purpose of this section of the Code is to impress on members what is expected of them in order to uphold the reputation and good standing of the BCS in particular, and the profession in general.

Professional Competence and Integrity

In many ways this is the section of the code that is most immediately relevant to the day-to-day activities of information systems professionals in the first few years of their career. It requires members of the Society to keep their professional skills up to date and to encourage those who work for them to do the same; to follow appropriate codes of practice and other standards; and not to claim to be competent in areas where they are not. Much of this section implies a commitment to continuing professional development, a topic that is developed further later in this chapter.

Status of professional codes of conduct

Most professional bodies have codes of conduct to which members are expected to adhere and most have procedures that allow them to take disciplinary action against members who break their code, with expulsion as the ultimate sanction. Where membership of the professional body confers a licence to practice, as in the case of the Law Society, this is a very serious punishment, since expulsion deprives expelled members of the right to earn their living in their chosen profession.

Most codes of conduct contain some very precise rules and some rather vague or aspirational ones. Clause 13 of the BCS Code of Conduct is an example of a very precise rule. It states:

> **You shall notify the Society if convicted of a criminal offence or upon becoming bankrupt or disqualified as Company Director.**

This is quite clear. There is little doubt about what it means and, in any specific case, it should be clear whether or not a member has complied with this rule.

Clause 2, on the other hand, is much more vague:

> **In your professional role you shall have regard for the public health, safety and environment.**

While no one can quarrel with this precept, it will not always be clear whether a particular development is or is not consistent with improvement in public health, safety and the environment. Some people would regard any work carried out for the nuclear industry as being detrimental to public health, safety and the environment. On the other hand, it is argued by others that the use of nuclear power stations to generate electricity is beneficial to the environment because it avoids carbon dioxide emissions. It would thus be unreasonable for the Society to take disciplinary action against members working in the nuclear industry, even though many other members might feel passionately that such work was dangerous to health, safety and the environment.

In practice, it is only possible to take disciplinary action in cases where the rule that has been broken is a precisely specified and objective one. This is because, if the sanctions imposed affect the member's right to practise, they can take the matter to the civil courts, which will expect the disciplinary proceedings to have been conducted in accordance with the rules of natural justice.

EDUCATION

The BCS promotes education in a number of ways:

- It runs its own system of professional examinations and grants approval to suitable organizations that provide courses to prepare students for them.
- It accredits degree programmes offered by institutions of higher education.
- It sets the syllabus for a range of vocational qualifications and accredits training organizations to provide the associated short courses.

The professional examinations

The Society's professional examinations were introduced in 1973. At that time there were only a few degree programmes in computing. The primary purpose of the BCS exams at that time was to provide a route by which those who had acquired professional skills in computing as a result of their experience could have these skills recognized and thus qualify for professional membership of the Society. In recent years, the increased availability of higher education in the UK and, in particular, the large number of courses in the various branches of computing have resulted in a substantial reduction in the number of UK candidates for the examination. However, this has been balanced by a substantial increase in the number of overseas candidates, a result of the success of the examinations and the international esteem in which they are held.

The BCS professional examinations consist of three stages, the *Certificate*, the *Diploma*, and the *Professional Graduate Diploma*. As well as the normal written examinations, projects are assessed at Diploma and Professional Graduate Diploma levels. The Professional Graduate Diploma and project is considered to be the equivalent of an honours degree.

A new development that is just starting is the European Certification of IT Professionals (EUCIP). This is an initiative of the Council of European Professional Informatics Societies (CEPIS); the BCS is licensed to operate the scheme in the UK.

EUCIP is intended specifically for those who wish to gain a professional qualification accepted throughout Europe. It is aimed at people with professional IT experience but no qualifications, those who have completed a non-IT education (at any level), and younger students interested in entering the IT industry.

A few other computer societies operate examination schemes. The Australian Computer Society has, for a number of years, operated its own system of examinations, somewhat comparable with the BCS Certificate and Diploma examinations but without the project. The IEEE-CS has recently introduced a scheme that allows someone with 9,000 hours of appropriate professional experience to take an examination set by the Society and, if successful, to be registered with the IEEE as a Certified Software Development Professional.

Accreditation and exemption

The term accreditation is used with a confusing variety of related meanings. In the context of engineering in the UK, it refers to a process carried out by professional engineering institutions on behalf of the Engineering Council. Under this process, specific academic awards made by specific institutions of higher education are recognized as satisfying the academic requirements, or part of the academic requirements, for registration as Chartered Engineer, Incorporated Engineer or Engineering Technician.

The requirements for accreditation are laid down in a document published by the Engineering Council entitled *The UK Standard for Professional Engineering Competence*, usually known as UKSPEC.

The typical situation for the BCS is that a university wishes to have several of its degrees accredited. It prepares a substantial submission to the Society. Detailed descriptions of the courses are required, as well as copies of recent examination papers and final-year student projects. Information is also required about the staff and laboratory resources available and the quality assurance procedures. A panel from the Society then visits the university to talk to the staff and students and inspect the facilities. Assuming that the requirements for accreditation are satisfied, accreditation is normally granted for a five year period. Accreditation may be granted at CEng or IEng level and it may be full accreditation or it may be partial accreditation. In the case of partial accreditation, holders of the qualification will be expected to gain some further academic qualifications before they can satisfy the educational requirements for registration as CEng or IEng.

In some instances, qualifications may not meet the Engineering Council's requirements for full or partial accreditation, but may be judged sufficient to allow graduates to be exempted from some or all of the Society's examinations.

Short courses

Through its Information Systems Examination Board (ISEB), the Society offers a substantial range of qualifications achievable through short courses. The courses are intended as training courses for staff working in the industry.

Typically, they last around 40 hours. The Society does not itself provide the training courses; they are provided by outside training organizations. ISEB determines the syllabus for each course, accredits training organizations that wish to run courses, and sets and marks the examinations.

Courses are available in a wide range of topics including, for example, Business and Management Skills, Data Protection, Information Security Management, Project Management, and Software Testing. ISEB also offers a series of diplomas in Business Systems Development.

At the level of the computer user rather than the systems developer, the BCS manages and promotes the European Computer Driving Licence® (ECDL) in the UK on behalf of the ECDL Foundation. This is a European-wide qualification that enables people to demonstrate their competence in computer skills. It is designed specifically for those who wish to gain a basic qualification in computing to help them with their current job, develop their IT skills, and enhance their career prospects. No computer skills or prior knowledge of IT are needed to study the ECDL. An advanced ECDL is also available.

CONTINUING PROFESSIONAL DEVELOPMENT

For many years, little attention was given to how professionals kept their knowledge up to date after qualifying. Thus it was possible for a doctor, a dentist or a solicitor to practise for 40 years without any formal requirement to update their knowledge. Of course, most professionals were aware of the need to do this and would take whatever opportunities were available. Nevertheless, these opportunities might not be readily available and the pressures of day-to-day work might make it difficult for busy professionals to take advantage of them.

The increasing rate at which new knowledge was becoming available and existing knowledge was being used in new ways led, in the 1970s, to increasing concern that professionals should keep their qualifications up to date and this process became known as *continuing professional development*. In October 1994, the Engineering Council defined continuing professional development (CPD) as:

> **The systematic maintenance, improvement and broadening of knowledge and skill and the development of personal qualities necessary for the execution of professional and technical duties throughout the individual's working life.**

In common with other professional engineering institutions, the BCS supports CPD both by providing a formal structure through which it can be recorded and assessed and by providing some of the means by which it can be achieved. This has been based on record cards and a log book, but from the end of 2004 it has become computer based.

CPD services to individual members

All members of the Society receive a copy of the Society's monthly publication, *The Computer Bulletin*. This is the basic mechanism the Society provides to keep its members aware of new developments and current topics of interest to the profession. Recent issues have included articles on such diverse topics as new applications of artificial intelligence, career development schemes for IT staff, common mistakes that endanger security, and project reviews as a way of improving the management of projects. Most professional bodies produce similar monthly publications for the same purpose. Through its branches, the Society provides its members with many opportunities for continuing professional development. There are some 40 branches spread across the UK, as well as a number of overseas sections in such countries as Hong Kong, Mauritius and Sri Lanka. The branches provide an opportunity for members to meet together to share experiences, talk about common problems and listen to talks about new developments, both technical and professional. They provide a valuable opportunity to keep up to date for members in areas away from the main metropolitan areas and for those who may be the sole information systems professional in a company.

Career development and CPD services to the industry

For many years, managing IT staff presented many problems to their employers. The chronic shortage of qualified and experienced staff together with the rapid pace of change made the problems particularly acute for large user organizations. Such organizations were faced with the problem of where to place IT specialists in their staffing structures. Because of their scarcity, such staff could command high salaries but, elsewhere in organization, such salaries would be associated with substantial managerial responsibility. IT staff were anomalies who provoked both envy and disdain among their colleagues.

The BCS started to tackle this problem in the mid-1980s with the development of the Industry Structure Model (ISM). The model took the form of a matrix of roles, with one dimension indexed by speciality (computer operations, network design, database design, programming, project management, and so on) and the other indexed by level, from 1 to 8. For each cell of the matrix, a description was provided that defined the criteria that a person should meet on entry to the role, the tasks an employee in that role is expected to perform and the level of competence expected, and a description of appropriate training and development activities. Such a model means that a large employer has a systematic way of structuring IT roles and is therefore in a much better position to address the problems referred to in the previous paragraph.

The ISM has recently been replaced with SFIAplus, an enhanced model based on the Skills Framework for the Information Age (SFIA). The SFIA is a common reference model for the identification of IT skills, which has been developed by the SFIA Foundation. The SFIA Foundation is a not-for-profit organization set up and owned by the BCS, the IEE, the Institute for the Management of Information Systems and e-skills UK, an industry body.

SFIAplus is embedded in a range of BCS tools designed to support both the individual practitioner and employer organizations in developing skills and careers. This includes the BCS Skills Manager, a software product to allow the IT skills within an organization to be identified and managed effectively. The Skills Manager itself is used as part of the BCS Career Development Framework. This is a software-based management system for applying structured and objective quality control to the training and development of individuals.

The BCS also provides a Career Development Accreditation service, which provides external, independent assurance that an organization's training programme not only meets the needs of the business and the trainee, but also complies with the best practice of the industry as a whole.

THE ADVANCEMENT OF KNOWLEDGE

The Royal Charter of the BCS states very specifically that one of its objectives is to advance knowledge of computing. Indeed, when the Society was founded in 1957, this was its main concern. Many professional bodies began in the same way and most include the advancement of knowledge among their objectives. In practice, however, much of the research that contributes to the advancement of knowledge takes place in universities and in research establishments both public and private. As a result, professional bodies tend to be more concerned with the dissemination of knowledge, through their publications, conferences that they organize or sponsor, and various other activities. The BCS and the IEE are both very active in this area, but they are inevitably small players in comparison with the ACM and the IEEE-CS.

One of the first actions of the BCS when it was formed was to establish *The Computer Journal*. The first issue was published in 1958 and it has been published regularly ever since. Currently, six issues a year are published. The *Journal* carries articles that present the results of research carried out in industry, in research establishments and in universities all over the world. The IEE publishes a journal entitled *IEE Proceedings: Software* (previously known as the *Software Engineering Journal*), which concentrates on new developments in information systems engineering.

Most of the articles in *The Computer Journal* and the *IEE Proceedings* are targeted at specialists. For the information systems professional who is not engaged in research and development, the three most useful publications are probably *Computer* (the flagship publication of the IEEE-CS), *IEEE Software*, and the *Communications of the ACM*. These contain authoritative articles on new developments and current issues written at a level that practising professionals can understand.

As well as the branches, the Society also supports a considerable number of specialist groups. These groups bring together people with interests in specific areas. They cover a wide range of specialist areas, from artificial intelligence to software testing, from human-computer interaction to law. They are particularly effective in spreading knowledge of good practice because they bring together practitioners from different organizations, all working in the same field, who learn from each other. Many specialist groups have gone on to develop an extensive range of resources, from books and reports to specialized software, to disseminate knowledge about their specialized topic.

Many of the specialist groups of the BCS organize or sponsor conferences. Conferences form a second important mechanism for disseminating advances in knowledge. Again, the ACM and the IEEE-CS are leaders in the field and sponsor or organize a large number of specialized conferences every year. However, the majority, though by no means all, of them are held in the USA. There is thus an important role for national societies in organizing national conferences. The BCS and its specialist groups regularly organize or sponsor conferences in the UK in such diverse areas as human–computer interaction, configuration management, healthcare computing, and IT security. The BCS and the IEE also collaborate to organize international conferences in the UK, such as the 2004 International Conference on Software Engineering, held in Edinburgh.

MEMBERSHIP GRADES

The BCS has three major membership categories: standard grades, professional grades and chartered professional status. Membership in the professional grades requires degree level qualifications in IT or substantial experience. For chartered professional status, both degree level qualifications and substantial experience are required.

The criteria for membership in the professional and chartered professional grades are flexible but, for that very reason, they are complicated. The descriptions given below are very much simplified and the BCS web pages should be consulted for precise and up-to-date information. Membership at any level requires a commitment to compliance with the Society's Code of Conduct.

Figure 3.1 shows an outline of the membership structure, which is described in more detail in the following subsections.

The standard grades

The standard grades are Affiliate, Companion, Student and Associate.

Affiliate status is open to anyone with an interest in IT who is prepared to commit themselves to complying with the BCS Code of Conduct and Code of Practice.

Companion status is open to members of other professional bodies with at least five years' work experience related to information systems and who are

FIGURE 3.1 *The BCS membership structure*

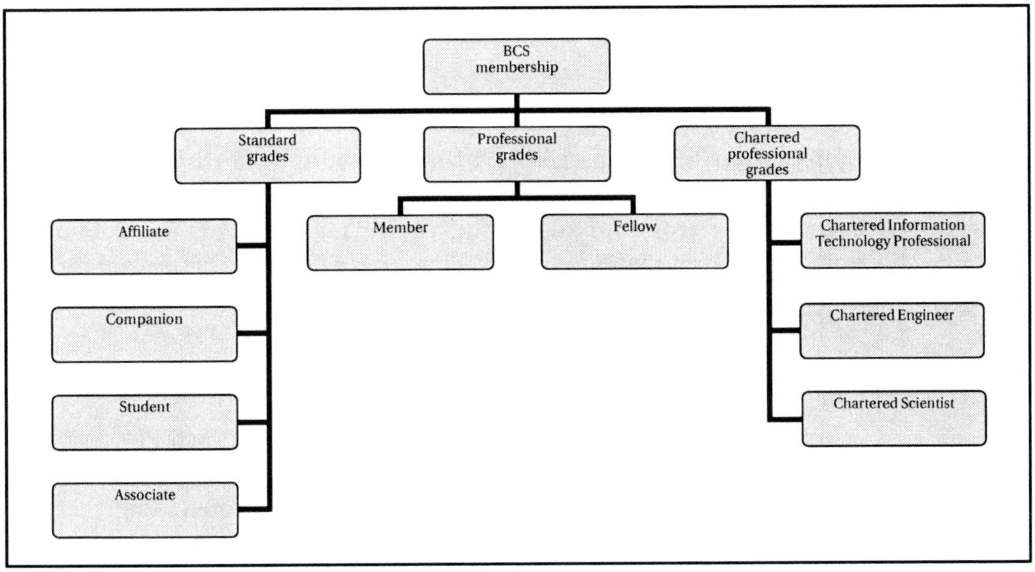

not eligible for BCS professional membership. Those with companion status are entitled to use the letters CompBCS after their name and to describe themselves as a Companion of the BCS.

Student membership is open to those following an approved course of study leading to a qualification recognized for admission to Associate or Professional membership of the Society.

Associate membership is open to anyone who has any of the following:

- more than one but less than five years of IT work experience;
- a Higher National Certificate in an IT-related field;
- a non-accredited degree with a significant IT content.

Associate members are entitled to use the letters AMBCS after their name.

The professional grades

There are two professional grades: Member and Fellow.

In order to qualify for membership in the professional grades, you must have one of the following:

- the BCS Professional Graduate Diploma including the project;
- an honours degree that gives you full exemption from the BCS examinations;
- five years of relevant professional IT work experience;
- some combination of academic qualifications and professional IT work experience that is judged to be equivalent to one of the above.

Members are entitled to use the letters MBCS after their name.

Fellow is the most senior professional grade. It is open to applicants who can demonstrate a minimum of five years IT practitioner experience and hold a senior IT position or who have an established reputation of eminence or authority in the field of IT. Fellows may use the letters FBCS after their names.

The chartered professional grades

In order to qualify for Chartered Professional status within the BCS, you must be a Member or Fellow holding the BCS Professional Graduate Diploma including the project or an honours degree that gives you full exemption from the BCS examinations and you must have five years of relevant professional IT work experience.

Chartered Professionals are entitled to use the letters CITP (for Chartered IT Professional) after their names, along with MBCS or FBCS, in the form MBCS CITP or FBCS CITP.

In addition, the Society is licensed to nominate Chartered Professionals who hold degrees accredited for CEng or IEng by one of the professional engineering institutions for registration as Chartered Engineer or Incorporated Engineer, as appropriate. It is also licensed by the Science Council to nominate suitably qualified members as Chartered Scientists.

The Professional Advice Register

As a service to the public and to its members the BCS maintains a register of those of its members who have the necessary knowledge and expertise to provide advice as consultants or security specialists, or to act as expert witnesses in court.

All applicants for inclusion in the register are assessed by one of the Society's assessors. The register currently contains some 100 names, most of whom have many years' experience in senior professional roles. In a few cases, non-members are included on the register but they must commit to accepting the Society's Code of Conduct and Code of Practice.

OFFICIAL ADVICE

Professional bodies are widely regarded as the source of the most authoritative advice on their disciplines. It is normal therefore for them to be consulted by the government about changes in the law as it affects the discipline or is affected by it. This consultation may extend over a period of several years, as happened, for example, when the BCS was consulted over the EU Directive on Data Protection and the 1998 Data Protection Act. As well as such official consultation, professional bodies are also regularly invited to talk to groups of members of parliament who are interested in their disciplines.

Professional engineering bodies are also routinely asked by standardization bodies, such as the American National Standards Institute or the British Standards Institute, to nominate members of committees developing standards in the field. Indeed, the IEEE itself runs the standards-making process in the area of local area networks through its Project 802.

EXAMINATION QUESTIONS

The examination questions below relate to the material covered in this chapter.

APRIL 2001 QUESTION 1

a) The Code of Conduct of the BCS is divided into four main sections. Explain what these sections are and describe briefly the issues addressed by each section.

[16 marks]

This is precisely the material included in 'Professional conduct' (page 26).

b) You have recently taken over responsibility for the maintenance of your company's accounting suite. While familiarizing yourself with it, you realize that the modules that handle sales contain a systematic error that will lead to the company paying less taxes than it should. When you point this out to your manager, he tells you to leave it as it is because that is the way the company wants it.

Which clauses in the Code of Conduct are relevant to this situation and how might the Code affect what you do?

[9 marks]

The most obviously relevant clause is Clause 4, which requires members to have knowledge of relevant legislation, regulations and standards, and to comply with them. You have now been instructed to break the provisions of the clause. Clause 1 states that if your professional judgement is overruled, you should point out the likely consequences. While you have already pointed out the problem to your manager, you should make sure he is aware of the possible consequences of this; in your own interests it would be best to do this in writing.

Whether you should take the matter any further depends on the seriousness of the situation. If the sum of money involved is only a tiny fraction of the company's tax bill, it would be difficult to justify taking further action. If it is more substantial, then the Clause 4 requirement to comply with the law requires you to do something more. Clause 8 requires you not to disclose confidential information relating to your employer without permission, unless ordered to do so by a court. Your next step should therefore be to raise the matter with higher management, perhaps the Financial Director, since this will not violate Clause 8. If this proves ineffective, it may be necessary to violate Clause 8 and disclose the information to the Inland Revenue. In the case of a serious violation of the law, the public interest and the requirement to comply with the law may override the requirement not to disclose confidential information.

(Note that the Public Interest Disclosure Act 1998 (see 'Redundancy, dismissal and grievance procedures' in Chapter 10) is also relevant to this question. Note also that candidates are not expected to be able to quote clause numbers.)

APRIL 2001 QUESTION 2(b)

Explain the roles and characteristics of the BCS as a professional body.

[10 marks]

The following list covers what was expected:

- sets standards of professional competence;
- promotes educational provision to assist in achieving these standards;
- defines standards of professional conduct and enforces these standards within its membership;
- promotes and supports the continuing professional development of its members;
- actively supports the advancement of knowledge in the field of information systems engineering, through its publications and sponsorship of conferences;
- advises the UK Government on relevant legislation.

APRIL 2003 QUESTION 6

Describe the membership structure of the BCS as a 'professional engineering body'.

[6 marks]

See 'Membership grades' (page 34). At the time that the question was set, the membership structure was simpler than it now is.

APRIL 2003 QUESTION 1(b)

a) The Code of Conduct of the BCS is divided into four main sections. Explain what these sections are and describe briefly the issues addressed by each section.

[12 marks]

See 'Professional conduct' (page 26).

b) Your company is due to deliver a new water processing facility to a national water company. The facility includes real-time

monitoring of chemicals and pollutants. This is a major contract for your company, but it is behind schedule and late delivery will result in heavy penalty costs. You have just been told that the company has assigned you to the project to work on the real-time monitoring subsystem. Assuming that you are an experienced programmer but have little experience of real-time systems, discuss which clauses in the Code of Conduct are relevant to this situation and how the Code might affect what you do.

[13 marks]

The most relevant clauses are:

In your professional role you shall have regard for the public health, safety and environment (Clause 2). The system you are going to work on clearly has the potential to affect all these. You must therefore take your responsibilities very seriously.

You shall seek to upgrade your professional knowledge and skill, and shall maintain awareness of technological developments, procedures and standards which are relevant to your field, and encourage your subordinates to do likewise (Clause 14). Since you have little experience of this field, you have a duty to try to learn as much as you can about it. You can certainly expect your company to send you on relevant courses or provide training in other ways but you should expect to spend some of your spare time on private study in the area.

You shall not claim any level of competence that you do not possess (part of Clause 15). You must make sure that your company understands that you have little experience in the area of real time programming.

APRIL 2003 QUESTIONS 1(b) AND (c)

b) Identify four key roles and/or responsibilities of the BCS and, using examples, explain how these are fulfilled.

[12 marks]

c) One of the responsibilities of being a member of the BCS is to maintain your own knowledge and professional competence. Identify two examples of how being a member of the society would help to achieve this goal. Discuss each example in detail.

[8 marks]

FURTHER READING

The IEEE-CS and the ACM have jointly produced a Code of Conduct for software engineers. This is a comprehensive and largely aspirational code, but it is well worth studying and comparing with the BCS Code of Conduct. It is available at the website:

www.computer.org/tab/seprof/code.htm

The codes of some other professional computing bodies are available on the web as follows:

- Australia: www.acs.org.au/national/pospaper/acs131.htm
- Hong Kong: www.hkcs.org.hk/ethics.htm
- India: www.csitvm.org/ethics.html
- Singapore: www.scs.org.sg/cgi-bin/cgiwrap/scsorg/scs/scs.cgi?aboutus&codeofconduct

The codes of conduct of professional bodies in other fields are readily available on the web and are worth studying. Here are a few examples:

- Royal Institute of British Architects:
  www.architecture.com/go/Architecture/Using/Conduct_346.html

- Royal College of Veterinary Surgeons: www.rcvs.org.uk (Click on Veterinary surgeons and then Guide to Professional Conduct)

- Institute of Physics: www.about.iop.org/Iop/member/conduct.html

- Institution of Mechanical Engineers: www.imeche.org.uk/membership/pdf/Code%20of%20Conduct.pdf

The BCS's website:

www.bcs.org.uk/

contains much information about the Society, including the text of its royal charter. It also contains the text of the new Code of Conduct.

The website of the SFIA Foundation can be accessed at:

www.sfia.org.uk

4 What Is an Organization?

After studying this chapter you should know and understand:

- *the different ways in which an organization can become a legal entity;*
- *the situations for which the different types of legal entity are appropriate;*
- *what a limited company is and why it is the preferred legal form for a commercial organization;*
- *the most important ways in which the law regulates limited companies.*

INTRODUCTION

An organization is a group of people working together in a formal way. Our life in a modern society is dominated by our interactions with organizations. We go to school and to college; schools and colleges are organizations. We or our friends and relatives go to hospital; a hospital is an organization. We have a bank account; a bank is an organization. We take the examinations of the BCS; it is an organization. And we work for a company or a government department, both of which are organizations. We may even set up a business of our own and thus create an organization ourselves. However, as we mentioned in Chapter 1, organizations need to have a legal existence. In this chapter we describe the different ways in which an organization can acquire a legal existence, concentrating on the idea of a limited company, because this is the most important type of commercial organization.

A very broad distinction can be made between commercial organizations, which are in business to make money, and public organizations or other non-profit-making bodies. This distinction is reflected in the different procedures used to set up the organizations and the different ways in which they are governed. Most of this chapter is concerned with commercial organizations but in the section 'Non-commercial bodies', we look briefly at non-commercial organizations.

COMMERCIAL ORGANIZATIONS

The law offers several different ways of setting up and operating a commercial organization. Depending on the circumstances, the business may be operated as a *sole trader,* a *partnership,* a *cooperative,* or a *limited company.*

A sole trader is an individual who runs their own business. There are no legal formalities attached to becoming a sole trader; you become a sole trader simply by starting to run a business. If the income of your business is large enough, you will need to register with Customs and Excise for VAT (value-added tax) purposes, and you may need to negotiate with the Inland Revenue about your income tax status, but neither of these is necessary simply in order to become a sole trader.

A sole trader is personally liable for all the debts of the business so that all the trader's assets, including the family home, are at risk if the business fails. For this reason, anyone who is in business in anything other than a very small way should not operate as a sole trader. It is usually better to form a limited company, as discussed later in this chapter.

If a group of people carry on a business with a view to making profits, and the business is not a limited company, then the law will treat them as being in a *partnership*. This will happen whether the people in question intend it to or not. The legal framework governing partnerships was established in the Partnership Act 1890 and has since been changed only in minor ways. The Act has important consequences for people going into business together.

The most important consequences are that the liability of the partners is unlimited and that the partners are *jointly* and *severally* responsible for the partnership's liabilities.

What does this mean in practice? Suppose that you and a friend are working together to write software for local company. Your friend is doing most of the work and you have agreed that he will get most of the money. Unfortunately, his software doesn't work and the company decides to claim damages for the harm it has suffered because of the defective software. You own a house and a car and have money in the bank; your friend doesn't. The company can sue you for the entire amount of the damages, despite the fact that it was your friend's software that didn't work.

A second problem with partnerships is the difficulty of making changes in the ownership. If one of the partners wishes to leave the partnership, perhaps to retire, how much money are they entitled to receive in return for relinquishing their share of the partnership? And how do the remaining partners raise this money? In the extreme case that one of the partners dies, how much is due to their estate?

Partnerships are mainly used in professions such as the law, medicine or architecture. The bodies that govern these professions have often insisted that their members practise in partnerships because the draconian rules regarding liability are seen to be a way of discouraging recklessness and ensuring the probity of the professionals concerned.

Cooperatives are another way in which an organization can acquire a legal existence. They are important in fields such as agriculture and enjoy a special legal status. They are, however, unusual in the information systems industry and we shall say no more about them.

By far the commonest form of commercial organization is the limited company. It is also the most suitable form of organization for most businesses. Most of the remainder of this chapter is dedicated to describing this type of organization.

LIMITED COMPANIES

There are three principles that are fundamental to the concept of a limited liability company:

- The company has corporate legal identity, that is, it is a legal person, completely separate from the people who work in it or the people who own it.
- The ownership of the company is divided into a (usually large) number of shares. These shares can be bought and sold individually. The people who own these shares are known as the members of the company or shareholders.
- In the event that the company incurs debts or other legal liabilities, the owners of the company have no obligation to pay these. The most that shareholders stand to lose is the money they paid for their shares.

The UK recognizes two main types of limited company, the public limited company (plc) and the private limited company. The essential difference is that a plc can, if it so wishes, offer its shares for sale to the public, but a private limited company cannot. The name of a private limited company will end with the word Limited or Ltd, e.g. Augusta Technology Ltd, while the name of a plc will end with plc, e.g. Lloyds TSB Bank plc.

In return for the privileges, particularly limited liability, that the status of being a limited company confers, a limited liability company has certain obligations. It must provide details about itself to Companies House, where they are available to the general public, and these details must be kept up to date. It must produce annual accounts (see Chapter 6) and an annual report; again these must be submitted to Companies House and will be publicly available. Some of the reporting requirements are eased for small companies, while there are more stringent requirements for companies whose shares are quoted on a stock exchange.

Until the middle of the 19th century, the only way to create a limited company was through an Act of Parliament or the issue of a Royal Charter, both very slow and expensive routes. The modern idea of the limited company was developed through a number of Acts of the UK Parliament in the middle of the 19th century and was rapidly taken up in other countries. It has played a very important part in subsequent economic development, which would probably have taken place much more slowly if the convenient mechanism offered by the limited company had not been available.

It can be safely said that the three principles stated at the start of this section hold in any country that recognizes the concept of a limited company. Within this framework, however, the details vary very widely from country to country. Several countries (e.g. New Zealand, Canada, Australia) have enacted legislation in recent years that simplifies the law relating to companies. While the UK government is currently reviewing this body of law and has announced that it intends to produce proposals for simplifying it, this has not yet happened. Note also that terminology differs from country to country; in particular, the term corporation is commonly used in the USA to denote a (large) limited company.

THE CONSTITUTION OF A LIMITED COMPANY

In order for a company to be registered, it must have a constitution. This consists of two documents: the *memorandum of association* and the *articles of association*.

The memorandum of association is a fairly short and straightforward document. It states:

- The name of the company: The choice of name for a company is subject to a number of rules. The most obvious one is that the name must not already be in use by another company. There are many words that cannot be used in company names without special permission. The list includes words that might give the impression that the company has some sort of official status, such as 'Parliament' or 'England', and words implying a representative role, such as 'Association'.

- The country in which its registered office will be located – England and Wales, Wales (to the exclusion of England) or Scotland.

- The objects of the company: This is a statement of the type of business in which the company will engage. This may simply state that its object is to carry on business as a general commercial company, without being any more specific.

- A liability clause: In the case of a company limited by shares, this clause merely states that the liability of the members is limited.

- The company's authorized share capital and the number and nominal value of its shares: The authorized share capital is the maximum amount up to which the company can issue shares. The company need not, and usually will not, issue all its shares. New companies are often started with an authorized share capital of £100 divided into 100 shares with a nominal value (or par) value of £1 each. The nominal value is the value written on the share, which is normally the money paid to the company when the share is first purchased; it bears no necessary relation to any subsequent market value of the share. In order to be registered as a plc, a company must have an issued share capital (that is, the nominal value of the issued shares) of at least £50,000.

In addition, the memorandum will conclude with a *declaration of association* along the following lines:

> We, the several persons whose names, addresses and descriptions are written below, are desirous of being formed into a company in pursuance of this Memorandum of Association, and we respectively agree to take the number of shares in the capital of the company set out opposite our respective names.

The articles of association are much more complicated and technical. They relate to such matters as the number of directors, how directors are appointed and removed, what their powers are, what happens when new shares are to be issued, what process is required in order to modify the articles, and so on. In order to simplify the setting up of companies, the Companies Act 1948 included a specimen set of articles of association, which have been regularly updated; these are known as *Table A*. Most companies now adopt Table A as the basis of their articles of association and specify only the way in which their articles differ from Table A.

Once a company has been registered, the memorandum of agreement and the articles of association are deposited at Companies House and are public documents, in the sense that anyone may visit Companies House and inspect them. It often happens in private companies that the shareholders wish to conclude a further agreement among themselves. Such an agreement is called a *shareholders' agreement*. Unlike the memorandum and the articles, this is not a public document.

DIRECTORS

In small companies, it may well be that the shareholders run the company directly but this is not feasible if there are more than a handful of shareholders; in any case, some shareholders may not wish to be involved directly in the day-to-day operations of the business. The law requires that the shareholders appoint directors to take responsibility for running the company on their behalf.

In small companies, the shareholders may actually be directors or at least be in regular contact with them. In large public companies, however, the shareholders have very little opportunity to influence the directors. To compensate for this, the law makes directors subject to certain obligations.

Directors must have regard to the interests of both the company's employees and its shareholders. Until the Companies Act 1985, directors were only required to act in the best interests of the shareholders, and theoretically at least, could have been sued if they took into account the interests of the employees to the detriment of the shareholders.

Directors must act in good faith and for the benefit of the company. Suppose, for example, that you are a director of a small company that writes software and that someone approaches you to have some software written. If you decided that you could do this yourself in your spare time rather than having it written by the company, you would not be considered to have acted in good faith for the benefit of the company and you could be required to pay the company compensation for the loss of the contract.

Directors must exercise the skill and care in carrying out their duties that might be expected from someone of their qualifications and experience. This means, for example, that a director with long experience of purchasing computers who signed a contract to buy a computer system that was not suitable for the use the company intended to make of it might be ordered by a court to pay back to the company the cost of the computer. Furthermore, directors must take the same care as an ordinary person might be expected to take on their own behalf.

A director who has an interest in a contract made with the company (e.g. owning an office cleaning company that the company is thinking of employing) must disclose this interest to the board of directors. Table A stipulates that the director must not be allowed to vote or be counted in the quorum when the matter is discussed but, in the case of a small company, this may well be varied by the articles.

The obligations described above can be described as domestic; that is, they are obligations owed to the company. In addition, there are certain external or legal obligations that the directors must fulfil.

First, directors are required to keep themselves aware of the company's financial position and not allow it to continue to incur debts when they know or should have known that the company will be unable to repay them. If they fail to do this, a court can make them personally liable for the company's debts.

Secondly, the directors are responsible for drawing up the company's annual report, including its accounts, and for filing this report with Companies House. In particular, they are responsible for selecting suitable accounting policies.

Thirdly, the directors are responsible for ensuring that the company complies with all relevant provisions of the law. While the company itself, having a legal existence, can be prosecuted for criminal breaches of the law, in some cases directors can be made personally responsible. Thus the Health and Safety at Work Act 1974 provides that in appropriate circumstances a director or other senior manager can be criminally liable if a company is found to be in serious breach of the Act.

Many companies have both *executive* directors and *non-executive directors*. Executive directors are normally also employees of the company, with specific responsibility for certain areas of its activities. Non-executive directors are directors who act in an advisory capacity only. Typically, they attend monthly board meetings to offer the benefit of their advice and are paid a fee for their services and serve on committees concerned with sensitive issues such as the pay of the executive directors and other senior managers. It is important to realize that, legally, the duties and responsibilities of non-executive directors are precisely the same as those of the executive directors.

Every company must have a company secretary. The company secretary is legally responsible for keeping the various records that the company has to maintain and for submitting various statutory returns to Companies House in Cardiff. They will normally also take responsibility for a variety of related matters. The company secretary is often also a director. Small companies often appoint an outsider, typically a solicitor or accountant, as company secretary, because such people are likely to have the necessary professional expertise.

SETTING UP A COMPANY

A limited company is created by a group of people each agreeing to subscribe a certain amount of money to set up an organization to pursue some stated goal and to register the organization as a limited company in accordance with the law.

In the UK, the process of setting up a limited company is straightforward and it can be done quite quickly and cheaply. It is not necessary to employ a lawyer or an accountant, although this may be advisable if you have little experience of dealing with formal documents. The commonest way of setting up a company is to buy an 'off-the-shelf' company. There are a number of company formation agents that set up companies with a standard constitution; they hold a stock of such companies, which never actually trade, and they sell them to customers wanting a company through which to run their business. Once the customers have bought the company, they can make changes to its constitution, including its name, at their leisure.

The alternative is to create a company specifically to meet the requirements of the business. The process of registering the business is quick and cheap; the Registrar of Companies offers a same-day service for less than £100. In practice, however, there are decisions to be made and forms to be completed, with the result that the process is likely to be slower and more expensive than buying an off-the-shelf company.

There are only a few countries in which companies can be set up as cheaply and as conveniently as in the UK or the USA. At the other extreme, in some countries it can take up to six months to register a new company and the cost can run into several thousands of pounds.

NON-COMMERCIAL BODIES

Many of the organizations with which we are most familiar come into existence by statute, that is, by Act of Parliament. Such organizations are often known as statutory bodies. Frequently the organizations themselves are created by secondary legislation. In the terminology of object-oriented programming, the Act of Parliament defines a class of 'organizations', specifying their structure, their duties and their powers. Secondary legislation is then used to create objects belonging to that class, that is, specific instances of it. Thus, in the field of local government, the Local Government Act 1992 created the class of unitary authorities together with a body, the Local Government Commission, which would make recommendations for the creation of specific unitary authorities; these authorities would then be created by secondary legislation.

In the UK, the government has, on the whole, preferred to entrust the provision and delivery of state services to free-standing statutory bodies rather than having these services provided directly by government ministries. This preference is shared by most English-speaking countries. British universities, for example, (and those in most Commonwealth countries and in the USA) are independent organizations. They are created by Royal Charter and are free to plan their own programmes. In many cases, the state provides some or all of the money required to run the university and is therefore able significantly to influence the university's behaviour, but this control is indirect.

Most of mainland Europe prefers a centralized system in which government ministries directly control and operate state services. Nowhere is this clearer than in the case of universities. In contrast to British universities, universities in continental Europe are typically regarded as a part of the government. Their employees are civil servants, albeit of a rather special kind, and the titles and content of the programmes they are allowed to offer are centrally regulated.

As well as statutory bodies, there are very many organizations whose activities are generally seen to be in the public interest and which are not intended to be profit-making. Such organizations include professional bodies, such as the BCS or the Institute of Physics, charities such as Oxfam or Christian Aid, political parties, and so on. Such organizations usually take the legal form of a company limited by guarantee. In this case, rather than subscribing for shares, the members agree to pay a small fixed amount (typically £1) to cover liabilities in the event that the body has to be wound up. A company limited by guarantee is not allowed to distribute its profits to its members. It can apply for charitable status and for the grant of a Royal Charter.

EXAMINATION QUESTIONS

The examination questions below relate to the material covered in this chapter.

APRIL 2000 QUESTION 5(a)

Write short notes on FIVE of the following:
a) the advantages and disadvantages of limited company status;

[5 marks]

The main advantages of limited company status (as opposed to trading as a partnership or a sole trader) are:

- part-ownership of the company can be transferred comparatively easily through the sale of shares;
- the principals' personal assets are not at risk;
- in most fields, a limited company is perceived, rightly or wrongly, as a more serious undertaking.

The disadvantages are:

- the disclosure requirements and the cost of meeting them;
- the responsibilities and liabilities that the law lays on the directors;
- more generally, the burden of company law.

APRIL 2001 QUESTION 4(a)

You and a few friends are thinking of going into business together to offer software development and system integration services to small businesses.

Explain why it would be wise (or, alternatively, why you think it would not be wise) to form yourselves into a limited company.

[15 marks]

APRIL 2002 QUESTION 2(a)

Boards of directors are answerable to the shareholders and to the law. Their responsibilities fall into two main categories, namely legal and domestic. Explain the legal responsibilities and the domestic responsibilities of the directors.

[13 marks]

This is covered explicitly in 'Directors' (page 45).

APRIL 2002 QUESTION 5

a) Explain the following terms:
- *sole trader*
- *partnership*
- *company*

[12 marks]

A sole trader is a business owned by a single individual who is fully entitled to the revenue of the business and is fully responsible for any losses the business suffers.

A partnership is a business arrangement in which two or more people jointly own a business, share the profits and are jointly and severally responsible for any losses.

A company is an organization legally allowed to produce and trade. It has a legal existence distinct from that of its owners. Ownership is divided among shareholders.

b) Shareholders of a company have limited liability. Explain this term and contrast it with the liability of sole traders and partners.

[7 marks]

Limited liability means that the most shareholders can lose is the money they have invested in shares. Unlike sole traders and partners, shareholders cannot be forced to sell their personal possessions if the business cannot pay its debts.

c) Two existing firms can join together in two different ways. One firm may make a takeover bid for the other, or a merger may occur.

Contrast a takeover bid with a merger.

[6 marks]

When a firm makes a 'takeover bid', it offers to buy out the shareholders of the second firm. Managers of the second firm will usually put up resistance, as they are likely to lose their jobs. Shareholders of the second firm are likely to accept the offer if it is sufficiently attractive. In contrast, a merger is the voluntary union of two companies where they think they will do better by amalgamating.

OCTOBER 2003 QUESTION 5(b)

Describe the liability and responsibility of the board of directors of a company.

[7 marks]

See 'Directors' (page 45).

FURTHER READING

Companies House has a very informative website that gives more detail about many of the topics covered in this chapter. Its address is:

www.companieshouse.gov.uk

A code of best practice concerning the duties of directors can be found at:

www.ivis.co.uk/pages/gdsc6_1.html

There are a large number of websites that offer services for setting up companies and these sites can be very helpful and informative but remember that they are commercial sites whose primary objective is to sell their services.

5 Financing a Start-up Company

After reading this chapter you should:

- *understand why start-up companies need capital;*
- *know what is required in a business plan;*
- *understand the different ways in which capital can be raised and the advantages and disadvantages of each.*

INTRODUCTION

New graduates in computing are often tempted by the idea of setting up their own company. They might, for example, decide to try to use their skills in website design and programming to offer services to small organizations wanting to establish a web presence. Or they may have ideas for a software package or perhaps a computer game, which they hope to develop into a commercial product. However modest the group's initial ambitions, it is likely that they will need some money to start the venture. This chapter is concerned to explain why that money is needed and how it might be raised.

WHY CAPITAL IS NEEDED

It is very difficult to start any commercial venture without having some money in hand, because your customers will not be willing to pay you until you have provided them with the service or the product they are buying. You, however, have to buy the things you need to make the product or to provide the service, and you have to live while you are making or doing it.

To take a very simple example, suppose that you are setting up in business painting houses. You need to buy paintbrushes, paint, ladders, and so on. It may take you two weeks to paint a house and during this time you have to live. You will only get paid when you've finished painting your first house. Indeed, you may well find that your customers don't always pay immediately but take another two or three weeks to pay. The amount of money you need may not be very large but you will find yourself in difficulties if you haven't got it.

If you are setting up a company to build websites, you are likely to need much more money. First, because your customers are likely to be other companies, it will take you longer to get paid. In normal commercial practice, invoices for services are issued at the end of a month to cover the work that has been done during the month. A client is unlikely to pay an invoice within less than one month of receiving it. Two months is more likely with commercial clients and three months is not uncommon; some large companies are notorious for not paying invoices for as much as 6 or even 12 months. The result is that you need enough cash in hand to be able to live for at least three months. Additional money will be needed for the expenses of starting the company.

If you intend to develop a package, the sum of money needed is likely to be even larger. While the package is being developed, there will be no revenue coming into the company. For this period cash will be needed for:

- salaries, however small, for the founders and for any other staff they may need to employ;
- rent, rates, heating and lighting of the premises used;
- equipment and consumables;
- costs of advertising and marketing the products;
- miscellaneous expenses, ranging from company stationery to travelling expenses for any trips that may be necessary;
- interest on any money borrowed.

While it is often possible to carry out the early stages of development in the founders' spare time, working from their homes, this is not usually satisfactory once commercial sales have started. However successful the development of the packages, it will take some months before sales reach a level sufficient to cover the company's ongoing costs, so, even after development is complete, more cash will be needed.

THE BUSINESS PLAN

The first step in raising the money is to produce a *business plan*. This is a document that explains your plans to potential funders and tries to convince them that these plans are well thought out and realistic and that the venture is likely to be successful. It should contain:

- a description of what the company will be doing, together with information to show that it is technically feasible and that the founders of the company have the necessary expertise;
- a description of the market the company is aiming at, an estimate of its size, and an assessment of the competition. It might contain statements like the following:

> The company's target market will be small firms providing repair and maintenance services to householders, within a radius of 15 miles of the centre of Llanafan. So far as can be estimated from the data provided by the Llanafan Chamber of Commerce, there are around 1,200 such firms in the area, only 16 of which have websites. There are two other companies offering website design and hosting services in the area but neither appears interested in this market.

- a prediction of the financial performance of the company. This will include budgets, cash flow predictions, and projected balance sheets and profit and loss accounts. These are dealt with in the chapters that follow.

Armed with the business plan, you are in a position to approach people who might be willing to lend you money, invest money in your company, or even give you money.

It is a mistake to think of a business plan as a prediction of what will happen when and if you succeed in starting your company. It should be seen much more as a scenario that demonstrates that your company has a reasonable chance of success. The attempt to produce a business plan will often show that what a new company is trying to do has very little chance of succeeding. This should have been true of many of dot.com companies that failed in the crash of 2001. Their predictions of the size of their market were quite unrealistic and any shrewd investor might have seen this.

SOURCES OF FINANCE

Government policy in the UK has, over recent years, strongly encouraged the growth of small companies and, as a result, there are many possible sources of funding. However, they can all be grouped under three headings: grants, loans, and sale of equity. Many other countries have similar policies, but there are big differences between countries in the way that the policies are implemented and policy within a single country can swing violently over time.

Grants

A *grant* is a sum of money given to the company; while the company is obliged to demonstrate that it has been used for the purposes for which it was given, it is not intended that the grant should ever be paid back to the organization which gave it. Not surprisingly, grants are only available from government (local or national) and EU sources or, very occasionally, from charities. Very often, grants are limited to a certain proportion of the money spent on a particular development and are conditional upon the remainder being raised from other sources.

The availability of grants and other help for new companies depends very much on where the company is located, how many people it expects to employ, and on government policy at the time. Typically, in the UK, a new company, setting up in an area where maximum assistance is available, might expect to be provided with premises rent free or at half rent for the first 12 months; it might also expect a grant of £15,000 to £20,000, once it is employing five or six people, and a second similar grant when the number of employees reaches 10 or a dozen. (Very much larger grants are available to established companies intending to make substantial investments that will lead to the creation of many jobs.)

These grants are usually:

- intended to assist with capital investment, typically investment in premises and equipment;
- subject to a number of conditions, in particular the raising of capital from other sources;
- limited to a certain proportion of the capital investment that the company can prove it has made.

This means that they are often of limited usefulness to small software companies, whose investment more usually takes the form of employees' time.

A variety of programmes, both national and European, offer grants to assist in the development of high-technology products. These are likely to be particularly helpful to start-up companies aiming to develop new packages. Examples are the European Community Framework VI programme and the research and development grants available to small and medium-sized businesses from the UK Department of Trade and Industry. Depending on the programme, it may be a requirement that the proposed development is collaborative, that is, involves more than one company, and, in the case of European programmes, that the collaboration involves companies from at least two member states of the European Union. The assistance is almost invariably limited to 50 per cent of the cost of the development and often to less.

Loans

While grants are undoubtedly very helpful, their effect on company finance is short term. The major sources of finance are loans and the sale of equity.

A loan is a sum of money lent to the company; interest is payable on it, at a rate that may be fixed or variable, and the loan is usually for a fixed period. The company has to pay back the loan eventually and, if it goes into liquidation, the lender is entitled to recover the loan from the sale of the assets of the company. In most cases, security is required for the loan. In other words, the company agrees that if it fails to make repayments, the lender is entitled to sell some of the company's assets in order to make up for the shortfall, rather in the same way that, if you borrow money to buy a house and then fail to keep up the repayments, the lender can sell the house to recover the loan.

It often happens that small companies do not have sufficient assets to cover the loan they are looking for. In this case, the lender may ask for personal guarantees from the directors of the company; this may mean that the directors have to use their own homes or other property as security for the loan.

It is usual to divide loans into overdrafts and long-term loans. An overdraft is the most flexible form of loan. Overdrafts are offered by banks; they allow a company (or an individual) to spend more money than is in its account, up to a specified maximum. Interest is only payable on the amount actually owed and the rate is normally comparatively low; it is usually fixed at a certain number of points above the bank base lending rate, the precise figure depending on the bank's view of the credit-worthiness of the borrower. While overdrafts are the most flexible and usually the cheapest way to borrow, there is a price to be paid. A bank can withdraw overdraft facilities without warning, possibly for reasons of general policy that have nothing to do with the borrower. Many small companies have been forced into liquidation unnecessarily as a result of such action by banks.

In contrast, long-term loans are usually made for a fixed period at a fixed rate of interest. The borrower receives the capital (the amount of the loan) at the start of the period of the loan and is committed to paying interest on that amount throughout the period of the loan. Provided the borrower pays the interest on time, the lender cannot call in the loan. The borrower must repay the capital at the end of the period.

As a result of various government initiatives, a 'soft loan' may be available; this is a loan on terms that are less onerous than those that prevail for commercial loans. Soft loans are usually only available to start-up companies; the interest rates may be lower than commercial interest rates and security is not demanded.

Loans are usually provided by banks or similar institutions. Even if a soft loan is available as part of a government initiative, it will usually be channelled through a commercial bank. In some instances, start-up companies are able to borrow money from relatives or friends of the founders – or, indeed, the founders may be able to lend the company money themselves. In such cases, it is important that the loan is put on the same sort of formal basis as a commercial loan. If it is not, and things go wrong for the company, there is real danger that confusion will lead to bitter arguments and will end up by spoiling personal relations.

Equity capital

Equity capital is money paid to the company in exchange for a share in the ownership of the company, as described in the previous chapter.

The founders of a new company often find the initial capital from their own resources or from friends and family, but few are able to continue raising capital in this way. If a company looks to have good prospects but needs to raise more capital, it will usually need to resort to *business angels* or *venture capitalists*.

Business angels are wealthy individuals who provide equity capital for start-up companies and small firms that are seeking to grow rapidly. They are usually interested in investing in firms operating in areas of which they have some experience and, as well as providing capital, they will usually expect to offer advice on management and other business issues. Business angel networks are organizations that bring business angels together and provide mechanisms to assist small companies to find suitable business angels and vice versa. The networks usually operate at national or regional (i.e. sub-national) levels.

Venture capitalists are companies whose business is investing in small companies with high growth potential. They are usually only interested in fairly substantial investments, from, say, £500,000 upwards.

If the company is already operating, the shares issued to business angels or venture capitalists will usually be new shares, taken from the difference between the issued capital and the authorized capital. The new investors will probably be paying substantially over the par value of the shares.

Both business angels and venture capitalists aim to make money by help-ing the company to expand and become successful and then selling their shares at a profit. Of course, many of their investments will not be very suc-cessful and a significant number may fail completely. They aim to offset these losses by very substantial gains in the most successful cases; often this may happen when the company has grown enough to be floated on a stock exchange, so that its shares become publicly traded.

GEARING

The relationship between loan capital and equity capital in a company is important. It is known as *gearing* or *leverage*. Shareholders are at a much greater risk of getting a poor return on their capital or even losing it com-pletely than are lenders, but, in compensation for this, they stand to make a greater profit than lenders if all goes well.

Suppose a company is started with a share capital of £100, owned by its two founders, and that it has a fixed term loan of £100,000, at an interest rate of 10 per cent. If, in its first year the company makes an operating profit of £10,000, the interest charges will consume all the profit and the shareholders will receive nothing. If the company's operating profit doubles, to £20,000, the lender will still receive £10,000 but, neglecting taxation and assuming that all the profit is distributed to the shareholders, the shareholders will receive £10,000, a very handsome return on an investment of £100. Furthermore, as the profits increase, the value of the company, and hence the value of the shares, increases. If the company is sold, the shareholders will get much more than their original £100 investment, but the lenders will still only be entitled to their original £100,000, plus interest. If, on the other hand, the company is unsuccessful and goes into liquidation, the lenders will be at the front of the queue of people to whom money is owed, whereas the share-holders will get nothing until everyone else has been paid in full.

Such high levels of gearing are undesirable both from the point of view of the shareholders, because so much of the company's income is committed to interest payments, and from the point of view of the lenders, because share-holders may encourage the company to trade recklessly in the knowledge that they have little to lose and a lot to gain. Most lenders will be reluctant to lend money if a company seems too highly geared.

FURTHER READING

The UK Department of Trade and Industry has a website:

www.businesslink.gov.uk

that includes financial and other advice on setting up a business and gives valuable guidance on producing a business plan.

The website of the National Business Angels Network (NBAN):

www.nban.co.uk

and the website of the European Business Angels Network (EBAN):

www.eban.org

both contain more information about business angels.

There are innumerable books on accounting and finance that will take the reader beyond what is covered in this book; most of them are, however, intended for budding accountants. A good treatment for non-specialists will be found in:

Peter Atrill and Eddie McLaney (2004) *Accounting and Finance for Non-Specialists*, 4th Edition. Pearson Education, Harlow.

This covers the material in this chapter and the next three.

6 Financial Accounting

After studying this chapter, you should understand the purpose of the three most important items in the annual report:

- *the balance sheet;*
- *the profit and loss account; and*
- *the cash flow statement.*

These are known as the financial statements and together they provide a picture of the overall financial health of the business. You should be able to interpret them in simple cases.

INTRODUCTION

The proprietors of limited liability companies are privileged, precisely because their liability is limited – they can lose no more than the money they invested in the company. In return for this privilege, the law requires that, every year, the company produces an annual report, which must be filed at Companies House. The annual report contains information about the company and its activities during the preceding year. In particular, it contains information about its financial health so that those who are considering dealing with the company can judge whether it is likely to meet its obligations. If the company is a public one, that is, if its shares are available for purchase by the public, through trading on a stock exchange, the stock exchange will impose additional *disclosure requirements*. In other words, it will require the company to make more information public. In recent years, a series of scandals has led to calls for greater openness and more extensive disclosure of companies' activities, which has, in turn, led to the inclusion of further statements and more extensive notes in companies' annual reports. Some are required by stock markets and some have simply become regarded as good practice. On the whole, but by no means universally, software companies set good examples in this regard.

THE BALANCE SHEET

The purpose of the balance sheet is to show what the company owns – its *assets* – and what it owes – its *liabilities*. It is a snapshot of the state of the company at a particular point in time, normally at the end of the last day of the company's financial year.

Balance sheet for a student

Perhaps the easiest way to get to understand the idea of a balance sheet is to look at the balance sheet not of a company but of an individual. We take an imaginary student called Jemimah Puddleduck and, as is usual, we show her present position side by side with the position a year ago, so that it is easy to make a comparison (see Table 6.1). Notice also the common accounting convention of putting a number in parentheses to indicate that it is negative, rather than using a negative sign as is normal in science or mathematics.

TABLE 6.1 *Balance sheet for a student*

Jemimah Puddleduck

Balance Sheet

As at 31 October 2004

	2004	2003
ASSET		
Cash in hand	25	40
Cash at bank	361	220
Pre-paid accommodation	300	200
Debts owed by friends	18	0
Computer	400	600
CD player	160	180
Total assets	1,264	1,240
LIABILITIES		
Credit card bill	174	64
Student loans	4,800	1,900
Total liabilities	4,974	1,964
NET WORTH	(3,710)	(724)

Jemimah's most obvious asset is money. She has, let us say, £25, in cash in her purse and another £361 in her bank account.

The next two items are less obvious. The accommodation item refers to the fact that Jemimah has paid a term's fees to the hall of residence in advance; since the balance sheet refers to the position on 31 October, some 60 per cent (6 weeks out of 10) of this accommodation has not been used. Depending on the regulations of the hall, if the accommodation is no longer required, the student may be able to get a refund on the unused period or sell it to another student; in other words, the student has paid for the right to live in hall for a further six weeks and this right can be converted into cash and is therefore an asset. In a similar way, the debt of £18 owed by friends can be turned into cash and is also therefore an asset.

The next two items are more complex because they represent capital items. Jemimah owns a computer, which cost £800 including the software when her parents bought it for her, two years ago. She owns a CD player, which she bought for £200 at the start of her 2003 year. These are examples of fixed assets, that is, assets that she will continue to own and to use for a fairly long period.

Standard accounting practice is to reduce the value of fixed assets each year to reflect the likely lifetime of each asset; the fall in the value of the asset from one year to the next is called the *depreciation*. Thus, Jemimah will probably keep her computer for four years before it becomes obsolete and she has to replace it with a new one. The simplest and commonest way of calculating the depreciation is to assume that it falls in value uniformly, that is, that it loses value at a rate of £200 per year. Hence after one year, it is worth £600, after two years £400, after three years £200, and at the end of the fourth year it no longer has any value. CD players typically have a longer life than computers. We have assumed that the CD player will have a life of 10 years, so that its value drops by £20 each year.

The figure given for 'other assets' covers the many personal items that everyone owns, including clothes, books, and CDs. We simply take an approximate figure for these, because the calculations involved in dealing with them precisely would be far more extensive than the value of the items justifies.

The valuation of assets can be a contentious issue. For the moment we shall simply accept the figures given in the balance sheet but we shall have much more to say on this topic when we come to look at a commercial balance sheet.

Jemimah's liabilities are more straightforward. She owes money on her credit card and she has a student loan. The credit card debt is an example of a short-term debt; she is expected to repay it fairly quickly, although she may incur other debts against it. The student loan is a long-term debt, which does not need to be repaid until she graduates and is earning a reasonable salary.

As its name suggests, a balance sheet must balance: the total assets and total liabilities should be equal. To achieve this we need to include a balancing item on one side or the other; it is often labelled 'excess of assets over liabilities' but in this case we have chosen to call it 'net worth' because it represents the amount of cash which Jemimah would have if all her assets were sold and all her debts paid off – in other words, how much, in financial terms, she is 'worth'. The net worth plus the liabilities together equal her total assets. In her case, as with many students, her net worth is negative.

Commercial balance sheets: Assets

Commercial balance sheets are prepared on precisely the same basis as we have just described but the assets and liabilities are grouped into various categories and a single figure is given for each category. There will be several 'notes' to the balance sheet describing the basis of the accounts and giving more detail about certain items; such items will cross-reference the notes. Table 6.2 is an example of such a balance sheet for an imaginary software services company.

Assets are classified as current assets and fixed assets. The essential diffeence between the two is that fixed assets contribute to the company's productive capacity and are held primarily for the purpose of creating wealth, while current assets are items which are bought and sold in the course of its day to day trading activities. The fixed assets are further subdivided into investments (e.g. shares in other companies), tangible assets (assets that have some physical existence) and intangible assets (assets such as copyright in software or ownership of brand names that have no physical existence).

In most cases, the difference between fixed assets and current assets is easily perceived. A new file server bought to support program development facilities in a software house or a machine tool used to produce satellite dishes are clearly examples of fixed assets; a stock of paper for the laser printer is equally clearly a current asset. It should be borne in mind, however, that the treatment of the same item may vary from organization to organization or even within the same organization. Thus, if a company buys a car to enable one of its salesmen to operate more effectively, this is a fixed asset but, if a car dealer buys a car in order to resell it as part of his business, this is a current asset. If the software house buys a computer on which it will implement special software before delivering the whole system to a client, the computer is a current asset, not a fixed one.

The rules of accounting state that current assets are shown on the balance sheet with a value that is the lower of what they cost and what it is expected they could be sold for. Suppose a company has a stock of 1,000 user manuals for a piece of software that it sells. The manuals sell at £10 each but cost £2 each to produce. Then they will appear on the balance sheet as worth £2,000, the cost price, rather than £10,000, the resale price. On the other hand, a stock of printer paper that cost £5,000 would only be saleable for a lower figure, say £2,000. It would therefore appear on the balance sheet at the resale price, because this is lower.

In contrast to current assets, fixed assets are not expected to be sold in normal trading operations and their resale value is irrelevant; what is needed is a measure of their value to the company. In practice, this is done by reducing their value each year in accordance with the company's depreciation policy. Much the commonest way of doing this is the so-called straight line method we described in connection with Jemimah's computer. We first decide how many years the asset will continue to be useful for. We then divide its initial cost by that number to get the annual depreciation. Each year, we reduce (or *write down*) the value of the asset by the amount of the annual depreciation until the value of the asset reaches zero. Suppose a company buys a large database server costing £100,000 and expects to use it for five years. Then the annual depreciation will be £20,000 (£100,000/5) and the values shown in the balance sheet will be £80,000 at the end of year 1, £60,000 at the end of year 2, £40,000 at the end of year 3, £20,000 at the end of year 4, and zero at the end of year 5. It is customary to depreciate all items of the same type over the same period and this will be stated in the notes to the accounts, which might include statements such as: 'It is the company's policy to write off all computer equipment over a period of three years and office furniture over a period of 10 years.'

Assets are generally valued on the basis of historic cost, that is, their original monetary cost. In times of high inflation, this can be seriously misleading. The value of certain types of fixed assets, in particular land and buildings, may increase rather than decrease. Some companies therefore arrange to have their property revalued from time to time and include this valuation in the balance sheet.

TABLE 6.2 *Balance sheet for a services company*

XYZ Software Ltd		
Balance Sheet		
As at 31 October 2004	2004	2003
	£'000	£'000
Fixed Assets		
Intangible assets	475	–
Tangible assets	960	770
Investments	50	82
Total fixed assets	1,485	852
Current assets		
Work in progress	550	621
Debtors	3,400	2,580
Cash in hand and at bank	2,491	1,770
Total current assets	6,441	4,971
Creditors: Amounts falling due within one year	(3,210)	(2,601)
Net current assets	3,231	2,370
Total assets less current liabilities	4,716	3,222
Creditors: Amounts falling due after one year		
Borrowings	(154)	(61)
Provisions for liabilities and charges	(7)	(16)
Net assets	4,555	3,145
Capital and reserves		
Called-up share capital	318	308
Share premium reserve	350	145
Profit and loss account	3,887	2,692
Shareholders' funds – equity	4,555	3,145

Tangible fixed assets have to be recorded in the company's fixed asset register and, from time to time, their presence will be physically checked. Each year, depreciation must be calculated and, if a fixed asset is sold for a sum higher than its depreciated value, the company must show the difference as income. Because of these complicated procedures, it is usual to treat all purchases of less than, say, £1,000 as expenses in the year in which they are incurred.

There are some items that are difficult to classify. Software is one example. Consider a payroll package. A company buys such a package because it will help it to carry out part of its day-to-day operations more efficiently. The package will be bought with the intention of using it for some time, at least 5 years and probably 10 or 15. Logically, the package should be treated in the same way as a piece of machinery. It should be treated as a fixed asset and the initial cost depreciated over its useful lifetime. The rules of accounting allow this to be done. But, because software is intangible, most companies treat the cost of buying it as current expenditure.

The treatment of research and development is a particular problem. Logically, resources spent on developing new products should be regarded as an investment that will produce a fixed asset, that is, something that will allow the company to operate more effectively. However, the results of research and development are always uncertain and often prove to be worth very little; to treat all the costs as investment would be misleading. In practice, most software companies in the UK treat expenditure on research and development as current expenditure rather than as investment, although the accounting rules allow for more flexible treatment. In the USA, there are strict rules regarding the capitalization of software that is developed for sale; these rules are based on a rather unrealistic model of the product life cycle.

Intangible fixed assets are the source of much discussion in the accounting profession. Software is generally regarded as an intangible asset, but it is more tangible than many items, brand names, for example, which are often shown as intangible assets. An item that frequently appears under intangible assets on the balance sheets of software product companies is goodwill. This might arise, for example, if XYZ Ltd purchased another company, PQR Ltd, that owned the rights in a profitable package. If, as is likely, the package was not shown as an asset on PQR's balance sheet, XYZ would probably have paid much more to buy PQR than the value of its net assets. The difference between the price paid for PQR and the value of its net assets represents XYZ's estimate of the value of the rights in that package (and, possibly, other things such as the value of PQR's name). This needs to be shown on XYZ's balance sheet. While it would be preferable for the value of the package to be shown explicitly, this is not normal practice and the whole of the difference between the purchase price and the value of PQR's net assets is normally shown under the heading of goodwill. It will then, of course, need to be depreciated over a fixed period. The notes to a company's accounts will normally itemize any acquisitions and give details of the goodwill arising from each one. When internet companies change hands, a similar situation occurs but, in this case, the intangible assets may be much more difficult to identify; they are certainly less tangible than the rights to a package.

Readers who are football fans may be interested to know that football clubs that are organized as public companies – Manchester United, for example –

include among their intangible assets the rights to the services of players whom they have bought.

Commercial balance sheets: Liabilities and owners' equity

The entry under 'Current liabilities: Amounts falling due within one year' refers to debts that the company has and is committed to repaying within one year. These will include trade creditors, that is, outstanding invoices that the company has received but has not yet paid, in just the same way that the 'debtors' item refers to invoices that the company has issued but which have not yet been paid. They will also include any bank overdraft, as opposed to a long-term loan.

The figure obtained by subtracting the current liabilities from the current assets, referred to as 'Net current assets' in Table 6.2, is also known as the working capital. It represents the amount of money invested in the day-to-day operations of the company, as opposed to its infrastructure.

'Creditors: Amounts falling due after one year' refers to long-term debts. These may be long-term borrowings or they may be liabilities, that is, sums that the company expects to have to pay at some time in the future.

When the total liabilities are subtracted from the total assets, we arrive at a figure called the 'Net assets'. These are balanced by items under the heading 'Capital and reserves'. There are a number of ways in which these may be shown. First, there is the item labelled 'Called-up share capital'. This is the amount raised from the par value of the shares that the company has issued. When a successful company decides to issue more shares, these are often sold at more than their par value. The extra is known as the share premium and the money raised from this is shown under the next heading, as the 'Share premium reserve'. In our example, the remainder is labelled as 'Profit and loss account', indicating that it results from the accumulated surplus on the profit and loss account over the life of the company.

The total under the heading of 'Capital and reserves' is often known by names such as shareholders' equity, owners' equity, or owners' claim. It notionally represents the value of the company to its shareholders.

THE PROFIT AND LOSS ACCOUNT

The *profit and loss account* shows how much money has been received and how much has been spent in a given period – usually the organization's financial year. In the case of non-profit-making organizations it is usually called an *income and expenditure* account. Table 6.3 shows such an account for our imaginary student. It does not include money borrowed or received from the sale of equity nor does it include expenditure on acquiring fixed assets.

It is important to observe that the excess of expenditure over income, that is, the amount that the student has overspent, is the same as the difference in her net worth between 2003 and 2004. This will usually be the case in simple situations where there has been no capital investment. In more complicated cases, particularly with commercial organizations, other items enter into the relationship.

Just as in the balance sheet, there is a certain arbitrariness about the way in which items have been aggregated. We could, for example, have lumped together 'Food' and 'Entertainment' under the heading 'Living expenses' or split 'Transport' into 'Road' and 'Rail'. We have chosen to show the income from the summer job net (i.e. the take-home pay) rather than show it gross (i.e. before deductions) with tax and national insurance on the expenditure side.

TABLE 6.3 *Income and expenditure account for a student*

Jemimah Puddleduck Income and Expenditure Account Year ended 31 October 2004	2004	2003
INCOME		
Contribution from parents	1,500	1,300
Income from summer job (net)	1,840	1,682
Total income	3,340	2,982
EXPENDITURE		
Course fees	1,050	1,025
Hall fees	2,100	1,980
Books	30	25
Clothes and personal items	179	120
Transport	134	112
Food	1,400	1,247
Entertainment	1,303	840
Depreciation	220	220
Total expenditure	6,416	5,569
EXCESS OF INCOME OVER EXPENDITURE	(3,076)	(2,587)

Some explanation of the depreciation item is required. The net figure at the bottom of the profit and loss account should reflect the extent to which the organization – or, in this case, the individual – is better or worse off at the end of the year than at the beginning. Clearly, a fall in the value of the assets tends to make it worse off. Depreciation, although it is not an expenditure in the sense that cash is paid out, reflects this decline and is therefore shown as an expenditure. The figure of £220 arises from the depreciation on the computer and the CD player.

Commercial profit and loss accounts

The example of a profit and loss (or income and expenditure) account that we saw in the last section is typical of the account that might be produced by a small club. A commercial profit and loss account looks very different, even though precisely the same ideas underlie it. Table 6.4 shows an example for a fictitious computer services company. Just as with the balance sheet, we see that items have been aggregated into very broad categories; the notes to the accounts will usually provide more detail. A package company, for example, might show in the notes how much of its income came from sales of packages, how much from training and consultancy, and how much from maintenance contracts.

TABLE 6.4 *Profit and loss account for a services company*

XYZ Software Ltd		
Profit and Loss Account	2004	2003
Year ending 31 October 2004	£'000	£'000
TURNOVER		
Continuing operations	14,311	11,001
Acquisitions	407	
Total turnover	14,718	11,001
Cost of sales	(11,604)	(8,699)
Gross profit	3,114	2,302
Other operating expenses	(1,177)	(805)
OPERATING PROFIT	1,937	1,497
Interest payable	(23)	(27)
Profit on ordinary activities before taxation	1,914	1,470
Tax on profit on ordinary activities	719	480
Retained profit for the year	1,195	990

A number of points about this statement need to be explained. First, the turnover for a company acquired during the year is shown separately from the turnover from continuing operations, that is, operations that were carried on in 2003 and 2004. This is to facilitate the comparison between the two years. In the same way, if part of XYZ Ltd had been disposed of in 2003, its turnover would have been shown under the heading 'discontinued operations'.

A second point is the distinction between 'cost of sales' and 'other operating expenses'. This distinction is an uncertain one and some companies do not show the items separately. However, for a package software company, there is a real difference between, on the one hand, expenditure on selling, printing documentation, installing software, and so on, all of which are the costs of sales, and expenditure on the development of new versions of existing packages or on new products, which would come under the heading of other operational expenses.

The bottom line shows the retained profit, that is, the profit not paid out in tax or dividends to shareholders; this is added to the retained profit in the previous year's balance sheet to give the value of the retained profit that is shown in the new balance sheet.

The profit and loss account itself gives very little information about where the company's revenue during the year has come from or how it has spent its money. Such information is normally given in the notes to the accounts. The Notes to the Accounts in the 2003 Annual Report and Accounts of LogicaCMG plc, for example, gives a breakdown of turnover by geographic area – UK, Benelux (Belgium, Holland, Luxemburg), Germany, France, the rest of Europe, and the rest of the world. It shows numbers of staff and expenditure on wages and salaries, on social security costs, and pension costs and other costs are also broken down into a number of categories. Package companies will often also show a breakdown of revenue into licence fees, maintenance charges, and consultancy fees – see, for example, the 1998 Accounts of London Bridge Software Holdings plc. On the whole, software companies are fairly open in revealing information in the notes to their accounts, but the level of detail provided in other sectors varies enormously from company to company.

THE CASH FLOW STATEMENT

As we have already pointed out, the income and expenditure account does not show expenditure on capital items, only their depreciation; capital expenditure affects the balance sheet but the balance sheet does not give sufficient information to deduce how much this expenditure amounts to and how it was funded. The link that ties the balance sheet and the profit and loss account to the capital expenditure is the cash flow statement. A moment's examination of our student's financial statements will reveal that, because there is no cash flow statement, there is no explanation of where the money to purchase her CD player came from.

Cash is defined as 'cash at bank and in hand and cash equivalents less bank overdrafts and other borrowings repayable within one year of the accounting date'. In Jemimah's case, this means £361 (the money in her bank account) plus £25 (the notes and coins in her possession) less £174 (her credit card debt), that is, £212. The previous year, the figure was £(220 + 40 − 64) = £196. One function of the cash flow statement is to explain this difference of £16.

The most obvious source of a change in the amount of cash Jemimah holds is her profit and loss account. She appears to have spent £3,076 more than she received. This is her major cash outflow. In fact, not all of this sum is a cash outflow. The item of £220 for depreciation corresponds to a reduction in the value of her capital assets, but not to any outflow of cash. To take this into account, we add the depreciation back in as a cash inflow. The only other cash outflow is the £18 that she has lent to a friend. This is not expenditure, because it is repayable. Nevertheless, it represents cash that has been paid out. If she had bought her CD player during the year, its cost would also appear as a cash outflow.

We see from her balance sheet that Jemimah's student loan increased by

£2,900 from 2003 to 2004. This means that she received £2,900 in cash from that source. While it is an inflow of cash, it is not income, because it will have to be repaid; hence it does not appear as income on the income and expenditure account.

These changes are summarized in Table 6.5, which shows Jemimah's cash flow statement.

TABLE 6.5 *Cash flow statement for a student*

Jemimah Puddleduck Cash flow statement Year ended 31 October 2004	2004	2003
Cash inflow		
Addition to student loan	2,900	1,900
Add back depreciation	220	220
Total cash inflow	3,120	2,120
Cash outflow		
From income and expenditure account	3,076	2,587
Loans made to friends	18	0
Total cash outflow	3,104	2,587
Increase/(Decrease) in cash over the year	16	(467)

Jemimah Puddleduck's cash flow statement tells us very little more than we could deduce from her other financial statements. In the case of a company, however, the cash flow statement has much more to tell us, because there are many more sources of cash flows.

FIGURE 6.1 *Sources and destinations of cash flows*

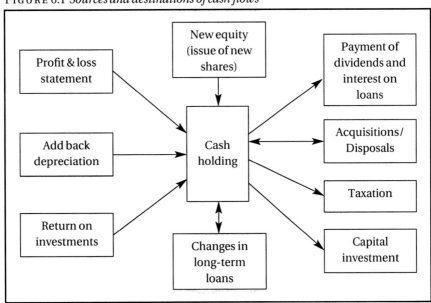

Figure 6.1 shows the cash flows that are captured in the cash flow statement of a typical company. The arrows show the normal direction of the flow in a profitable company, but it is always possible for the flows to be in the opposite direction. Table 6.6 shows the cash flow statement for our example company.

TABLE 6.6 *Cash flow statement for a software company*

XYZ Software Ltd		
Cash Flow Statement	**2004**	**2003**
Year ending 31 October 2004	**£'000**	**£'000**
Net cash inflow from operating activities	2,105	1,620
Returns on investments and servicing of finance	(23)	(27)
Capital expenditure and financial investment	(320)	(265)
Taxation	(719)	(480)
Acquisitions and disposals	(380)	
Equity dividends paid		
Cash outflow before financing	(1,342)	(772)
Net cash inflow before financing	763	848
Financing		
Issue of share capital	215	100
Repayment of long termlong-term loan	(50)	
Net cash inflow from financing	165	100
Increase in cash in the year	928	948

The first source of cash is the operating profit before tax generated during the year. This needs to be adjusted for certain items which may appear in the profit and loss account but do not involve the movement of money in or out of the company. The most obvious of these is depreciation. This was entered in the profit and loss account to reflect the extent to which the life of the fixed assets was consumed during the year; in no way did it reflect the movement of money out of the company and so it must be added to the profit.

Following the adjusted figure for the operating profit, there are a number of items that may lead to cash flowing out of the company for reasons that are nothing directly to do with its operations. Taxation, interest payable and dividends paid are obvious examples. Capital investment in equipment or premises is another reason for which cash may flow out of the company, as is the purchase of another company. In some circumstances, for example, the disposal of a subsidiary company, these items can give rise to an inflow of cash. When all these items are added together and subtracted from the operating profit, we arrive at a total figure for the inflow or outflow of cash into or out of the company before taking into account any changes in the financing of the company. The final section of the cash flow statement shows the effect on the cash position of changes in the financing of the company. The company has issued new shares and raised £215,000 through this; it has also paid off £50,000 of long-term debt. Both of these, of course, affect its cash position and the bottom line of the cash flow statement reflects this; it gives the overall change in the company's cash position over the year.

The alert reader will recall that XYZ's balance sheet shows that, despite the fact that a loan of £50,000 has been paid off, the long-term debt has increased from £61,000 to £154,000 and that there is nothing in the cash flow statement to account for this. It almost certainly arises from the acquisition of another company. The statement shows that £380,000 was spent on acquisitions; the likelihood is that the company bought substantial debts, which were taken over by XYZ as part of the deal. This would be explained in the notes to the accounts.

At this point we should make clear that the financial statements for XYZ Software Ltd show a vigorous company growing very rapidly in an expanding market; they are typical of many IT services companies in the 1990s, but not typical of many other industries.

THE OVERALL PICTURE

The balance sheet, the profit and loss account, and the cash flow statement can none of them be understood or interpreted in isolation. Their relationship to each other needs to be understood and they need to be looked at together when assessing the financial state of a company.

The balance sheet shows a snapshot of the financial position of a company at the end of an accounting period (usually the company's financial year), while the profit and loss account and the cash flow statement describe what has happened during the accounting period and thus explain the

FIGURE 6.2 *The relationship between the three financial statements*

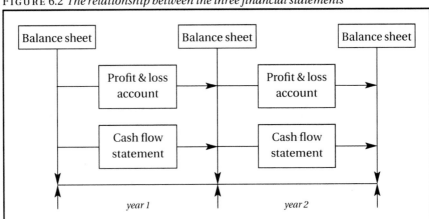

relationship between successive balance sheets. This is illustrated in Figure 6.2. The profit and loss account explains the relationship between the owners' equity in the two balance sheets, while the cash flow statement explains the relationship between the cash item shown in the two balance sheets. This is illustrated in Figure 6.3.

FIGURE 6.3 *How the cash flow statement and the profit and loss account affect the items in the balance sheet*

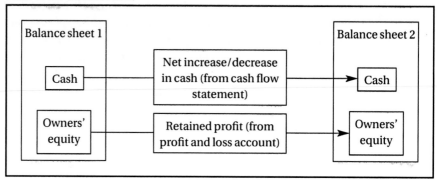

EXAMINATION QUESTIONS

The examination questions below relate to the material covered in this chapter.

APRIL 2000 QUESTION 4

Explain the meaning of the terms fixed assets and current assets, illustrating your explanation with suitable examples.

[10 marks]

Fixed assets are items owned by a company that contribute to its productive capacity and are expected to be retained over a long period. Examples include:

- equipment such as computers or machine tools used in the company's operations;
- premises used by the company or let on a long-term basis;
- rights to computer software or brand names.

Current assets are items that are bought or sold in the course of the company's normal day to day trading operations. Examples include:

- consumables, such as printer paper,
- items bought from suppliers with a view to resale;
- items manufactured for sale.

Describe how the two types of asset are valued for balance sheet purposes, using as an example the following assets owned by a company that writes and sells software packages:

- **a stock of 500 user manuals for version 1 of a package, version 2 of which is to appear shortly. The company paid £5,000 to have 1,000 manuals printed and has been selling them at £25 per copy;**
- **a file server costing £15,000 that is used by the software development teams.**

[15 marks]

Current assets are valued at the lower of cost and resale value. The user manuals have been produced specifically to be sold to customers – they come under the heading of items bought from suppliers with a view to resale – and should therefore be treated as current assets. The cost price of the stock is £5 × 500 = £2,500, while its resale value would appear to be £25 × 500 = £12,500. At first sight, therefore, the stock should be valued at the lower of these two figures, that is, £2500. However, given that a new version of the package is about to appear and will, presumably, require a new edition of the user manual, it may be that most of the stock will be unsaleable. If we assume that only 50 of the remaining manuals can be sold, their resale value is £25 × 50 = £1,250. This is lower than the cost price and should therefore be taken as the value of the stock.

Fixed assets are valued by assuming that their value declines from the initial purchase price to zero over their useful life. The file server that is to be used by the software development team clearly contributes to the productive capacity of the company and is therefore to be considered as a fixed asset. If we assume that its useful life will be three years, its value will fall by £15,000/3 = £5,000 per year. The value will therefore be £10,000 at the end of the first year, £5,000 at the end of the second year, and zero at the end of the third year.

APRIL 2001 QUESTION 4(b)

Your company is about to spend £25,000 on a powerful database server that is expected to be in use for the next five years. Explain the different ways in which it will affect the company accounts over that period.

[10 marks]

The purchase will affect the balance sheet, the profit and loss account and the cash flow statement.

The effect on the balance sheet will be to increase the value of the fixed assets by £20,000 at the end of the first year, £15,000 at the end of the second, £10,000 at the end of the third, and £5,000 at the end of the fourth.

The effect on the profit and loss account will be to increase the depreciation item under expenditure by £5,000 at the end of each year from the first to the fifth.

The effect on the cash flow account will be to increase the figure reported under the capital investment heading by £25,000 in the first year and to increase the figure added back under the heading of depreciation by £5,000 in years 1 to 5.

APRIL 2002 QUESTION 4

a) Explain the meaning of the terms fixed assets and current assets, illustrating your explanation with suitable examples.

[8 marks]

b) Describe how the two types of asset are valued for balance sheet purposes, using as an example the following assets owned by a company that writes and sells software packages:
  i) a stock of 1000 CD-ROMs containing version 1 of a package, version 2 of which is to appear shortly. The company paid £1,000 to have the CD-ROMs prepared and has been selling them at £100 per copy;
  ii) an uninterruptible power supply costing £15,000 for the computer room housing the main servers.

[17 marks]

OCTOBER 2003 QUESTION 2(b)

XYZ plc is a large import/export organization. It owns computer and communications equipment that cost some £45,000 in total when it was bought. The equipment was bought from ABC plc; some of it was held in stock at ABC and some of it was specially ordered by ABC.

Compare and contrast the way that the equipment would be treated in the accounts of the two companies.

[15 marks]

FURTHER READING

To get a feeling for company accounts and for the way the software industry works, it is worth reading the annual reports and accounts of software companies. Many of them are available directly from the companies' websites. As a starting point we suggest looking at LogicaCMG, the Sage Group, Admiral and IPL, all of which are readily available on the Web.

The book by Atrill and McLaney recommended at the end of Chapter 5 also covers the material in this chapter.

7 Management Accounting

After reading this chapter, you should, in simple cases:

- *be able to calculate the cost of labour;*
- *understand the concept of overheads and the different ways in which they may be distributed;*
- *be able to determine how much it costs to produce a particular product or provide a specific service;*
- *understand how to produce a budget and a cash flow forecast, and how to monitor them.*

INTRODUCTION

In the last chapter, we were concerned about the financial state of the company as a whole and about the way in which this has to be presented to satisfy the requirements of the law and of stock exchanges. Such information is intended primarily for potential investors and trading partners. It is not very useful in the day-to-day running of the company. Furthermore, it is concerned with the past, with what has already happened. Managers need to know what is likely to happen in the future, while recognizing, of course, that knowledge about the past is likely to be much more accurate than predictions of the future.

COST OF LABOUR

Suppose you decide to set up a company that makes computers. The company buys items like processor boards, memory chips, hard disks, and so on. It then assembles the machines, installs and configures the software, and delivers the computer to the customer. There is, in principle, no problem in working out the cost of the components that go into the computers – although it is only too easy to forget to add in the cost of the odd small component. What is more difficult is working out the cost of labour.

The cost of employing someone is more than just the cost of their salary. In most countries, employers are required to pay a tax for every employee. This tax usually goes by a name such as *employers' national insurance contribution* (in the UK) or *social security contribution*; it is proportional to the employee's salary. In some countries, this contribution may be as large as 60 per cent of salary, while in others it is very much smaller. In the UK the rules for calculating the national insurance contribution are complicated and change frequently, but for the purposes of this chapter we shall take it as simply 10 per cent of salary.

There may be other costs associated with an employee, depending on the law and the practices of the individual country. In the UK, it is common for larger companies to operate a pension scheme of their own, to which the company makes a contribution on behalf of each employee. The company may pay for medical insurance for its employees. Senior employees may be provided with a car or other benefits. The total cost of employing a person, that is, the salary plus employers' social security contributions plus any other costs associated directly with the employee, is sometimes known as the employee's *payroll cost* or *direct cost*. Consider a technician who is employed to assemble the computers and suppose that he is paid an annual salary of £20,000. His payroll costs are £22,000.

To calculate the cost of the time the technician spends assembling a computer, the annual payroll cost is not very helpful. What we need to know is the cost per hour. This is not so simple to calculate as might be expected. First, we need to calculate how many days we can expect the technician to work. There are 52 weeks in the year. Assuming the company works a five-day week, there will be 260 week days. However, the company will be closed for public holidays and the technician will not be working. The number of public holidays varies from country to country and even within a country. In England and Wales there are eight public holidays a year; there are also eight in Scotland but they are different; in Northern Ireland there are 10. There are 10 public holidays in the USA and in Pakistan, 11 public holidays in Singapore, and 16 in Sri Lanka and Mauritius.

In addition to public holidays, employees are generally entitled to a certain amount of paid leave. Within the EU, most employees are, by law, entitled to 20 days of paid annual leave in addition to public holidays. (This is generous by international standards. Indeed, in many countries there is no requirement to grant paid annual leave.)

In addition to their annual leave, employees may miss some working days because of sickness. While we cannot predict accurately how much time will be lost in this way, it is usual to guess at a reasonable average of, say, five days per employee. Finally, it may well be that there are some days in the year when, because of scheduling difficulties, there will be no revenue-earning

TABLE 7.1 *Calculation of the number of revenue-earning hours in a year*

Total number of weekdays (1)	260
Public holidays (2)	10
Annual leave (3)	20
Sick leave (4)	5
Unproductive time (5)	10
Total non-revenue-earning time (2) + (3) + (4) + (5) = (6)	45
Total number of revenue earning days (1) − (5) = (7)	215
Total number of hours available (7) × 7	1505

work available for the employee. Table 7.1 shows how all these factors can be taken into account to obtain a figure for the number of revenue-earning working hours can be expected from an employee over the period of one year.

The direct cost of the technician is £22,000 per year so that the direct cost of an hour of their time is £22000/1505 = £14.62.

OVERHEADS

On the basis of the calculations above, we might reason as follows. If the components of a computer cost £200 and it takes 10 hours of a technician's time to assemble the computer, install the software and configure it, then the cost of constructing the finished product is £200 + 10 × £14.62 = £346.20.

Unfortunately, there are many costs that we have ignored. Even if our technician works as a sole trader, with no assistance, there will be other costs he has to pay.

Costs that cannot be directly associated with a particular product are known as overheads. Because they are costs that ultimately the business has to pay, they have to be added to the direct costs of the products in one way or another. In a large business, there are many ways in which overheads can be spread over the different activities the business performs; there is no single 'right' way of doing this.

Consider a company that is in the business of assembling computers and selling them on to customers. The owner runs the company and it employs three technicians and a part-time secretary. It makes three models of computer, the Basic, the Advanced, and the Professional. It owns a van that it uses for delivering computers to customers. Table 7.2 shows the cost of the components for each model, the number of hours of technician time to build one, and the expected sales of that model over the next year.

TABLE 7.2 *Direct costs and expected sales for the different computer models*

Model	Cost of components (£)	Technician time (hours	Expected sales
Basic	£200	10 hours	200
Advanced	£300	12 hours	100
Professional	£400	15 hours	50

In the next section we show how this scenario might lead to annual overheads of £63,500, which the company has to recover from its sales. There are at least three commonly used ways that we might spread these overheads over the computers sold.

The simplest way is to allocate the same overhead to each computer sold, regardless of the cost of the components or the amount of labour involved.

Since we expect to sell 350 units, this means £181.43 per computer. This means that the Basic model would cost

£181.43 + £200 + 10 × £14.62 = £527.63

The Advanced model would cost

£181.43 + £300 + 12 × £14.62 = £651.83

and the Professional model would cost

£181.43 + £400 + 15 × £14.62 = £802.23

The second way of allocating the overhead is to make it proportional to the number of hours of labour involved. This means adding an overhead component to the cost of an hour of a technician's time. Since we have three technicians, each supplying 1,505 hours of productive labour per year, we need to add

£63500/(3 × 1505) = £14.06

to the cost of an hour's labour, making it up to £14.62 + £14.06 = £28.68. Now the cost of the three models comes out at:

£200 + 10 × £28.68 = £486.80 (Basic)
£300 + 12 × £28.68 = £644.16 (Advanced)
£400 + 15 × £28.68 = £830.20 (Professional)

Finally, we can distribute the overhead in proportion to the total cost, that is, taking into account the cost of components as well as the cost of labour. This means that we take the direct cost (components and labour) and add on a fixed percentage. To calculate this percentage we divide the total overhead by the total direct cost of all the units we expect to sell, that is, 63500/(200 × 346.20 + 100 × 475.44 + 50 × 619.30) = 0.43. This means the cost of the Basic model is £346.20 × 1.43 = £495.06, of the Advanced model, £679.88 and of the Professional model, £885.60.

Table 7.3 summarizes the cost (to the nearest pound) of the three different models according to the three different ways of distributing the overheads.

TABLE 7.3 *Effects of different overhead calculations*

	Fixed overhead	Overhead proportional to labour content	Overhead proportional to total direct cost
Basic	528	487	495
Advanced	652	644	680
Professional	802	830	886

The costs calculated in this way can form the basis for pricing the computers. Certainly, computers should not normally be sold at prices that are lower than the costs. More commonly, the prices will be set on the basis of 'what the market will bear', that is, how much customers will be willing to pay, and this depends very much on the competition. The cost calculations will, however, show us where our costs lie and how to go about reducing them so that we can sell our products more cheaply. It is essential that we ensure that the overheads are covered.

BUDGETING

A budget is a financial plan showing the expected income and expenditure for an organization over a specific period, typically one year.

As a simple example, we consider the company that assembles and sells computers. Table 7.4 shows an estimate of the company's costs and its income over a year of operations.

TABLE 7.4 *An example budget*

Overhead Expenditure	
Owner's payroll costs	42,000
Secretary's payroll costs (part time)	8,000
Costs of van (including depreciation)	3,500
Internet connection, telephone, postage, etc.	1,000
Advertising	2,000
Premises (heating and lighting, rent, rates, etc.)	4,500
Professional fees	1,000
Insurance	500
Total overheads	63,500
Operating costs	
Technicians' payroll costs	66,000
Bought-in components	90,000
Total manufacturing costs	156,000
Total costs	219,500
Sales income	
Basic model (200 @ £595)	119,000
Advanced model (100 @ £795)	79,500
Professional model (50 @ £895)	44,750
Total sales	243,250
Profit	24,750

Most of the entries for overhead expenditure are obvious enough, but two items may require some explanation. We have said that the company is run by its owner. For many reasons, to do particularly with taxation and social security, owners should treat themselves as employees and pay themselves a salary, rather than attempt to live on the company's profits. This accounts for the item labelled 'Owner's payroll costs'. Unless the owner is an experienced accountant, the services of an accountant will be necessary to help prepare the annual accounts and possibly to give advice from time to time. The advice of a lawyer may also be necessary from time to time. These items are covered under the heading 'Professional fees'. Finally, employers are legally required to carry insurance to cover any claim against them for injuries suffered by employees during the course of their employment; other insurance, against theft from the company's premises for example, may also be necessary. This explains the heading 'Insurance'.

The total figure of £63,500 for overheads is the figure that we used in the previous section when calculating the costs of the different models of computers. This figure corresponds to what are sometimes called 'fixed costs', that is, costs that the company incurs even if it doesn't sell a single computer. The cost of components, in contrast, is a variable cost and will increase if we sell more computers than we expect, or decrease if we sell fewer. The cost of the technicians can also be adjusted to match the sales volumes, though less easily, by recruiting another technician or making a technician redundant.

The sales income is based on the company's best estimate of how many computers it can sell and at what price. We note that the prices are not directly related to the costs (by whatever method of calculation).

Once a budget has been agreed, it should be used to monitor the company's financial progress. The first step is to break it down to show monthly income and expenditure – a budget broken down in this way is sometimes called a *profiled budget*. At the end of each month, the management then compares what has actually happened during the month with what was planned in the budget. Where there are exceptions, that is cases where income or expenditure differ significantly from what was planned, the management will investigate the reasons for the exceptions and decide what action, if any, to take. If, for example, sales income is 30 per cent lower than predicted, managers might decide to mount a further advertising campaign or they might decide to cut costs by reducing staff. The point is that they will be made aware of the problem as soon as it appears and can take appropriate action quickly.

CASH FLOW FORECAST

A company may be very profitable but unable to pay its bills. For that reason, it may be forced into receivership. This apparent paradox typically arises because bills have to be met, in particular staff have to be paid, before the income they generate is received. In order to avoid this difficulty businesses need to prepare cash flow forecasts, that is, estimates of the amount of money that will flow into and out of the company each month.

Table 7.5 shows a cash flow forecast for our example company's operations. In order to keep the overall picture clear, we have only shown a six-month forecast. In practice, companies normally try to forecast twelve months ahead. We have also made the rather unrealistic assumption that the company is launching into its operations at full stretch from day 1. Finally, because sales and energy costs are both seasonal, we have assumed that the company is starting operations on 1 January.

The figures in each cell show the amount of cash entering or leaving the company during that month, under the heading given at the left-hand end of each row. Thus the figure of £500 given in the 'January' column and the 'Insurance' row means that an insurance premium of £500 will be paid sometime in January. The figure of £7,000 in the 'March' column and the 'Income from trade sales' row means that £7,000 will enter the company's bank account in March as a result of trade customers paying invoices.

The timing of the payments is important and it depends on commercial practice. Thus rents are normally paid quarterly, in advance. Hence the rent payment will be made at the beginning of January and the beginning of April. Components will probably be bought against credit accounts with one or more suppliers. Under such arrangements, invoices for components delivered in one month will be issued at the end of that month and customers will be expected to pay the invoice within 28 days of its being issued. Similar arrangements will probably apply to energy costs but these will reduce as we move from the cold winter months into the warmer season.

TABLE 7.5 *A six-month cash flow prediction*

Month	Jan	Feb	March	April	May	June
Cash outflow						
Rent and property taxes	500			500		
Energy costs		400	400	300	200	200
Payroll costs	9,666	9,666	9,666	9,666	9,666	9,666
Communications		83	83	83	83	83
Insurance	500					
Components		4,000	7,000	10,000	10,000	10,000
Advertising		500		250		500
Road tax and insurance on van	700					
Professional fees			300			
Van operating costs	100	100	100	100	100	100
Monthly cash outflow	11,466	15,349	17,549	20,899	20,049	20,549
Cash inflow						
Income from retail sales	5,000	5,000	5,000	5,000	5,000	5,000
Income from trade sales		5,000	7,000	10,000	15,000	18,000
Monthly cash inflow	5,000	10,000	12,000	15,000	20,000	23,000
Net monthly cash flow	(6,466)	(5,349)	(5,549)	(5,899)	(49)	2,451
Cumulative cash flow	(6,466)	(11,815)	(17,364)	(23,263)	(23,312)	(22,861)

We have assumed that retail sales, that is sales to individuals, are paid for immediately and that these run at a steady level of £5,000 per month throughout the period. Trade sales, that is sales to businesses, are typically paid for in the month following delivery. We expect these sales to increase steadily during the period. The total cash received for the six-month period is estimated to be £85,000. Since trade sales made in month 6 will not appear in this figure, it looks as though the sales for the period are estimated to be around £105,000. The budget (Table 7.4) is based on total sales of £243,250, leaving £138,250 to be earned in the second six months. This is not unreasonable; demand both from consumers and from businesses is traditionally at its highest in September, October and November.

Assuming that the estimates are realistic, this forecast shows that, at no time during the period, will the cash received come close to balancing the cash paid out. At the worst point, at the end of month 5, the cash paid out will be £23,312 more than the cash received. This has nothing to do with the company's profitability; it could well be that the company is on track to meet the budget in Table 7.4 and make a respectable profit. Nevertheless, the company will need to have at least £23,312 available in cash if it is to keep operating through this period. Prudence suggests that it should plan on requiring £30,000 to allow for things going wrong.

The amount of cash required to allow the company to continue to operate over a period is known as its cash requirement. It is also often referred to as working capital, although, as we saw in 'The Balance Sheet' in Chapter 6, this term is more correctly used to refer to the difference between current assets and current liabilities. The two concepts are related but they are not identical. The traditional way of funding a company's cash requirement is through a bank overdraft, but banks are not always eager to lend to small companies and loans from other sources may be necessary.

An initial cash flow forecast is an essential part of a business plan but a well-run company will maintain a rolling 12-month cash flow forecast. That is, each month it will produce a new cash flow forecast for the next 12 months, the first 11 months of which will be an updated version of the figures in the previous month's forecast. Such forecasts will provide early warning of any prospective cash shortage and banks will generally respond well to a request for an increase in overdraft facilities that is made well in advance and based on detailed cash flow predictions.

At first sight, cash flow forecasts and budgets seem very much the same thing. It is important to understand the difference. Cash flow forecasts deal with the flow of cash or its equivalents in and out of the company. Budgets deal with income and expenditure. If our company delivers computers worth £100,000 to a large customer today and sends it an invoice, this will immediately appear as income when we are monitoring the budget. However, it may be three or for months before the invoice is paid and the corresponding sum appears as cash. The difference can be crucial.

EXAMINATION QUESTIONS

The examination questions below relate to the material covered in this chapter.

April 2003 question 3

a) Explain what is meant by the terms *working capital* and *cash flow*.

[5 marks]

Strictly speaking, working capital is the difference between current assets and current liabilities. It is often used loosely, particularly by those who are not trained accountants, to mean the amount of cash required to finance the operations of a business.

Cash flow is commonly used to refer to a period and it means the difference between the cash (or cash equivalents) received during the period and the cash expended during the period.

b) Three people who recently completed the BCS Diploma successfully have established a small company to set up websites for third parties and, if required, to host the website on a computer in their office.

They have already won one significant contract that will provide them with about three months' work and they have a number of other promising sales leads.

  i) Making reasonable assumptions, which should be stated, about the costs and revenues involved, produce a cash flow forecast for the first six months of operation.

[15 marks]

  ii) Explain how you would use this forecast to estimate the amount of working capital required.

[5 marks]

This question is asking candidates to reproduce the example in 'Budgeting' above, with the assumptions about costs and sales modified to fit the new scenario.

October 2003 question 2(a)

a) Employees of Syniad Software plc work a five day week. They are entitled to 20 days holiday a year in addition to public holidays. On average, each employee loses 10 working days per year through sickness. Syniad aims to allow each employee 15 days per year for training. Experience shows that employees spend an average of five days a year unproductively, as a result of scheduling problems. In accordance with government regulations, employers must pay social security contributions equal to 6 per cent of salary.

> **Calculate the average direct cost of one day's work from an employee earning £20,000 per year. State explicitly any assumptions you make.**
>
> [10 marks]
>
> The payroll costs of an employee earning £20,000 per year will be £20,000 + 0.06 × £20,000 = £21,200. The number of revenue earning days per year is 260 less 10 days (public holidays) less 10 days (sickness) less 15 days (training) less five days (unproductive), giving 220. Hence the cost of one day's work is £21200/220 = £96.36.

FURTHER READING

The book by Atrill and McLaney recommended at the end of Chapter 5 also covers the material in this chapter.

8 Investment Appraisal

After reading the chapter, you should:

- *understand what is meant by the* time value of money;
- *be able to carry out a discounted cash flow analysis to assess the viability of a proposed investment proposal;*
- *be able to interpret a discounted cash flow analysis in commercial terms.*

INTRODUCTION

Successful companies are always looking at ways in which they can change and develop. The senior management will be faced with a number of different proposals, ranging perhaps from the development of a new product to establishing a company presence in a new part of the world. The company will only have a limited amount of money of its own available and lenders and investors will only be prepared to offer limited amounts. The management is therefore faced with the need to decide which of the proposals to support.

There is no single way of assessing and comparing the different proposals; factors that must be taken into consideration include, for example:

- the extent to which the proposals are consistent with the company's long-term plans;
- the risk attached to the proposals;
- the availability of the necessary resources even if the money is available.

One important criterion, however, is the financial one: which of the proposals will give the best return on the investment? The usual way of determining this is to use the method known as discounted cash flow (DCF) and this is what we describe in this chapter.

It is important to realize that DCF is a tool that is used for many different purposes, for example:

- by investors on the stock market to assess whether the share price of a company reflects accurately its financial prospects;
- to assess whether it is better to purchase capital equipment or to lease it;
- to decide which of several possible projects is the most financially appealing;
- to decide whether a proposed capital project will be worthwhile.

In this chapter we concentrate on the third and fourth bullets in this list.

THE TIME VALUE OF MONEY

Advertisements for cars often make offers like the following:

> New Wolsey Hornet
>
> £8995 or
>
> only £500 down and £400 per month for 24 months

Suppose that you have £8,995 available so that you could pay cash if you decided to. Would you be better off at the end of three years paying cash at the beginning or taking the easy payment terms? We show how to answer this question a little later. For the moment, we consider a simpler situation.

Suppose that you have £100. You can choose to deposit it with a bank or some other savings organization. If the rate of interest is 3 per cent, then in a year's time you will have £103. In other words, the promise of £103 in a year's time is worth the same as £100 now. This simple example illustrates what is known as the *time value of money*. It forms the basis of discounted cash flow analysis.

In general, if the interest rate is r (expressed as a fraction such as 0.03, not a percentage), then the present value of a sum of money X due in t years time is:

$$\frac{X}{(1 + r)^t}$$

The quantity $1 \div (1 + r)^t$ is known as the *discount factor*. Table 8.1 shows the discount factors for periods up to five years for a range of interest rates.

TABLE 8.1 *Discount factors for periods up to five years*

Interest Rate (%)	1	2	3	4	5
3	0.9709	0.9426	0.9151	0.8885	0.8626
4	0.9615	0.9246	0.8890	0.8548	0.8219
5	0.9524	0.9070	0.8638	0.8227	0.7835
6	0.9434	0.8900	0.8396	0.7921	0.7473
7	0.9346	0.8734	0.8163	0.7629	0.7130
8	0.9259	0.8573	0.7938	0.7350	0.6806
9	0.9174	0.8417	0.7722	0.7084	0.6499
10	0.9091	0.8264	0.7513	0.6830	0.6209
15	0.8696	0.7561	0.6575	0.5718	0.4972
20	0.8333	0.6944	0.5787	0.4823	0.4019

To use Table 8.1, we look for the cell in the row corresponding to the discount (interest) rate and the column corresponding to the time period. The value in this cell gives the discount factor. Thus the discount factor for a discount rate of 8 per cent over a period of four years is 0.7350. This means that, if the discount rate is 8 per cent, the present value of a sum of £1,000 payable in four years time is £1000 × 0.7350 = £735.

We are now in a position to tackle the question of buying the car. The easy terms on offer mean we pay £500 now, £400 at the end of the first month, another £400 at the end of the second month, and so on until the end of the 24th month. Using the idea of discount factors, we can calculate the present value of each of those monthly payments. If we add the present value of all those payments to the £500 that we have to pay immediately, we shall obtain the present value of the total of the payments we have to make. If this is more than £8,995, we shall be better off buying the car outright immediately.

The discount rate that we need to use in doing our calculations is the rate of interest that we would receive on our £8,995 if we left it in our savings account. At the time of writing, this is around 3 per cent per year in the UK. We, however, need the equivalent monthly rate and this is 0.2466 per cent per month.[1] With this discount rate, the discount factors at the end of the months 1 to 3 are 0.9975, 0.9951, and 0.9926. The present values of the first three £400 payments are thus £400 × 0.9975 = £399.02, £400 × 0.9951 = £398.03, and £400 × 0.9926 = £397.05. The necessary calculations are tedious but, fortunately, spreadsheets such as Excel have a built in function for calculating the net present value of a series of payments at a given discount rate. The result of applying this function (NPV) to a sequence of 24 payments of £400 with a discount rate of 0.2466 per cent is a net present value of £9,310.30. To this we must add the £500 down payment. This shows that the NPV of the payments on easy terms is £9,810.30. Clearly we shall be much better off by buying the car outright for £8,995 if we have the money available.

APPLYING DCF TO A SIMPLE INVESTMENT PROJECT

The essence of investment is that money is spent now so as to produce benefits in the future; assuming those benefits can be quantified in monetary terms, we need to ask what is their present value. To do this, we calculate the net cash flows that the project will generate over each year of its life and convert these to a present day value. Then we add these up to get the NPV of the project as a whole.

As an example of simple DCF analysis, consider a small computer maintenance company. The company has one van that it uses for transporting computers that cannot be repaired on site to and from its workshop. When things are busy, the one van is not enough and the company often has to rent a second van. It is considering whether it is worthwhile to buy a second van.

A new van will cost £10,000. There will be annual costs of £500 for insurance and £150 for road tax. The cost of maintenance is estimated to be £200 in each of the first two years, £300 in year 3, £400 in year 4 and £500 in year 5. At the end of the fifth year, it is expected that the van will be sold for around £2,000. The interest rate that the company pays on its borrowings is 10 per cent. Van hire costs £30 per day and it hires a van for about 100 days a year. All the costs are subject to inflation, which is judged to be around 5 per cent over the period, but the resale value of the van is the cash figure expected at the time.

Table 8.2 shows the cash flows in the two cases. Most of the figures are in brackets, indicating negative cash flows, because the flows of cash are out of the company.

TABLE 8.2 *DCF analysis of van purchase versus leasing*

	Year 0	Year 1	Year 2	Year 3	Year 4
Buying a van					
Van purchase/sale	(10000)				2000
Tax and insurance	(650)	(683)	(717)	(752)	(790)
Maintenance	(200)	(210)	(331)	(463)	(608)
Annual cash flow	(10850)	(893)	(1048)	(1215)	602
NPV of annual flow	(10850)	(812)	(866)	(914)	412
Total NPV	(13030)				
Continuing to rent					
Annual costs	(3500)	(3675)	(3859)	(4052)	(4254)
NPV of annual costs	(3500)	(3341)	(3189)	(3044)	(2906)
Total NPV	(15980)				

The NPV of the cost of continuing to rent is £15,980, while the NPV of the cost of buying a van is £13,030. We conclude that the company will be better off by buying a van. This conclusion depends, of course, on the validity of the assumptions. The main uncertainty is in the number of days for which a van would have to be rented. If the company's business expands, so that it would have to rent a van more often, the cost of the rental option would increase so that buying would have more of an advantage. If, however, business declined or the company were able to use the existing van more efficiently, the cost of the rental option would decrease and the advantage of buying would be reduced or even disappear.

Timing of the cash flows

The analysis assumes that the cash flows take place at the start of each period, so that the discount factor for year 0 is 1. In other words, the first payments are at the start of project so that their NPV is their actual monetary value. This is realistic for the costs involved in buying the van; the cost of the van itself is due when it is bought, which is effectively the start of the project, while the insurance and the road tax are both due at that point and on the same date in succeeding years. Only the comparatively small maintenance costs occur at different points during the year.

This assumption about the timing of the cash flows is not, however, valid for the rental option. The maintenance company is likely to have an account with the rental company so that it receives monthly invoices for the rentals in the previous month and the cash flows are distributed throughout the year. If we assume that 'on average' the rental costs are paid half way through the year, we can correct for the result of assuming that the cash flows take place at the beginning of the period by applying a further six-month discount factor to the NPV. This factor is the square root of the annual discount factor, 0.9091, that is, 0.9535. The resulting NPV is £15,237. The advantage of buying the van is thus slightly less than in the original calculation but is still significant.

Cost of capital

We said that the company pays 10 per cent interest on its borrowings and we assumed that it would have to borrow the money to buy the van. This is an over-simplification.

Even if the company has the cash available to buy the van outright, there is still a cost because the company will lose the income it could have received by investing the money somewhere else, in a suitable interest bearing account for example. Such a cost is known as an *opportunity cost*. If the company is able to pay cash for the van, this is the interest rate it would be appropriate to use in the DCF analysis.

As we have seen in Chapters 4, 5 and 6, large companies raise money by taking loans, the rate of interest on which may be fixed or variable, by the issue of shares, on which dividends may be paid, or by retaining profits. When a large company invests in new projects, the money required is likely to come from a combination of these. The company's financial director is expected to carry out arcane calculations to balance the cost of money from these different sources and come out with a single figure for the cost of capital, which the company will use in appraising all investment proposals.

Handling inflation

Inflation in a financial context means the fall in the value of money over time. It is usually expressed as an annual percentage. Thus, for example, an inflation rate of 5 per cent means that in a year's time goods that today cost £100 will cost £105. In two years' time, they will cost £100 × 1.05 × 1.05 = £110.25. The inflation rate can vary very much from time to time and from country to country. Typically, in countries with a stable economy, it will be under 5 per cent, while in countries where the economy is disintegrating and out of control, it can rise to several thousand per cent.

The presence of inflation means that the 'monetary' rate of interest, that is, the rate that is normally quoted is something of a delusion. £100 invested at a quoted interest rate of 10 per cent will be worth £110 in money in a years' time. However, if the rate of inflation is 5 per cent this £110 will only buy as much as £110/1.05 = £104.76 would buy today. Thus the real rate of interest is only 4.76 per cent.

In the example, we initially estimated all costs in today's pounds. We then assumed an inflation rate of 5 per cent and adjusted the cash flows for future years to take this into account. We used the 'monetary' rate of interest rather than the 'real' rate. In normal economic conditions this is the simplest way to carry out a DCF analysis. It is perfectly possible, however, to carry out a DCF analysis ignoring inflation and using the 'real' rate of interest as the discount factor.

Financial cash flows

It is not necessary to include the cash flows associated with borrowing the money to buy the van, that is, the cash inflow when the bank loan is received and the interest payments made to the bank. The DCF analysis automatically takes these into account so that the same result is obtained whether or not they are included.

ASSESSMENT OF A SOFTWARE PRODUCT PROPOSAL

As a more sophisticated example, we consider a company that is assessing a proposal for the development of a software product. It is estimated that three people will be required for development in the first year and a further person and a half in the second year; suitable staff cost £35,000 per year, including the employer's pension and national insurance costs. The product will be released in the second year. After the second year, maintenance is expected to require one person, full-time. Sales and marketing costs are estimated to be £20,000 in the first year, rising to £30,000 for each of the next four years. The product itself is a fairly high-value but specialized product. It is expected that about 100 copies will be sold over this period, at around £5,000 a copy. Table 8.3 shows the DCF analysis of the project over a five-year period, using 10 per cent as the (monetary) cost of capital.

TABLE 8.3 *DCF analysis of a proposed software package development*

	Year 0	Year 1	Year 2	Year 3	Year 4
Development cost	105000	55125			
Maintenance			38588	40517	42543
Sales and marketing	10000	21000	22050	23153	24310
Number of sales		10	20	40	30
Revenue		50000	100000	200000	150000
Net cash flow	(115000)	(26125)	39363	136331	83147
Discount factor	1	0.9091	0.8264	0.7513	0.6830
Present value	(115000)	(23750)	32529	102425	56789
Cumulative present value	(115000)	(138750)	(106221)	(3796)	52993

In this table, we have shown additional entries for the *cumulative present value*. This is the NPV at the end of the first year, the NPV at the end of the second year (that is, the present value of the cash flows for the first two years), and so on. The NPV of the project over its five-year life is the cumulative present value at the end of year 4, shown in the bottom right-hand entry, £52,993, but there are other measures of a project's attractiveness that can be deduced from this table. One is the *pay-back period*; this is the time required for the project to achieve a positive net cash flow. For the project in the table, this is a little over four years, since the cumulative cash flow at the end of year 3 (£3796) is close to zero, and the cumulative cash flow is firmly positive by the end of the year 4. (The term *simple pay-back period* is sometimes used to refer to the pay-back period calculated without taking into account the time value of money.)

The pay-back period is important in a project like this one because predicting the sales of a software product three or four years ahead is a very uncertain activity. A project that promises a pay-back within two years will therefore usually be preferred to one whose pay-back period is four or five years. The same thing would not necessarily be true of a project in a more stable industry such as electricity generation, where it is quite normal to look 20 years ahead and to accept projects whose pay-back periods are 10 years.

It is also possible to calculate the *internal rate of return* (IRR) on the project. This is the cost of capital which would lead to the NPV being precisely zero. The calculation involves some difficult mathematics but, fortunately, most spreadsheets provide a function to calculate it. The IRR is the maximum cost of capital at which the project would be viable. For the figures in the table it is 23 per cent. The term *accounting rate of return* or *simple return on investment* is used to denote the average annual benefit as a percentage of the average investment.

There are times when interest rates can fluctuate quite violently, even in basically stable economies. This happened, for example, in the UK in the mid-1970s and again in the late 1980s. The IRR is a useful guide to the viability of a project in such an environment. An IRR of 23 per cent at a time when the company's cost of capital is 10 per cent means that the viability of the project will not be affected by any likely increase in interest rates.

A proposal will normally be rejected out of hand if its NPV is not positive, if its pay-back period is greater than some pre-set threshold or if its IRR is less than the current cost of capital. If there still remain projects between which a choice must be made, the organization should probably choose those that have the highest positive NPV. This, however, usually reflects a long-term view and other pressures may cause companies to accept the projects with the highest IRRs or the shortest pay-back periods.

PITFALLS OF DCF

Because of its apparently precise nature, there is a tendency to put too much trust in DCF analysis; however precise the calculations, the cash flow predictions are inherently uncertain. An example of the case where uncertainty is comparatively low is the replacement of plant or equipment in the manufacturing or process industries. If the new plant is installed and functioning correctly by the scheduled date and if market conditions do not change dramatically, the cash flow predictions should be reasonably accurate and the major source of uncertainty is the cost of capital; there are, of course, plenty of occasions when the assumptions about installation of the plant and market conditions will prove false but this is likely to be the exception rather than the rule.

If we use DCF analysis to assess a proposal for developing a software product, as we have done above, then the sources of uncertainty are very much greater. Although an NPV of £52,993 and an IRR of 23 per cent look attractive, we must take into account that:

- most software projects take more effort than expected;
- most software doesn't work very well when it's first released;
- we may not manage to sell as many copies as we expected;
- there is a considerable risk that a competitor will launch a similar product before ours is ready.

We need to assess how sensitive the project is to such risks. The way to do this is to carry out a series of DCF analyses with different estimates of the cash flows and the discount rate and see how the results change. If the project remains attractive under the different sets of assumptions, it is comparatively low risk; if it becomes unattractive under small changes, then it is high risk and should probably be re-thought. In the given example, if the sales in year 3 drop from 40 to 20, the cash flow never becomes positive. Predicting sales this far ahead is very uncertain, so the project should be regarded as high risk. On the other hand, if the price is increased to £6,000, the NPV rises to £117,420 and the pay-back period falls to two years. This sensitivity to changes in sales volumes and selling price is characteristic of software product developments.

EXAMINATION QUESTIONS

The examination questions below relate to the material covered in this chapter.

APRIL 2001 QUESTION 6

Bell and Sons are a specialist food wholesaler. They purchase products in bulk from producers around the world and sell to local shops across the country. Their stock control is currently done manually, but they have found as the company has grown that more problems have occurred with stock-outs and food items going beyond their sell-by date.

To solve this problem the company management is investigating two software options: a general stock control package (StockIT)

and a specialist food stock control package (FoodStore). StockIT could be installed on the organization's existing file server and does not require specialist customization, so it is cheaper than FoodStore to install. However, FoodStore provides a better match to the organization's requirements and therefore is expected to deliver greater benefit. The anticipated costs and benefits are shown in Table 8.4 below. The company is borrowing the money to finance the purchase of the software. The cost of capital is 20%. You should assume annual costs and benefits commence the year after the installation.

TABLE 8.4 *Anticipated costs and benefits of new software*

	StockIT	FoodStock
Installation Costs		
Purchase price	£2,000	£3,000
Consultancy costs	–	£2,000
Additional hardware	–	£2,000
Company time	£2,000	£3,000
Annual costs		
Licence/maintenance fee	£250	£500
Additional manual processing costs	£750	–
Annual Benefits		
Additional profit from sales from avoiding stock-outs	£2000	£2,500
Reduced cost of food wasted due to out of date	–	£2,000

Perform the following types of cost-benefit analysis to show which package Bell and Sons should buy.

a) simple payback analysis to show the length of the payback period;

[8 marks]

b) simple return-on-investment to show the average rate of return;

[8 marks]

c) net present value from the discounted cash flow over the four years after implementation.

[9 marks]

a) Simple payback analysis to show the length of the payback period. Ignoring the time value of money, the payback period is the installation cost divided by the annual benefit.

For StockIT, the net annual benefit is £1000 and the installation cost is £4000. Hence the simple payback period is 4000/1000, that is, four years.

For FoodStore, the net annual benefit is £4000 and the installation cost is £10000. Hence the simple payback period is 10000/4000, that is, 2.5 years.

b) Simple return-on-investment to show the average rate of return.

Ignoring the time value of money, the simple return on investment is the net annual benefit divided by the investment that is 1000/4000 = 25 per cent for StockIT and 4000/10000 = 40 per cent for Foodstore.

c) NPV from the discounted cash flow over the four years after implementation.

StockIT

Year	0	1	2	3	4
Cash inflow	0	2000	2000	2000	2000
Outflow	4000	1000	1000	1000	1000
Net cash flow	(4000)	1000	1000	1000	1000
Discounted cash flow	(4000)	835	696	580	483
NPV	(1406)				

FoodStore

Year	0	1	2	3	4
Cash inflow	0	4500	4500	4500	4500
Outflow	10000	500	500	500	500
Net cash flow	(10000)	4000	4000	4000	4000
Discounted cash flow	(10000)	3333	2778	2315	1929
NPV	(355)				

On all counts Food Store comes out best although StockIT would have a higher NPV if a shorter period were considered.

(Note that a calculator is unnecessary; only simple mental arithmetic is involved in the calculations. In each case, the net cash flows in years 1 to 5 are the same. The NPV of the year 1 cash flow is then obtained by dividing by 1.2, and the NPV of the year $n + 1$ cash flow is obtained by dividing the NPV of the year n cash flow by 1.2)

FURTHER READING

The following book is highly recommended. It contains a lot of more detailed material specifically concerned with the assessment of IT investment proposals, as well as some material covering other aspects of finance and accounting:

Blackstaff, M. (1998) *Finance for IT Decision Makers.* Springer Verlag, London.

The book by Atrill and McLaney recommended at the end of Chapter 5 also covers the material in this chapter.

Much of the other literature on discounted cash flow is aimed at investors on the stock market or in other financial markets. It is not therefore directly relevant to the appraisal of alternative investment proposals within a company.

NOTES

1. The equivalent monthly rate is not simply 1/12th of the annual rate because the interest is compounded. The monthly equivalent of a rate of r (as a fraction) is $(1 + r)^{1/12} - 1$.

9 Structure and Management of Organizations

After studying this chapter, you should be able, in the context of organizations with which you are familiar, to:

- *recognize how they are structured;*

- *suggest alternative possible structures and identify their advantages and disadvantages.*

INTRODUCTION

As we said at the start of the Chapter 4, an organization is a group of people working together in a formal way. What this means is that the work that has to be done is shared between these people and that there are rules about who does what. How the work is shared and how tasks and people are grouped together – the structure of the organization – will vary very much from organization to organization. It is surprising, however, that organizational structures have much more in common than might be expected. In this chapter, we describe the most common ways of structuring organizations.

ORGANIZATIONAL MODELS

The bureaucratic model

Organizational theory, the study of how organizations are structured and how they work, goes back to end of the 19th century. The founders of the theory were sociologists like Max Weber[1] and Mary Parker Follett,[2] and practical business people like Henri Fayol[3] and Lyndall Urwick.[4] They developed what is known as the bureaucratic model. In a modified form, this model still describes the organizational structures to be found in most large, and many smaller, organizations. (Note that *bureaucratic* here is simply descriptive; the pejorative sense developed later.)

The ideal bureaucratic organization was thought to have the following characteristics:

1. All tasks are split up into specialized jobs, in which jobholders become expert; management can thereby hold the jobholders responsible for the effective performance of their duties.

2. The performance of each task is governed by precise rules. This means

that there should be no variation in the way tasks are carried out and therefore no problems with the co-ordination of different tasks.

3. Each individual (and hence each unit) in the organization is accountable to one and only one manager.

4. In order to ensure that personalities and personal relationships do not interfere with the organization's performance, employees are required to relate both to other employees and to clients in an impersonal and formal manner.

5. Recruitment is based on qualifications and employees are protected against arbitrary dismissal. Promotion is based on seniority and achievement. Life-time employment is envisaged.

These ideas have proved surprisingly long lasting. Remnants even of item 4 above were certainly still to be found in banks and local authorities in the 1980s. In the 1970s, it was still the case in some companies that if two employees became engaged to be married then one of them would be required to resign.

It is an inevitable consequence of these rules that the organization will be hierarchical and that its structure can be represented as a tree.

Despite the obvious weaknesses of the approach (at least in this form), it brings many benefits and many companies were run successfully along these lines for many years. Modernized and liberalized versions are still to be found working successfully, particularly in production line industries. Much grief has ensued when companies whose main business is appropriately organized in this way have applied these ideas to software production, for instance by separating the tasks of writing code, compiling it and correcting compilation errors, and testing it and assigning them to three different groups of specialists.

The organic model

The best known alternative model is the *organic* model, particularly associated with Rensis Lickert.[5] He expresses the basic assumption of the model in the following (rather verbose) terms:

> **An organization will be effective to the extent that its structure is such as to ensure a maximum probability that in all interactions and in relationships within the organization, each member, in the light of his background, values, desires, and expectations, will view the experience as supportive and one which builds a sense of personal worth and importance.**

This view underlies the organizational structure of most small professional companies – software houses, advertising agencies, even solicitors' and GPs' practices; it is also common in academic institutions, both schools and universities. The view is not necessarily consciously articulated – nor is this view and the adoption of the structures it suggests sufficient to achieve effectiveness!

Proponents of the bureaucratic model claim that it is universally applicable. Proponents of the organic model make similar claims. It says little for common sense that those who hold the obvious view that each has its appropriate place should be christened adherents of the contingency school of organizational design.[6]

Matrix management

It is an essential feature of the bureaucratic model that every individual and every unit in the organization is responsible to only one manager. This is not realistic in the context of project-based, high-technology companies. A specialist in high-speed communications working for a systems integrator may well find themselves working on two or three projects simultaneously, as well as having a more general responsibility for maintaining the company's expertise in the area. In the past 30 years or so the idea of matrix management has become fashionable as a way of addressing such situations. It accepts that individuals may be responsible to more than one manager and requires rules that will enable possible conflicts to be resolved.

Some organizations and some management consultants have tried to formulate the matrix management model much more formally. The results are not encouraging.

STRUCTURING PRINCIPLES

The bureaucratic model tells us something about the way individuals and groups in an organization relate to each other. It tells us nothing, however, about how to group together the tasks and activities that have to be carried out. In practice, there are many different ways of doing this and we shall describe some of them in the sections that follow. It should not be thought that these models are mutually exclusive. In all but the smallest companies, different parts of the organization are likely to reflect different ways of producing a structure. Furthermore, the structures produced by the different criteria may be combined in a matrix structure.

Structure by function

In almost every organization, we can identify certain groups of activities that have to be carried out and that fit naturally together.

First of all, there are the activities that are the primary purpose of the organization. These activities are known as *operations*. The primary purpose of a school is to teach students. The primary purpose of a hospital is to cure sick people. The primary purpose of a software company is to provide software for its customers. In each case, these activities constitute the operations of the organization concerned.

Secondly, almost all organizations have to pay their bills and pay their employees. They need to ensure that the buildings they use are cleaned regularly. If they charge for their services, they may need to send out bills and ensure that these are paid. They will probably need to hire new employees from time to time. These activities are generally known as *administration.* While operations in different types of organization will be very different, administration varies much less.

Thirdly, many organizations will need to publicize their services or their products and try to persuade people to use them or buy them. In the business world these activities are usually known as *sales and marketing.* Strictly speaking, marketing means the activities involved in making potential customers aware of the products the business can offer; it also includes planning new products on the basis of what the company might provide and what customers would like. Selling or sales is the activity of persuading individual customers to buy from the company.

It is often thought that sales and marketing are activities restricted to commercial organizations. This is not the case. Health services try to persuade people to go for check-ups and to participate in screening programmes. Publicizing these services is a marketing activity; sending out specific invitations to individuals is a sales activity. In the UK, as part of the policy of giving parents a choice of schools for their children, schools are encouraged to compete for pupils. This means schools must produce publicity material, a marketing activity, and must try to persuade parents visiting the school to send their children to it, a sales activity.

Finally, many organizations need to be continually developing new products or services, or developing new ways to deliver them. These activities are known as research and development.

A structure based on functions, with an administrative division, an operations division, a sales and marketing division, and possibly a research and development division, is the commonest type of structure to be found in medium-sized companies. It is illustrated in Figure 9.1.

FIGURE 9.1 *A function-based structure*

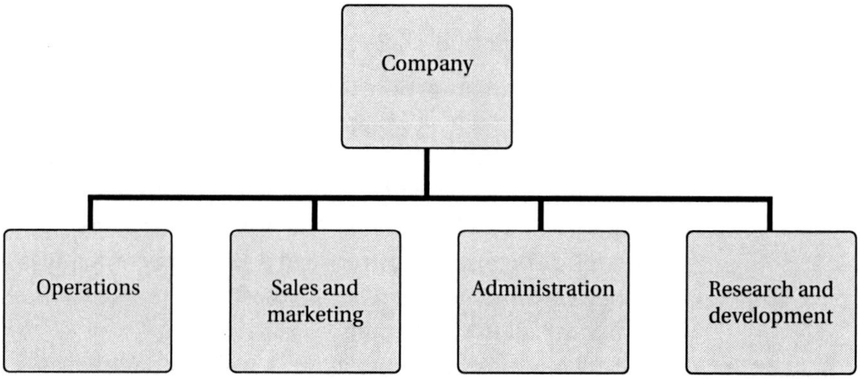

Structure by geography

In many cases it makes sense to group activities together on a geographical basis. Multinational companies, that is, companies that operate in a number of different countries, are usually forced to have some geographical elements in their structure. In most cases, in order to operate effectively in a country, they will need a permanent presence there, and this requires that they have a legal personality, usually in the form of a subsidiary company registered in the country but owned by the parent. The subsidiaries are subject to the laws of the countries in which they are registered, in particular, the laws regarding employment, accounting and taxation. These laws differ markedly from country to country so each subsidiary will need its own administrative capability. Linguistic and cultural factors will usually mean that sales and marketing have to be locally based; certainly this is the case if the company's customers are consumers.

Within a single country, geographical factors have become less important as a result of the development of modern communications and, as a result, geographical structures have been replaced by structures based on other factors. British banks, for example, operated through local branches that provided all but the very largest customers with all the banking services they required. The local branches themselves were under the control of regional management, based on geographical regions. Now that customers can do much of their banking online over the internet, the role of the local branch and the extent of its manager's authority are steadily declining. Instead, the banks have moved towards a product line organization, in which different banking services (current accounts, loans, investment advice, and so on) are provided by different divisions of the bank, independent of the local branches.

Product line structure

A product line structure is a structure that is based around the different types of product that an organization produces. This type of structure is very common in the engineering industry, for example, where a motor vehicle manufacturer organizes around types of vehicle.

Companies that produce and market a substantial piece of software for corporate customers – a multi-user accounting package, for example – often organize themselves into three main operational divisions: development and maintenance of the software, consultancy, and training. This should be regarded as a product line structure since the three types of activity, providing software, giving advice to companies in how to use it, and providing training for customer staff, can be considered to be different services that the company provides and they are typically provided by different teams of people.

Large multinational companies often show a mixture of functional, geographical and product line structures. A good example is Cadbury Schweppes, which produces beverages and confectionery. It has six global functional units: Human Resources, Legal, Finance, Supply Chain, Commercial Strategy and Science and Technology. It also has five operating units that are defined partly in geographical terms and partly in terms of the two major product lines, beverages and confectionery. Figure 9.2 shows the structure.

FIGURE 9.2 *The Cadbury Schweppes structure*

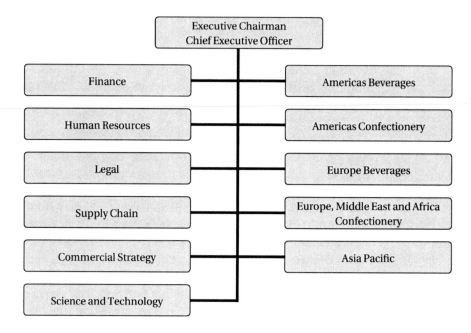

Structure by market sector

Structure by market sector means structure based on the different market sectors to which its customers or prospective customers belong. LogicaCMG, a large multinational provider, is organized into divisions.

This approach is very popular within the software industry. From the sales and marketing point of view it has the great advantage that each division can fairly readily identify its potential customers, and its staff, both sales and technical, are likely to be familiar with customers' problems and to speak a language that the customer understands.

There are two dangers with this approach. First, there is the risk one division may be unaware of technological expertise that exists in another division. This may lead to inefficient use of resources through unnecessarily hiring additional specialists or employing consultants, or, worse, to failing to learn from mistakes that have been made by other parts of the company.

The second danger with a structure based on market sector is that, by continuing to concentrate on its traditional areas even when these markets are becoming saturated, the company will miss new opportunities and will stagnate.

Structure by technology

A technology-based structure was once a favourite model for software companies. Thus, a company might have divisions specializing in artificial intelligence, communications, web-based systems, databases, and real-time systems. There are several problems with type of structure:

- it usually requires several different technologies to meet a customer's needs;

- there are many applications that cannot be said to require specific technologies;

- there are many competent software engineers whose expertise runs across a number of technologies;

- it is difficult, if not impossible, for sales and marketing staff to predict which potential clients will need which technology.

The last of these is particularly serious and companies that are primarily structured by technology have serious problems finding their clients. In marketing jargon, they are not sufficiently 'customer-focused' – they concentrate on selling the technologies that they have rather than finding out what the customer needs.

Operational structure

The actual operations of a company may be organized on a *project* basis or on a *production* basis, although the line separating the two may be vague.

A project is an activity that has specific objectives that have to be achieved within a fixed time period and with the expenditure of no more than some fixed quantity of resources. Every project is different from every other project. In some companies, nearly all the revenue-earning activities are project based. This is particularly true of companies that produce bespoke software or companies that carry out system integration work.

Project-based activity is not restricted to operations. Most research and development is organized on a project basis and such administrative activities as introducing a new accounting system or transferring a company's head office are also to be regarded as projects, in that they last for a fixed length of time, after which they should be complete.

Projects last a comparatively long time but the team carrying out the work only stays together for the length of the project. Production activities are comparatively short, but the team carrying them out stays in existence indefinitely. The central data processing operations of a company are organized on a production basis. There is a schedule of programs – payroll, accounts payable, accounts receivable, and so on – that have to be run regularly on specific dates. It is the job of the operations team to ensure that these activities are completed on schedule. Although the individuals in the team will change from time to time, the team itself will continue to exist.

From the point of view of the employee, the difference between project-based and production structures is very marked. On the whole, if activities are structured on a project basis, employees will find their working environment – their colleagues, their clients, and even the job they are doing – changing radically every few weeks or months, as they move from project to project. If they are working in a production environment, change will be slower and more gradual. One environment is not generally preferable to the other; much depends on the personality of the employee.

DEPTH OF STRUCTURE

The depth of an organizational structure is the number of layers in the structure – or, more precisely, the maximum number of layers, since not all parts of the structure will have the same number of layers. Organizational structures are often described as flat or, in contrast, deep or tall, according to whether the depth is small or large. For a given number of people, the depth of the structure will obviously depend on the number of people reporting directly to each manager; this is sometimes known as the manager's *span of control*. Figures 9.3 and 9.4 both show 15 people organized in a bureaucratic structure. In Figure 9.3, each manager's span of control is two and there are four layers in the structure. This means that the people at the bottom of the structure, such as H, have to pass through two managers (B and D in the case of H) before reaching the head of the organization, A. Figure 9.4 shows a flatter structure for the same number of people. Each manager's span of control is six but the number of layers is reduced to three, meaning that people at the bottom of the structure only have to pass through one manager to reach A. It is generally accepted that, in a bureaucratic structure, managers should not be expected to have more than six people reporting to them directly.

FIGURE 9.3 *Fifteen people organized into a four-level structure*

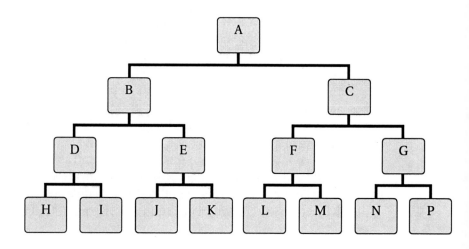

FIGURE 9.4 *Fifteen people organized into a three-level structure*

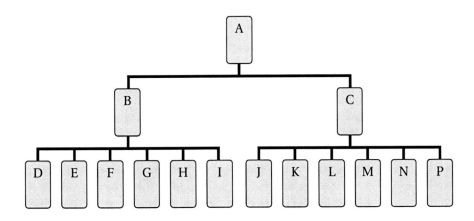

Obviously the structure of organizations with large numbers of employees will usually be deeper than that of smaller organizations. Professional staff generally prefer to work with flatter structures.

CENTRALIZATION

Organizations may be centralized or decentralized. In a centralized company, as much power as possible is kept at the top of the company, with delegation only when essential. In a decentralized company, as much power and control as possible is delegated to the lowest level. If we take a software company as an example, centralization might mean that there were company-wide rules that all programming should be done in C++ and that, whenever a database package was needed, Oracle should be used. Such a policy has the obvious advantages that programmers could be easily moved from one part of the company to another and that it would be possible to build up a close relationship with Oracle. On the other hand, it might mean that C++ and Oracle were used for projects that would have been much better done using Java and MySQL or Visual Basic and Access. Decentralization would allow the most suitable tools to be chosen for each project but might mean that the staff were very inflexible. It could also lead to a maintenance nightmare in the future, with maintenance staff needing to be familiar with large numbers of obsolete tools.

Drawing the correct balance between centralization and decentralization is important but difficult. Decentralization is commonly found in high-technology companies, where there is plenty of talent at lower levels. Centralization is commoner in large manufacturing companies and other long-established organizations. The ideal might be described as *flexible centralization,* in which rules and practices are laid down centrally but it is accepted that reasonable arguments for modifying them in specific cases will be readily accepted. Unfortunately, putting this into practice often proves difficult.

SETTING UP A STRUCTURE IN PRACTICE

In most cases, an organization of any size will have a structure that includes elements of several of the different types of structure described above.

Consider the case of a medium-sized UK-based company providing bespoke software development and consultancy in the UK and operating in several other western European countries through subsidiary companies there.

At the top level, the company is faced with a choice. It could adopt a market sector structure, with divisions corresponding to each market sector in which it operates. Each division would be responsible both for sales and marketing in that sector and operations, that is, carrying out projects for that sector. Alternatively, it could adopt a functional structure with a sales and marketing department and an operations department. In either case it seems sensible to have a finance and administration department, probably under the management of the Finance Director.

The functional structure would have the advantage of bringing together all the programmers, analysts, designers and project managers in one group and all the sales and marketing staff in another. This offers great flexibility and should enable the head of each group to deploy its staff efficiently. If this is done, however, it will probably be necessary to structure the sales and marketing division according to market sector, because sales and marketing activity is usually only effective if aimed at specific sectors.

In order to sell in a country, it is almost essential to speak the language and to be familiar with the culture. Furthermore, despite the gradual harmonization of business regulations in the EU, each country has its own laws, its own bureaucratic procedures and its own way of producing accounts. All these factors suggest a need for a country-based organization. The best way of doing this may be to set up a subsidiary company in each country, with a small office responsible for sales and marketing, and administration in that that country. The subsidiary will be able to call on the sales and marketing division in the UK for specialist help.

The organizational structure within the operations division presents other difficulties. While a project structure will obviously be used for carrying out individual contracts for customers, some higher level structure is required. Do we group projects by market sector or by technical characteristics? It may be that both are appropriate; that is, projects where the risks and problems are technical are grouped into one or more units, depending on the technology required, while projects where application considerations are more important are grouped into units depending on market sector.

Figure 9.5 shows an example of the sort of structure that such a company might adopt.

FIGURE 9.5 *An organizational structure for a bespoke software house*

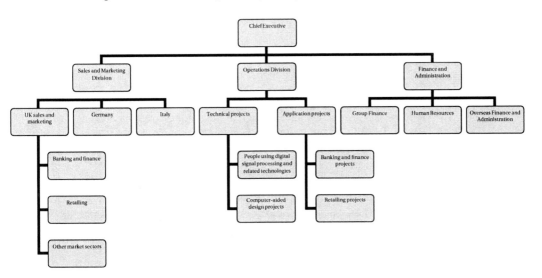

EXAMINATION QUESTIONS

The examination questions below relate to the material covered in this chapter.

> ### APRIL 2000 QUESTION 6
>
> **Pontevedro Software produces a range of packages for project management, accounting, and cost estimation in the construction industry. It is currently developing a new package for computer-aided drafting that will interface with the cost estimation package. It currently employs some 200 professional staff. The packages are sold in the UK, North America and Australia but the company is keen to expand into Asia and into mainland Europe. The organizational structure of the company is more or less the same as when it was a company with 20 staff, operating only in the UK, and the directors have decided that a fundamental reorganization is necessary.**
>
> **Discuss the main decisions that have to be taken before the new organization can be set up.**
>
> [25 marks]
>
> The fundamental decision is whether to structure the organization on the basis of function, product, or geography – or, rather, how to incorporate these aspects into a suitable structure.
>
> There is a strong argument for a functional structure at the top level, with a sales and marketing division, a development and production division, and an

administrative division. The sales and marketing division would then be organized geographically, with sections responsible for each of the main geographical areas.

The development and production division might be divided into three: customer support; maintenance and development of existing products; and development of new products.

The advantage of this structure is that, while sales and marketing probably requires a physical presence in each of the main geographical areas, production and development does not. Nevertheless, customer support may require a knowledge of local languages and local practices in the construction industry, and product development may involve producing versions of the product in other languages or reflecting local practices. If it is felt that this is the case, it may be necessary to attach a customer support unit to each sales unit and to have several product development centres in different regions.

APRIL 2002 QUESTION 2(b)

Syniad Software plc is a large and successful producer of professional level desk-top publishing packages. It operates globally and produces versions of its packages for eight different alphabets. Discuss the different ways in which the organization might be structured, paying particular reference to the relationship between the research and development function on the one hand, and sales, marketing and customer support on the other.

[12 marks]

FURTHER READING

There is an enormous literature on organizations and management. At one end of the spectrum are the popular but superficial books to be found on airport bookstalls. The biggest weakness of such books is not that they are wrong nor that that their prescriptions are often imprecise. It is that their authors' experience is usually restricted to one type of company, typically in the retail sector, and that this limitation is reflected in their text. At the other extreme, there are jargon-filled books of great length, usually written by those who have little experience of business or management, which present elaborate theories that are applicable, if at all, only to very large organizations.

Nevertheless, there is a great deal to be learned about the subject from books and this chapter has barely scratched the surface. One writer who avoids these two extremes and writes in a thought provoking way about the topics discussed in this chapter is Charles Handy. Two of his books that can be strongly recommended are as follows:

Handy, C. (1993) *Understanding Organizations.* Penguin, London.

Handy, C. (1995) *Gods of Management.* Penguin, London.

NOTES

1. German sociologist and historian, 1864–1920.

2. American academic, social worker and management consultant, 1868–1933.

3. French industrialist, 1841–1925. Trained as a mining engineer. Spent all his working life with the Commentry-Fourchambault company. Became managing director in 1888 when the group was on the edge of bankruptcy. When he retired in 1918, it was financially impregnable and was regarded as the best run company in France

4. British industrialist, management theorist and management consultant, 1891–1983.

5. His ideas are put forward in two books: *New Patterns of Management* (1961) and *The Human Organization* (1967).

6. But see Charles Handy, *Gods of Management* (1995) for a much more reasonable and eclectic approach. This book is also good in that it looks at a much wider range of organizations than most management texts, including schools, universities and professional practices.

10 Human Resources Issues

The purpose of this chapter is to explain some of the most important human resources issues that affect companies in the IT sector. After studying it, you should:

- *appreciate the complexity of the law in this area;*
- *understand the constraints under which management and human resources staff act;*
- *understand why and to what extent managers need to be aware of general human resources issues.*

INTRODUCTION

The term 'human resources' emphasizes the fact that the people who work for an organization are an indispensable part of the organization's resources and, very often, the most important part. For this reason, the organization will try to ensure that it always has available the appropriately skilled, qualified and experienced staff that it needs in order to exploit its other assets. This must be done without wasteful over-staffing and within the constraints of what is lawful. The cost of recruiting new staff is high and the loss of continuity when staff leave can also be very expensive. Accordingly the organization will want to keep staff turnover low. Many organizations (though by no means all) want to behave as a 'good' employer and will therefore try to follow the best of current employment practice.

Any organization that employs staff will be faced with the need to handle administrative issues relating to their employment. When the number of employees grows to, say, a dozen, one person will have to devote a significant proportion of their time to this. And by the time the number of employees reaches around 30, a full-time personnel officer or human resources manager will be required. However, managers cannot hand over all responsibility for personnel matters to specialists. This is especially the case in the information systems industry, where staff have high expectations and staff turnover is particularly high.

THE LEGAL CONTEXT

Human resources management is practised in an environment beset by legislation. Furthermore, since it is an area in which it is often difficult to legislate clearly, the practical effect of much of the legislation can only be assessed in the context of subsequent decisions by the courts and by tribunals. To make the situation worse, it is a political battleground so that changes in the legislation occur frequently – four Employment Acts and three Trade Union Acts in the UK between 1980 and 1993 – so that anything one reads is in danger of being out of date. This makes it very much a field for experts.

Throughout the 20th century, up to the end of the 1970s, industrial relations in the UK were based on collective bargaining and were conceived very much in terms of relations between trade unions and employers. In particular, the rights of trade unions received much more prominence than the rights of individual employees. The situation could be characterized by the following features:

- Industrial disputes leading to damaging strikes were common.
- Such strikes were often instigated by politically motivated left-wing members of the trade unions, against the wishes of the majority of members.
- Strikes were supported by aggressive picketing, that is, by large numbers of strikers gathering outside workplaces to 'persuade' other employees to join the strike.
- Secondary action was common, so that companies that had nothing to do with a dispute could find themselves subject to strike action or intimidatory picketing.
- The closed-shop (the system by which, through agreement between the employer and a trade union, all employees had to be members of that trade union) meant that expulsion from the trade union would cause the employee to lose his job. This meant that trade unions could discipline their members very effectively and made workers very reluctant to disobey their union's instructions, whatever their feelings.
- Nearly all trade unions imposed a 'political levy' on all their members, which was passed on to the Labour party, whatever the political views of the individual member.
- Elections for trade union officials were often rigged.
- Over-manning was preventing British industry from taking advantage of modern equipment, because trade unions insisted that the same number of people continue to be employed to carry out a task, whether or not they were required.
- Trade unions were effectively immune from legal action.

There had been attempts at reform through the 1960s and 1970s, most notably the plans put forward in the white paper 'In Place of Strife' by Barbara Castle[1] under the Labour government elected in 1966, but they had all failed because of the strength of the opposition from the trade unions.

The trade unions were to pay dearly for their opposition to the moderate reforms proposed by Mrs Castle. In 1979, a Conservative government under Margaret Thatcher was elected with a mandate for root and branch reform of the law relating to industrial relations and trade unions. The popularity of this policy was an important factor in the victory of the Conservative party at the next three general elections. The legislation passed under these four successive Conservative governments completely broke the power of the trade unions, aided, it must be said, by economic conditions that led to the decline of the heavy industries, which were the stronghold of trade union power. None of the nine bulleted statements above would be regarded as true any longer.

The erosion of the collective power of employees through the limitations on the rights of trade unions has been balanced by a significant increase in the rights of individual employees. This started in the 1960s with legislation to ensure equal pay for women. This is an example of anti-discrimination legislation; this topic is so important that it is dealt with in a chapter of its own (Chapter 11). The concept of unfair dismissal was introduced in the Industrial Relations Act 1971. Industrial or employment tribunals were introduced in 1964. These are special courts designed to handle cases concerning employment rights and related matters. They provide a cheap and comparatively speedy way for employees to take action if they consider that their rights have been breached.

The greater attention paid to the rights of individual employees and the need to comply with anti-discrimination legislation have very considerably increased the workload of human resources departments in the UK. The following list is a summary of the tasks they are expected to undertake within the overall aim of ensuring that the organization has the workforce that it needs:

- ensuring that recruitment, selection and promotion procedures comply with anti-discrimination legislation;
- staff training and development;
- setting up and monitoring remuneration policy;
- setting up and monitoring appraisal procedures;
- administering dismissal and redundancy procedures;
- dealing with contracts of employment;
- workforce planning;
- administering grievance procedures;
- being aware of new legislation affecting employment rights and advising management of what the organization must do to comply with it;
- dealing with health and safety;
- administering consultative committees.

RECRUITMENT AND SELECTION

Human resources managers often make a distinction between the two terms recruitment and selection, using recruitment to mean soliciting applications and selection to mean selecting the applicants to whom offers will be made.

Increasingly, the two are seen as separate activities and recruitment, particularly at professional level, is being outsourced to specialized agencies. Such agencies handle the advertising and, often, carry out initial screening of applicants, before presenting their clients with a shortlist of suitable applicants. They charge a fee that is normally based on the salary of the person appointed, typically something like 25 per cent of the first year's salary.

The best of these agencies are thoroughly professional and offer an excellent service, but the world of recruitment agencies is murky and some of them indulge in very questionable practices.

Before you employ a recruitment agency, you need a description of the job to be filled and the type of qualifications or experience you expect in the successful applicant; a good agency can help draw this up. Note that there are two clearly different situations: it may be that you need to fill a specific post, such as Manager of Feline Rodent Elimination Agents, or it may be that you are looking for as many good staff with experience of real-time system design as you can find. In the latter case, the job description is likely to be much less precise, specifying simply a range of activities that people appointed may be expected to carry out.

Selection is kept in the hands of the employer, although a member of the recruitment agency staff may sometimes be invited to advise. A wide range of selection techniques is available and is used in making professional appointments:

- A series of one-to-one interviews with senior management and senior technical staff: This can be a very reliable method of selection, particularly if records are kept so that you can look back and see how effective each individual's judgement has been. Unfortunately, this approach does not make it easy to demonstrate that equal opportunities legislation has been complied with.

- Interview by a panel: Despite extensive research evidence demonstrating its unreliability, this technique is widely used, particularly in the public sector. It tends to favour applicants who are smooth talkers. The panel may well contain a majority of people who are neither professionally competent nor operationally involved in the appointment. Such 'independent' members are commonly used, for example, in appointing school teachers and university staff; they are thought to help prevent nepotism and other forms of corruption, but the evidence suggests that they are often responsible for bad appointments.

- Assessment of references: Great importance is usually attached to references for academic posts and some other posts in public bodies. In contrast, commercial employers usually pay little heed to them and use them only as a final check that candidates are who they say they are. Legislation in many countries is making it possible for job applicants to demand to see references written about them and even to sue for damages if they consider the reference unfair. Employers, or others, who feel that they have been misled by a reference could also sue if they can show that the reference was written without proper care. Because of these legal dangers, references are being used less and less.

- Psychometric tests: These are of three types. *Ability tests* measure an individual's ability in a general area, such as verbal or numerical skills. *Aptitude tests* measure a person's potential to learn the skills needed for a job. Such tests can be fairly effective, provided that the ability they are assessing is well correlated with the ability you are looking for. In the past, these were widely used for recruiting trainee programmers. However, results can be spoiled if the candidates have had the opportunity to practise, and this is usually the case nowadays. It is difficult to design satisfactory tests for higher-level skills. *Personality tests* attempt to assess the characteristics of a person that significantly affect how they behave in their relationships with other people. Unfortunately, there are several competing theories of personality and, although the tests are widely used, their value is far from clear.

- Situational assessment: This is much used in selecting military officers and by prestigious multinational companies when recruiting new graduates. The shortlisted applicants are brought together and put into a variety of situations where their performance is observed and assessed by the other participants in the situations. It is expensive and is only suitable for use when a number of candidates for jobs can be brought together. However, the use of situational questions in interviews is valuable. The interviewer describes a scenario to the candidate and asks them what they would do in such circumstances.

- Task assessment: Candidates are asked to carry out some of the tasks that they will be required to do in the job, e.g. ask them to write a program. This works very well, provided that the tasks the successful candidate will be expected to undertake lend themselves to being assessed in this way. The trouble is that, where a job involves some skills that can be assessed in this way and some that can't, the former will tend to be over-emphasized. Thus the ability to write a short program can be easily assessed in this way, but the ability to write a 2,000 statement program cannot – it would take too long. Unfortunately, there are many people who can write short programs but not long ones.

The comments above apply to professional appointments; selection of, say, bar staff or cleaners is likely to be done just using a single interview, backed up by references.

To these formally recognized methods of staff selection we should add *nepotism* (choosing cousins, children or other family members) and *cronyism* (choosing friends or former colleagues). The latter, in particular, should not be rejected as unfair or ineffective. If one has worked with a person in the past and seen that they are effective in the role that one is now looking to fill, then to offer them the job is a low risk way of filling it.

As described in the Chapter 11, the need to comply with anti-discrimination legislation, and with codes of good practice associated with it, is of great importance and, in a large organization, the human resources department is likely to spend a good deal of effort in ensuring this compliance.

STAFF TRAINING AND DEVELOPMENT

UK management is frequently criticized for its lack of interest in staff training. By and large, these criticisms seem fair and they reflect also the comparative lack of concern for qualifications. In the USA, employers commonly encourage staff to undertake part-time masters degrees by paying the fees and buying the books needed for the course – and, most importantly, by not promoting people who don't have masters degrees. Such behaviour is rare in the UK.

Successive British governments and industry organizations have been well aware of this problem and there are a number of initiatives that provide positive encouragement and support to firms to invest in staff training. Some of these, such as the Modern Apprenticeships programme, are intended to give young employees the opportunity to acquire skills and obtain qualifications; others, such as Investors in People, are aimed at ensuring that employees are able to keep their skills up to date throughout their working lives. It usually falls to the human resources department to establish and administer a policy for staff training and development, particularly if government support is to be received through one of the programmes mentioned.

In general, these programmes are not aimed primarily at professional staff, although there is no reason in principle why continuing professional development should not be supported. Furthermore, unless the company is a specialist IT company, it is unlikely that internally organized courses will contribute very much to the CPD of the information systems engineer. For this reason, it may be up to individuals themselves, and their managers, to identify specific needs and seek out conferences or external courses through which these needs can be addressed. In this context, it is worth noting that Clause 14 of the BCS Code of Conduct not only requires members to maintain their own professional knowledge but also to encourage their subordinates to do so. This means that managers are expected to take some responsibility for the CPD of their staff.

Staff training and development are of particular importance in high-technology companies, where failure in this respect can threaten the company's raison d'être. It is unfortunate that, when money is tight, it is often the first thing to be cut.

REMUNERATION POLICIES AND JOB EVALUATION

One of the major sources of discord and staff dissatisfaction in organizations both large and small is perceived disparities in remuneration. (We use the term 'remuneration' rather than salary to indicate that other things, such as private health insurance or a company car, may be included.) It is the difficult task of human resources management to provide a framework for fixing remuneration that will avoid giving rise to such disparities.

In the public services, this is achieved by using fixed scales that employees move up by annual increments. The financial effect of a promotion is that you are moved to another, higher scale. Regular negotiation with trade unions leads to the scales as a whole being increased from time to time, possibly to reflect inflation and possibly to reflect increases in the aspirations of the employees involved or changes in the esteem in which the public or the government hold them. Some systems also include provision for allowances for specific responsibilities, e.g., being Dean or being in charge of keeping school premises tidy. By and large, as might be expected, any discord that arises under such systems arises from the allocation of jobs to grades. This is now often done by bureaucratic job evaluation schemes; these require the preparation of elaborate job descriptions that are then painfully compared against sets of criteria for each grade.

The trouble with such systems is that they have difficulty in coping with market conditions. Thus, the Civil Service has always had difficulty in recruiting and retaining good software staff because the grading system always landed up by paying them much less than they could get in private industry.

Formal bureaucratic systems of this type are also employed in some of the larger companies, albeit with, in most cases, much more flexibility to cope with market conditions. However, automatic annual progression up a fixed scale is uncommon. In professional environments it is more usual to fix salaries individually, within broad guidelines. Ensuring that these guidelines are adhered to is always difficult. I know of a recent case where someone threatened to leave, whereupon his annual salary was increased from £25,000 to £40,000. Either he was underpaid before or he is overpaid now; in any case it is very likely that this increase breached whatever guidelines the human resources department was trying to maintain.

Job evaluation is a technique that is often used for comparing the relative worth of jobs and allocating jobs to specific grades. Job evaluation must always involve an element of individual judgement, but the aim is to be as objective as possible.

Anti-discrimination legislation has led to the need for organizations to be able to demonstrate that they comply with the doctrine of 'equal pay for work of equal value'. Job evaluation has a valuable role to play here. In the private sector, mergers and acquisitions of one company by another lead to a need to harmonize remuneration policy and job evaluation is a valuable tool in these circumstances.

It also has a place in younger, rapidly growing companies, where it is used to underpin the reward system to provide clarity and consistency, while flexibility is maintained.

Many organizations are now using job evaluation as the basis for flatter, broad-banded pay structures. Having extended pay ranges means that the emphasis moves away from promotion as the only way of progressing, with an expectation that lateral movement between functions may be more common. It has often been the case in the IT industry that the only way in which highly competent designers could be rewarded adequately was by promoting them to managerial positions for which they were unsuitable – turning good designers into bad managers. Broad-banded pay structures allow the salaries of such staff to be increased without changing their roles.

To further facilitate career management, some companies are establishing generic role profiles, which follow the factors measured during the job evaluation exercise. This allows roles to be compared across the organization. Some companies seek to strengthen the links between job evaluation and other human resource activities by using competency frameworks as a unifying factor.

Job evaluation schemes may be *analytical* or *non-analytical*. Non-analytical schemes involve comparing whole jobs without considering the individual elements and skills that go to make up the job. There are a number of fairly simple non-analytical techniques in use. One technique that has been widely used in the public sector is known as job classification. Using this technique, the number of grades is decided first and descriptions of the characteristics of jobs in each grade are then produced.

Analytical job evaluation schemes assess each job on the basis of the different elements that are involved. Such elements might include financial responsibility, supervisory responsibility, degree of autonomy, decision-making powers, IT skills, linguistic skills, and so on. Each of these elements is given a weight to reflect its importance relative to the others. Each job is then assessed for each of the elements on a scale, typically of 0 to 4, with the criteria for each level specified as objectively as possible. Thus, for linguistic skills, one might ask which of the following statements most accurately describes the job, and award the score shown.

There is no requirement or opportunity to speak a language other than English.	0
Situations occasionally occur when it is helpful that the holder can speak a second language.	1
The holder of the post regularly has to use a second language in informal situations and the ability to do this is a requirement of the job.	2
The holder of the post is required to speak and read a second language fluently.	3
The holder of the post is required to be completely fluent in a second language, including being able to write it correctly and to act as an interpreter when required.	4

A score for the job is then calculated by adding the scores for each element, multiplied by the weight assigned to that element.

Analytical job evaluation is usually preferred because its (spurious) objectivity is considered to make it more likely to be successful against a claim for 'equal pay for work of equal value'.

It is always stated that job evaluation schemes are intended to evaluate the job and not the person currently doing the job. This is reasonable when there are a large number of people doing a more or less identical job. It does not make sense in an organization where every individual is doing a different job and where individuals are valued for their own contribution.

APPRAISAL SCHEMES

It is astonishing and contrary to all common sense that people should be able to spend 30 years in a professional job without anyone, colleague or superior, giving them any indication of how well they are doing the job or how they might improve. Yet, until recently, this was commonly the case for school teachers, university lecturers, many civil servants, and not a few managers in commercial and industrial organizations. It is still true of many doctors, solicitors, architects, and others. To be more precise, there are or were no procedures or regulations that ensured that there was any such feedback. In practice, many senior practitioners in these fields would try to keep an eye on new entrants to the profession and help and advise them; equally, the newcomers would commonly seek such help from their more senior colleagues. Nevertheless, there was no requirement that this should happen and very often it did not. Even when it did happen, it would probably cease to happen by the time the practitioners reached the age of, say, 35, and they would continue to practise for the next 30 years with no feedback, unless they were disastrously incompetent.

It falls to human resources management to design procedures to avoid this undesirable situation. Appraisal schemes are the usual formal way of doing this. They derive from the idea of Management by Objectives (MBO). This idea was developed by Peter Drucker, one of the most distinguished of management theorists, in the 1970s, and it rapidly became popular in industry. It was seized on by government in the 1980s as a way of dealing with what they saw as poor performance and indolence in many state-funded jobs.

The essence of MBO is that managers and their subordinates agree on a set of objectives for the subordinate to achieve over the next period, typically six months. These objectives should be precise, objectively verifiable and, ideally, quantifiable. In other words, objectives like 'increase the turnover of your division by 10 per cent while maintaining its present level of profitability' are preferable to objectives like 'improve the public image of your products'. At the end of the period, the manager and subordinate meet and discuss the extent to which these objectives have been achieved. If the objectives have not been achieved, they will discuss the obstacles that have prevented them from being achieved and how these obstacle might be overcome. They then agree a revised set of objectives for the next period. The process filters down from the highest level of management, where the overall objectives of the organization are set. At each level, managers take their objectives and break these down into more specific goals. From these goals, they delegate tasks by negotiating goals for their subordinates.

The strength of MBO is that it makes managers and others aware of what the organization's objectives are and how they are expected to contribute towards achieving them. Its main weaknesses are:

- Not all legitimate objectives can be easily specified in precise and quantifiable terms. Such objectives are often therefore ignored when using MBO. This is particularly a problem in the public sector.

- The insistence on quantifiable objectives can distort behaviour. For example, setting specific targets for cutting the length of waiting lists in the British National Health Service can lead to doctors choosing patients for treatment on the basis of the effect on the waiting list rather than on their clinical needs.

- MBO tends to emphasize short-term objectives at the expense of long-term strategic objectives.

Modern management practice has moved away from the idea of setting rigid, formal objectives, while maintaining the general principles of MBO. The emphasis is now on *empowerment*; that is, telling employees at all levels what is expected of them but then leaving it to them to decide how to achieve this.

Appraisal schemes usually involve an appraiser and an appraisee meeting regularly (every six months, every year, even every two years) to discuss the employee's performance and career development under a number of headings. The result is a report signed by both parties; if they cannot agree on certain points this will be recorded in the report. There is an obvious similarity to MBO, all the more so because many schemes seek to identify objectives to be achieved by the time of the next appraisal interview.

There is no doubt that such schemes are useful. Professional staff (in the widest sense) are usually willing to listen to ways in which they can improve their performance and will usually accept that someone else can throw new light on the way they do their job; they also provide a good opportunity to review career plans and ambitions and to assess training needs. A good appraiser will do all these things. (From an employee's point of view, it is worth noting that appraisal reports, assuming they are favourable, can provide valuable ammunition in unfair dismissal cases.)

However, the process has many weaknesses. It often seems artificial and appraisal interviews can be rather uncomfortable affairs. Appraisals are supposed to be non-judgemental but this may be difficult to achieve when the appraisee is not felt to be pulling their weight. The training typically given to appraisers is derisory and many of them prove unable to perform satisfactorily in the role. There is the difficult question about whether appraisals should have any link with promotion or salary increase. Too close a link may mean that they are not conducted with the openness and frankness that is essential if the participants are to get the best out of them; if there is no link – and perhaps the appraiser has no influence on the promotion procedure – then appraisees may regard the process as a farce: if your appraisals for the last five years have said that you are ready to become a project manager but you have never been given that opportunity, you can be forgiven for doubting the usefulness of the appraisal system.

A good appraisal process provides an effective framework for fulfilling the requirements of the BCS or other professional body as regards CPD, both from the point of view of the senior member, who has a duty to ensure the continuing development of less senior members, and from the point of view of the less senior members who need advice on how their professional development should proceed.

REDUNDANCY, DISMISSAL AND GRIEVANCE PROCEDURES

It normally falls to the human resources department to ensure that, when staff are made redundant or are dismissed, the proper procedures are followed. Failure to follow the proper procedures can lead to the organization facing the embarrassment of actions for unfair dismissal in an industrial tribunal. This is expensive in terms of staff time as well as money and is bad for an organization's image. Unless the dismissal or redundancies are seen to be fair as well as lawful, the effect on the morale of the remaining staff will be bad.

Unfair dismissal

In order for a dismissal to be fair, the reason for the dismissal must be a fair one and the dismissal procedure itself must have been carried out fairly. If either of these conditions is not satisfied, an employee can take action in an industrial tribunal alleging unfair dismissal. If the tribunal finds in favour of the employee, it will usually order the employer to pay compensation to the employee who has been unfairly dismissed. The amount of compensation awarded depends very much on the circumstances of the particular case; in a few cases it can reach £63,100. A tribunal can also order reinstatement of the employee, that is, order the employer to take the employee back. In practice, tribunals are reluctant to do this.

The law accepts a wide variety of reasons as justifying dismissal. Specifically, it accepts:

- lack of capability;
- misconduct;
- breach of the law – not by the employee (that would be covered by misconduct) but that the employer would be in breach of the law if he continued to employ the employee, for example, because the employee is a foreign worker whose work permit has expired;
- redundancy (see below).

Furthermore, it allows for 'any other reason'! However, there are many reasons that cannot be used to justify a dismissal. These include anything excluded by anti-discrimination legislation (see Chapter 11), taking legal action against an employer to enforce your employment rights, taking part in trade union activities, and so on.

In the UK, new regulations came into effect in October 2004 regarding dismissal and the handling of grievances. The most important effect of these is that dismissals will be *automatically* considered to be unfair unless the statutory dismissal procedure has been followed. In other words, no matter what the employee has done or has not done, if the employer has not followed the statutory procedure in dismissing them, an industrial tribunal will judge the employee to have been unfairly dismissed and will award them compensation.

The statutory dismissal procedure is not, on the face of it, unreasonable. It requires the employer to give the employee a written statement of why dismissal is being considered; the employer must then arrange a meeting at which both sides can state their case. Following that meeting, the employer must inform the employee of the decision. If it is decided to go ahead and dismiss the employee, then the employee must be given the opportunity to appeal, with the appeal being considered by a more senior manager where this is practicable.

Until the regulations have been in operation for some time, it is difficult to know how tribunals will react to claims from employees such as:

- the statement of why dismissal was being considered did not provide enough detail or was not provided far enough in advance of the meeting for the employee properly to consider their response;
- the employer was too slow in following the procedures;
- that the meeting was conducted in such a way that the employee did not have a reasonable opportunity to state their case.

For this reason, it is very important for human resources departments to lay down detailed procedures to ensure that such claims are not successful.

Of course, the fact that the statutory procedures have been followed does not automatically mean that a tribunal will consider a dismissal to be fair. Most of the reasons for which an employer might reasonably consider dismissing an employee – inability to do the job, misconduct, persistent absenteeism, and so on – are, in principle, acceptable, but the employer has to show that appropriate training was offered or warnings given, and so on.

Redundancy

Essentially, dismissal because of redundancy ('retrenchment' in the USA) occurs when employees are dismissed because the employer no longer needs people to do their jobs. In these circumstances, most employees will be entitled to compensation based on their age, salary and years of service. The law lays down a minimum level of compensation that must be paid. In practice, many employers pay more than this.

If the employer is intending to make 20 or more employees redundant over a period of 90 days or less, the employees or their representatives have a right to be consulted.

Rather confusingly, however, there are two definitions of redundancy used in British law and they are not equivalent. For the purposes of entitlement to compensation, redundancy occurs when an employee is dismissed because the employer no longer needs employees to do that job in that place. In determining the right to consultation, however, redundancy is defined as occurring when the dismissal is for a reason or reasons not related to the individual concerned.

In most cases of redundancy, the employer will be seeking to reduce the number of workers in a particular job category rather than dismiss all such workers. The question of how to select the employees to be made redundant therefore arises. It is common practice to use the 'last in, first out' principle, that is, the most recently recruited employees are the first to be made redundant. While there are many reasons for feeling that this is not a desirable policy, it is acceptable to the trade unions and to the courts. Dismissal for redundancy can easily become unfair dismissal if individuals are selected for redundancy in some other way. There is a very long list of criteria that are not acceptable in this context, ranging from participation in trade union activities to sex, racial or ethnic origin, sexual orientation, religion, and so on.

Constructive dismissal

It sometimes happens that an employer behaves towards an employee in such a way that the employee feels that they have no option but to resign. If the employer's behaviour amounts to a substantial breach of the contract of employment, the law may regard the employer's behaviour as tantamount to dismissal. This situation is known as constructive dismissal and can be the subject of unfair dismissal proceedings, although the fact that it is constructive dismissal does not automatically make it unfair dismissal.

The following are a few examples of circumstances that might lead to employees resigning in circumstances that would probably amount to constructive dismissal:

- the employer moves an employee's place of work to somewhere 400 km away, at short notice and without consultation;
- the employer requires someone who was employed as an accountant to spend their time acting as a receptionist;
- a senior manager repeatedly countermands instructions issued by a more junior manager.

The 2004 regulations regarding dismissal procedures also lay down statutory grievance procedures to be used if an employee has a grievance against the employer. Furthermore, employees are required to make use of these procedures before they can claim constructive dismissal.

Takeovers and outsourcing

It frequently happens in modern commerce and industry that one company takes over another; this is particularly frequent in the IT industry. It also happens when an organization outsources its IT activities (or any other activities). In these circumstances, staff involved are usually transferred to the new employer. This could mean a major change in their employment conditions. In particular, if IT activities are being outsourced from a government department to a private company, there are likely to be major changes affecting security of employment and pension rights.

There are specific regulations in the UK and other countries of the EU governing what happens to employees when an undertaking or part of an undertaking is transferred from one employer to another. These are known as the Transfer of Undertakings (Protection of Employment) (TUPE) regulations. The purpose of the regulations is to maintain the employees' conditions of employment in these circumstances. They provide that:

> Employees employed by the previous employer when the undertaking changes hands *automatically* become employees of the new employer on the same terms and conditions. It is as if their contracts of employment had originally been made with the new employer. Thus employees' continuity of employment is preserved, as are their terms and conditions of employment under their contracts of employment (except for certain occupational pension rights).
>
> Representatives of employees affected have a right to be informed about the transfer. They must also be consulted about any measures which the old or new employer envisages taking concerning affected employees.
>
> DEPARTMENT OF TRADE AND INDUSTRY (2003)
> *Transfer of Undertakings: A Guide to the Regulations*

Public interest disclosures

Until comparatively recently, an employer could dismiss an employee for revealing publicly that, for example, the employer was consistently and wilfully breaking the law. There were a number of well-known cases in which senior employees revealed that their employers were breaking the law in areas such as price fixing or the disposal of toxic wastes. The employees (so-called *whistle blowers*) were dismissed and, furthermore, because of the high profiles of the cases, they found it impossible to get other jobs in the industry.

The enquiries after two serious accidents – the sinking of *The Herald of Free Enterprise* and the Clapham Junction rail crash – revealed that employees had been aware of the risk of such accidents occurring, but had not disclosed them for fear of the consequences such disclosures might have for their jobs. This, rather than the more publicized cases of whistle blowing, was the immediate reason for bringing legislation before Parliament.

The Public Interest Disclosure Act 1998 (PIDA) applies to people at work who raise concerns about criminal behaviour, certain types of civil offences, miscarriages of justice, activities that endanger health and safety or the environment, and attempts to cover up such malpractice.

The Act protects employees who make disclosures about such malpractices to their managers or to certain prescribed regulatory bodies such as the Health and Safety Executive or the Financial Services Authority, provided the disclosure is made in good faith and that the employee has reasonable grounds for making the allegation.

If an employee makes the disclosure more widely – to the media, to the police or to an MP, for example – the disclosure will be protected provided it was not made for personal gain, and the whistle blower:

- reasonably believed he would be victimized if he raised the matter internally or with a prescribed regulator;
- reasonably believed a cover-up was likely and there was no prescribed regulator; or
- had already raised the matter internally or with a prescribed regulator.

Employees who are dismissed for making a protected disclosure, can take the matter to an Employment Tribunal, which can award unlimited damages and order their reinstatement. The tribunal will consider all the circumstances of the disclosure and it is by no means certain that judgement will be given in favour of the whistle blower. Tribunals have taken a very strict view of the conditions. Any employee thinking of relying on the Act will be well advised to consult a solicitor at the earliest opportunity.

Wrongful dismissal

For the sake of completeness, we should mention wrongful dismissal. This is significantly different from unfair dismissal. An action for wrongful dismissal is an action for damages brought by an employee against an employer for breach of the contract of employment. It is an action under the common law and for this reason is not subject to the maxima laid down by statute for unfair dismissal. It is typically brought by very senior or highly paid employees who can make a reasonable case for very substantial compensation resulting from their employer's breaking of the contract.

CONTRACTS OF EMPLOYMENT

Under British Law, every employee has a contract of employment, whether or not it is written down. What this means is that the agreement between an employee and their employer can be enforced in a court of law. The law requires that, if the contract is not written down, the employer must provide the employee with a statement of the major conditions of the employment, including grievance procedures.

A good contract of employment should be written in terms that are easily understood and should avoid legal jargon. Prospective employees should not need to consult a lawyer in order to understand it. They should, however, read it carefully before signing it.

An example of a contract of employment, with some explanatory comments, is included as Appendix D.

HUMAN RESOURCE PLANNING

If the human resources department is to ensure that the organization always has available the staff it needs, it must be able to forecast the needs some time ahead. This is extremely difficult, particularly in software companies. As we move through the spectrum of organizations, from software houses through banking, manufacturing and retailing to policing, health care and the operation of lighthouses, the uncertainty, although always present, is reduced and it becomes possible to predict staff needs much more precisely.

In a software house, there are three inputs to the human resource planning process:

- Human resource plans from existing projects, showing how many staff of each grade and with which specialized skills will be required in each of the following months.

- Sales forecasts: These are subject both to the whims of potential clients and the judgement, good or otherwise, of the sales staff. Sales staff are asked to identify all active sales situations, that is, situations in which they are talking to potential clients about their actual needs, not just trying to establish the company's credentials. They then estimate the staff needs for doing this work in terms of numbers of staff in the various grades and any special skills required, and assign a probability to winning a contract to carry out the work. The probabilities are carefully defined in something like the following manner:

    0.9   negotiations concluded successfully but no signed contract yet received;

    0.7   the company has been offered the business, subject to negotiation on price, contractual conditions, etc;

    0.5   the company has submitted a proposal for the business and has been short-listed, or for other reasons, are in competition with no more than two other companies;

    0.3   the company has been asked to submit a formal proposal;

    0.1   the client has an identified requirement that is expected to be met by commissioning a software house.

- Forecasts of the likely staff losses in the coming months: In the software business this depends very much on the buoyancy of the market for software developers. This, in turn, seems to depend on the economic cycle, being, like other capital goods industries, sensitive to growth rates rather than to the overall production of the economy. However, it is also very strongly affected by events such as decimalization in 1972 and the problems associated with the year 2000. Such events generate an enormous demand for staff in the year or two leading up to them, and are followed by an equally large fall, leading to much temporary unemployment, particularly among contractors.

From these inputs, we can try to predict how many staff will be required each month, with their grades, qualifications and experience, and how many will be available. We can then proceed to produce a plan for recruiting staff if necessary.

In practice, human resource prediction in project-based companies never works very well and there are good statistical reasons why it never will. If we are summing 1,000 weighted predictions, the uncertainty in the sum will be quite small, even though the uncertainty in each prediction may be quite large; this follows from what is called the Law of Large Numbers. But if we are summing over only 20 predictions, the uncertainty will still be very large. This suggests that human resource planning should be easier in larger companies and to some extent this is so. However, few project-based companies, even large ones, ever have as many as 100 live sales situations referring to the same pool of staff at any one time. Furthermore, most such companies depend for their success on specialized skills; this means that you cannot treat every employee in a given grade as the same – the fact that you have a grade 5 expert on communications available does not help the project that needs a grade 5 expert on data modelling. And you cannot turn one into the other by sending them on a two-week training course. As a result of all these difficulties, most project-based organizations find themselves see-sawing between being desperate to get new staff for the projects they've won and being desperate to get new projects for the staff they've got.

JOB DESIGN

Setting up an organizational structure implies designing jobs. As soon as a one-person organization becomes a two-person organization, it has to decide who does what; in other words it has to design jobs. In project-based organizations, jobs get designed when the project team is set up and when the project plan is produced. The jobs are ephemeral – they last only as long as the project – and the technical nature of the project determines exactly what tasks the jobs have to cover. Nevertheless, this job design is done within an established framework: a project-based organization will (or should!) have procedures that lay down the way in which project teams are to be structured; such procedures may mandate the use of chief programmer teams in certain circumstances or specify the maximum span of control and the responsibilities of team leaders and project quality assurance (QA) staff in a hierarchically organized project. The tasks to be carried out will probably be defined by the development methodology that the company uses.

In many large organizations structured along bureaucratic lines, job specialization leads to very narrow and tightly defined jobs. As a result, the people carrying out those jobs find them dull and unsatisfying. This in turn leads to poor performance and high turnover. In an effort to alleviate this problem, companies have tried three different ways to provide more interesting and satisfying jobs: job rotation, job enlargement, and job enrichment.

Few jobs in the software industry suffer from the extremes of job specialization that are found in production line jobs for example. Nevertheless, the manager should bear in mind that a software engineer who is expected to spend a full year on testing a system may well be moved to apply for other jobs and that efforts to reduce staff turnover are unlikely to be successful if staff are expected to spend most of their time in activities that they find dull or unpalatable.

The basic ideas of job design become of major importance when we are designing information systems. The introduction of the system can have a considerable impact on the jobs of its users. Very often this may involve an element of deskilling; that is, the jobs under the new system demand fewer skills or less knowledge from the people doing them, which tends to reduce job satisfaction. The way in which the system is designed can ameliorate this situation or exacerbate it. Clause 1 of the BCS Code of Conduct states: 'You shall carry out work or study with due care and diligence in accordance with the relevant authority's requirements, and the interests of system users.' This implies clearly that the information systems engineers should be concerned with the effect the system they are building will have on the work of its users.

Job rotation, that is, rotating staff through a series of jobs, is the most obvious way of preventing employees from becoming bored with a very narrow and specialized task.

Consider the handling of creditors' invoices in a large accounts department with a very specialized regime, An analysis of the process might identify the following tasks, which then might be allocated to the individuals named:

1. Receive incoming invoice and match to purchase order (Freda).
2. Confirm price calculations and despatch to receiving department for confirmation that goods or services have been received (Gareth).
3. Receive confirmation from department and pass for payment (John).
4. Produce payment (Peter).
5. Handle queries arising at any of the above stages (Julie).

Job rotation could be introduced very simply by arranging that in week 1, Freda does task 1, Gareth, task 2, and John, task 3; in week 2, Freda moves to task 2, Gareth to task 3 and John to task 1; and in week 3, Freda moves to task 3, Gareth to task 1, and John to task 2; and in week 4 they return to the tasks they carried out in week 1. Some extra training would be required, but any cost would be more than balanced by the added *resilience* of the department, that is, by its increased ability to handle absence through sickness or holiday. Including tasks 4 and 5 in the cycle is not so easy. The principle of separation of responsibility as a means of reducing fraud means that the payment function should not be given to anyone who is involved at any point in authorizing payment. Task 5 is inherently a more sophisticated task requiring both greater intelligence and more experience.

Job enlargement means redesigning a job so that it includes more tasks at essentially the same level of skill and responsibility. Thus, in the case of the example cited in the previous paragraph, Freda, Gareth and John might each be asked to handle all three of tasks 1, 2, and 3. This might be done by allocating each of them responsibility for invoices from certain suppliers or perhaps for orders from certain departments. In this way, they would see more of the whole process and would be more likely to build up relationships with the departments or suppliers with which they deal; this, in turn, is likely to encourage them to take a pride in their work.

Job enrichment means redesigning jobs so that the amount of responsibility, discretion and control required of the employee is increased. In the accounts office example, this might mean encouraging Freda, Gareth, and John to try to handle simple queries themselves, rather than refer them all to Julie. Care is necessary here. Some staff may be reluctant to take on extra responsibility, either because they fear that they may not be competent to handle it or because they like a simple and quiet life.

In the context of professional jobs in the software industry, job enlargement and job enrichment usually turn out to be synonymous. Since almost all tasks involve an element of discretion, judgement and decision making, adding an extra task will always increase the extent of the job holder's discretion. However, whichever term we use, the idea can be an important and valuable one. Software maintenance is a notoriously unpopular task; it is common for an analyst to analyse and specify users' requests for changes, while a programmer implements them. The job can be made much more attractive, and also valuable from the point of view of staff development, if the job is enlarged so that one individual analyses user requests for changes, specifies the changes and obtains change control board approval, as well as implementing the changes and re-testing the system.

EXAMINATION QUESTIONS

The examination questions below relate to the material covered in this chapter.

APRIL 2000 QUESTION 1

Many organizations undertake regular job performance appraisals. Appraisal systems can vary in purpose and style.

Explain the different purposes of an appraisal system.

[4 marks]

Appraisal systems have three main purposes: monitoring performance, career planning and assessing training needs.

Describe a suitable generic appraisal process, showing how this might affect the style of the appraisal.

[15 marks]

The generic appraisal process consists of three phases: preparation, the appraisal process itself, and documenting the appraisal.

Preparation should be, in part, a continuing process involving consideration of agreed objectives and keeping an account of relevant actions and events since the last appraisal. Preparation for the appraisal meeting itself will involve writing up this material and thinking ahead to the following period.

In the appraisal meeting there will be a discussion of past performance, review of how it might have been improved, and a discussion of training needs, both to improve performance and to fit the appraisee for other tasks. The appraisee's career progression should be reviewed and new or revised objectives agreed.

The appraisal should be documented by one or other of the parties. It is then reviewed before being signed off by both.

The style of the appraisal is likely to be affected by what management sees as the primary purpose of the appraisal process. If it is staff development and career planning, then it should be possible to have a very open exchange. If it is more concerned with monitoring progress or with pay and promotions, then there is likely to be less openness and more scope for disagreement or conflict.

What influence would your membership of the BCS have on the preparation for your own appraisal?

[6 marks]

The code of conduct makes professionals responsible for their own development and for keeping themselves informed of new technologies, practices, and so on. They need to be competent to do the job, looking to improve, aware of own limitations and accountable for their responsibilities. These are issues that professionals should make sure are covered in their appraisals. CPD provides some structure for this and encourages documentation, of which the appraisal documentation might form part.

APRIL 2001 QUESTION 3(a)

Explain the ideas of job rotation, job enlargement and job enrichment, illustrating your explanation by showing how they might be applied to the following scenario.

Peter, Paul and Mary work in the suppliers' invoices section of the accounting department of a university. Peter's job is to receive incoming invoices from suppliers, enter them into the invoice register, match them to purchase orders, and send them to the relevant department for confirmation that the goods had been received. Paul's job is to receive the invoices back from departments, mark them in the invoice register as approved by the department and code them according to the nature of the expense. The invoices are then passed to Mary who checks that everything is in order, marks them in the invoice register as passed for payment, and passes them to the payments section.

[15 marks]

This scenario is essentially the one discussed in 'Job design' (page 127).

APRIL 2002 QUESTION 5

a) Birchall (1975)[2] states that 'job enrichment is aimed at increasing the worker's involvement in the organization and/or the job'. In the case of a computer programmer having their job enriched by including team leader responsibilities, list five issues that management needs to consider.

[5 marks]

The following is one possible list:

- training needs;
- acceptability to other team members;
- motivation;
- need to reflect greater responsibilities by an increase in pay and/or other benefits;
- succession planning.

b) The project team structure lends itself to job rotation, insofar as project team members move between different projects and hence different tasks. What are the advantages of such a structure to project team members and management?

[10 marks]

From the point of view of the team member, the movement from project to project brings the following advantages:

- variety, which both broadens experience and makes work more enjoyable;
- skills and knowledge are likely to be extended and updated by the range of demands of a variety of projects;

- the team member is exposed to wider aspects of the business, and is thus better qualified for assuming management positions;
- the broader view that results is likely to increase the team member's motivation.

From the management point of view, the movement from project to project results in:

- a more flexible workforce;
- greater resilience, that is, the organization becomes less dependent on key individuals because of the wider experience of the workforce as a whole;
- the need for expensive formal training is reduced because individuals have more opportunity to learn from each and to learn by experience;
- the need for restructuring is reduced.

c) MegaBuys is a large retailing company with a small IT department. It is proposing to carry out a job evaluation programme and is concerned about the way that salaries in the IT department should be determined following completion of this programme. Discuss the possible approaches to this issue and indicate the one you consider is most appropriate.

[10 marks]

First, the issue may be approached from the point of view of internal or external comparisons. Internal comparison involves looking at other jobs within the organization that require comparable levels of skill, qualifications, motivation and responsibilities. The need to ensure that the 'equal pay for equal work' criteria are satisfied means that there must be an element of internal comparison in the scheme. Secondly, in most cases, it will be necessary to ensure that salary levels are comparable to those for similar staff in other companies in the same geographical area. They should not be significantly lower, because that would lead to loss of staff. There may be cases where it is better to pay more than the going rate in the area but this may mean unnecessary expenditure. It is difficult to use job evaluation for external comparison because it is difficult to know precisely what the responsibilities of staff in other organizations are. For this reason, it usually necessary to identify comparable jobs on the basis of job title and an outline description.

The most appropriate way of determining salaries will be to use external identification, moderated by internal comparisons to ensure equal pay for equal work.

OCTOBER 2003 QUESTION 5(a) AND (c)

a) Describe the system of *Management by Objectives*.

[8 marks]

c) Describe some of the strategies used by organizations to improve job satisfaction and employee motivation.

[10 marks]

FURTHER READING

The ACAS advisory handbook *Discipline and Grievances at Work* and its advisory booklet *Redundancy Handling* are the best sources of information on the material covered in 'Redundancy, dismissal and grievance procedures' (page 121). They are available on the ACAS website at www.acas.org.uk.

Information about contracts of employment is also available on the ACAS website.

NOTES

1. Department of Employment and Productivity (1969) In place of strife (Cmnd.3888). HMSO, London.
2. Birchall, David (1975) *Job design: A planning and implementation guide for managers.* Gower, Epping. Note, however, that this book is now out of print.

11 Anti-Discrimination Legislation

After reading this chapter you should understand:

- *in general terms what anti-discrimination laws are trying to do and how they will affect you as an information systems engineer;*

- *why your employer has codes of practice that you are expected to follow in order to avoid breaching the legislation;*

- *that if you become involved with discrimination issues at any deeper level, you should seek advice from a professional in the field, sooner rather than later.*

INTRODUCTION

Three hundred years ago, the laws of England contained many specific statutes embodying discrimination on grounds of sex, religion and wealth. In order to vote, you had to be male and own property. In order to be admitted to either of the two universities, you had to be male and a member of the Church of England. If you were a woman, when you married all your personal property became the property of your husband.

From 1700 to the 1950s, almost all these explicit examples of discrimination enshrined in the law were slowly but surely abolished. With a very few exceptions, men and women, whatever their religion and however rich or poor they might be, were treated by the law in the same way. This did not, how-ever, eliminate discrimination. There were, for example, golf clubs that would not admit Jews, medical schools that were very reluctant to admit female students, and professions into which it was difficult for anyone not from a wealthy background to enter.

The past 50 years have seen a steady stream of legislation aimed at making such discrimination unlawful. It is one thing to make a law giving women the vote, but it is quite another to legislate effectively to ensure they are treated on an equal footing with men in all matters concerned with employment, not to mention other matters such as getting a mortgage. Furthermore, even if effective legislation can be framed – itself a difficult task – legislation, of itself, is not enough; time is required to bring about the changes of attitude that are necessary if discrimination is to be eliminated.

Information systems engineers need to have an appreciation of anti-discrimination legislation for two reasons. First, as professionals, they will inevitably find themselves in managerial and supervisory positions and the law requires people in such positions to prevent the people they supervise from behaving in a discriminatory manner and to avoid such behaviour themselves. Secondly, the obligation to avoid certain sorts of discrimination, in particular discrimination on grounds of disability, should influence the way in which information systems are designed and constructed.

It should be emphasized that what is presented here is a very simplified picture of the law in an area that is complicated and subtle.

WHAT IS DISCRIMINATION?

Discrimination means treating one person or one group of people less favourably than another on the grounds of personal characteristics. The law in Europe, the USA and many other countries prohibits discrimination on grounds such as:

- sex;
- race, colour, ethnic origin or nationality;
- disability;
- sexual orientation;
- religion;
- age.

Much of the law and much of the debate on discrimination issues relates to employment and related matters. However, the legislation relates to discrimination in other contexts as well.

Discrimination can be *direct* or *indirect.* Direct discrimination occurs when one person is treated less favourably than another specifically because of their sex or race, and so on. Here are some examples that, on the face of it, would constitute direct discrimination:

- A woman does exactly the same job as a man but is paid less than he is.
- A doctor refuses to treat a Chinese patient on the grounds that he has no room for any more patients but then accepts an English patient.
- A company advertises for a secretary and automatically rejects all the male applicants.
- A company advertises for 'a mature woman to act as the Chief Executive's personal assistant' or 'a strong young man to work as a trainee zoo-keeper'.

Industrial tribunals have increasingly taken the view that racial or sexual harassment constitutes direct discrimination. Harassment is defined as 'engaging in unwanted conduct which has the purpose or effect of violating another person's dignity or is creating an intimidating, hostile, degrading, humiliating or offensive environment'. However, harassment is, anyway, unlawful under the Harassment Act 1996.

Indirect discrimination occurs when an employer imposes conditions that apply to all employees or all applicants but have a disproportionate effect on one group. Here are a few examples that might constitute indirect discrimination:

- Advertising a job with the requirement that applicants must be at least 180 cm tall. In the UK, there are many men over 180 cm tall but very few women. The result is that few women can apply for the job.

- When allocating public housing, a local authority has a policy of giving priority to the children of existing tenants.

- An employer insisting that all employees work on Saturdays. This might be held to be indirect discrimination against those who practice Judaism, since Saturday is their Sabbath. This would be discrimination on grounds of religion but, since the practitioners of Judaism are overwhelmingly of the Jewish race, it might also be regarded as racial discrimination.

Where it is associated with employment, indirect discrimination can be justified if the employer demonstrates that there is a genuine occupational requirement that the offending condition be satisfied.

DISCRIMINATION ON GROUNDS OF SEX

Most people under 50 are surprised when they are told about the position of women workers in the 1960s. Where formal salary scales were in operation, there would either be separate, lower scales for women or there would be additional allowances for men, especially for married men. A female employee who got married might lose her job or might be transferred to the 'temporary' staff, making her ineligible for bonuses or additional holiday entitlement for long service. Women who had babies were not normally expected to return to work and had no legal right to do so. Outside a few professions such as nursing and teaching, promotion prospects for women were very poor and there were few women in senior positions. Indeed, it was very difficult for women to gain entry to academic and professional courses in fields such as medicine or the law that would have qualified them for senior positions. Discrimination also existed outside the field of employment. Some hotels would refuse to let rooms to unaccompanied women. Building societies applied much stricter criteria when considering whether to offer a mortgage to a single woman than to a single man.

In the UK, this situation was dramatically changed by two Acts of Parliament: the Equal Pay Act of 1970 and the Sex Discrimination Act of 1975. Although these acts have been repeatedly amended to extend their scope and to clarify what constitutes sex discrimination, they form the cornerstone of the present position. The most recent amendment at the time that this was written was the Sex Discrimination (Indirect Discrimination and Burden of Proof) Regulations 2001. The 1975 Act has been used as a model for much subsequent legislation to make other types of discrimination unlawful.

The most important features of the law as it stands can be summarized as follows:

Employment

- It is unlawful for an employer to discriminate against a person on grounds of their sex or marital status in terms of the arrangements made for recruitment and selection and the terms on which employment is offered (not just pay but also holiday entitlement, sick pay, notice period, and so on). The Act specifically makes unlawful advertisements that explicitly or implicitly suggest that only persons of one sex will be considered.

  The courts have interpreted the principal of equal pay for equal work as applying not just to men and women doing the same jobs but also to men and women doing jobs 'of equal value'.

- It is unlawful for an employer to discriminate against an employee on grounds of their sex or marital status in regard to opportunities for promotion, transfer or training or to any other benefits.

- It is unlawful for an employer to discriminate against an employee on grounds of their sex or marital status in regard to dismissal or redundancy.

- It is unlawful for an employer to victimize an employee for bringing a complaint of sex discrimination or for giving evidence in support of another employee's complaint.

- It is unlawful for any of the following to discriminate against a person on grounds of sex or marital status: a trade union, a professional body, a registration authority (e.g. the Architects Registration Board, see 'Reservation of title and function' in Chapter 2), an employment agency or a provider of vocational training.

Contract workers are covered by the legislation.

There are a few exceptions to these provisions. The most important is where there is a genuine occupational requirement for a person of a specific sex, as, for example, in the case of recruiting actors to play roles of a specific sex.

Education

It is unlawful for a provider of education (public or private, school, college or university) to discriminate against a person on the basis of their sex, in offering admission to the establishment or to specific courses, and in providing access to the other benefits and facilities it offers.

The main exceptions to this are that allowance is made for single-sex establishments and that provision for physical education may be different for the two sexes.

Provision of services

- It is unlawful to discriminate on grounds of sex in the provision of goods, facilities or services. The Act gives a number of examples including accommodation in a hotel, facilities for entertainment, recreation or refreshment, banking and insurance services, and so on.

- It is unlawful to discriminate on grounds of sex in selling or letting property.

The main exception to these provisions are for charities that have been founded with the purpose of helping a specific group of people who are all of the same sex, for example, single mothers.

Remedies

A person who believes that they have been discriminated against in their employment because of their sex – whether by being refused a job, refused promotion, paid less, not given training opportunities or anything else – can bring the matter to an employment tribunal. If the tribunal finds in favour of the complainant, it can award damages and make recommendations to the respondent. If the respondent fails to act on the recommendations, the amount of the damages may be increased.

An individual who feels that they have been the victim of sexual discrimination in the other areas covered by the legislation can take action in the civil courts for damages.

The Equal Opportunities Commission is a government body set up to promote the cause of equality between the sexes. It provides advice and assistance to complainants who feel that they have been subjected to discrimination on grounds of their sex, whether in their employment or elsewhere. Anyone considering a formal complaint of sex discrimination is well advised to start by consulting the Commission.

DISCRIMINATION ON RACIAL GROUNDS

The first race relations legislation in the UK was the Race Relations Act 1965, which made it unlawful to discriminate on grounds of race or colour by banning people from using public services or entering places such as bars, cinemas or theatres. It also created a new criminal offence of incitement to racial hatred by inflammatory publications or speeches. In 1968, a further act was passed making it unlawful to refuse housing, employment or public services to people because of their ethnic background. This act also established two new bodies, the Race Relations Board, to deal with complaints of discrimination and the Community Relations Commission to promote 'harmonious community relations'.

The present law is based on the Race Relations Act 1976 and subsequent amendments to it. It makes it unlawful to discriminate on grounds of race, colour, ethnic origin or nationality. It introduced the idea of indirect discrimination based on race. And it established the Commission for Racial Equality by the merger of the Race Relations Board and the Community Relations Commission.

The specific provisions of the law relating to discrimination on racial grounds are very similar to those already described relating to discrimination on grounds of sex, and the Commission for Racial Equality has, in the field of racial discrimination, a mission very similar to that of the Equal Opportunities Commission in sex discrimination.

There is one major difference, however, that makes the implementation of racial discrimination legislation much more problematic than that of sex discrimination legislation. With a very few exceptions, the human race is divided into two sexes; a person can only belong to one sex at one time; and it is clear to which sex any given person belongs. (The Sex Discrimination Act does, in fact, make specific provision for persons who change their sex.) The same is very much not true of race, colour, ethnic origin or nationality. The Act attempts to define these terms but the definitions are imprecise and ambiguous. Are the English, the Irish, the Scots and the Welsh to be regarded as different racial groups? Is a person whose parents were Afro-Caribbean, but who was born and brought up in Cardiff to be regarded as belonging to the Welsh, British, or Afro-Caribbean racial groups, or perhaps to all three? These considerations go far beyond what it is relevant to consider here, but they illustrate the difficulty of legislation in this area.

DISCRIMINATION ON GROUNDS OF DISABILITY

From the 1970s onwards, government had been encouraging the recruitment of disabled employees into the Civil Service and encouraging employers to take on disabled workers by withholding government contracts from companies that could not demonstrate a commitment to offering opportunities to the disabled. It was not, however, until almost 20 years after the 1976 Race Relations Act that anti-discrimination legislation was extended to cover discrimination on grounds of disability, in the Disability Discrimination Act 1995. This was followed in 2001 by the Special Educational Needs and Disability Act, which extends the provisions of the earlier act to cover education. To support the legislation, the Disability Rights Commission has been established, analogous to the Equal Opportunities Commission and the Commission for Racial Equality.

The Act makes it unlawful to treat a disabled employee or applicant less favourably because of their disability without justification. The justification must be serious and substantial. Thus it would be justified to reject a blind applicant for a job as a bus driver or a paraplegic for a job as a lifeguard, and it would probably be justified to reject a dyslexic applicant for a job as a copyeditor. However, the Act requires the employer to make reasonable adjustments to meet the needs of disabled applicants or employees. This might include adapting a bus so that a disabled applicant could drive it safely or providing a work station with special hardware and software to make it suitable for use by a partially sighted employee.

The Act also makes it unlawful for businesses and organizations providing goods and services to treat disabled people less favourably than other people for a reason related to their disability, and service providers are required to make reasonable changes to make it possible for disabled people to use their services.

The requirement to make reasonable adjustments could certainly include adapting information systems so that they can be used by a blind or partially sighted employee, provided this can be done at reasonable cost. The requirement for service providers to make reasonable adjustments certainly requires that reasonable adjustments should be made to the way that services are provided over the web. The Disability Discrimination Act thus has a direct effect on information systems professionals in a way that other anti-discrimination legislation does not: it directly influences – or should influence – the way in which information systems are designed. In practice, for the ordinary information systems developer (as opposed to specialists working in areas such as text-to-speech conversion) this translates into the need to make systems usable by the blind, those whose vision is impaired, those whose hearing is impaired, those suffering from lack of manual dexterity (and so unable to use a mouse, for example), and those suffering from dyslexia. This need is most apparent, and most likely to be enforceable, when the system includes publicly accessible web pages.

In 1999, the World Wide Web Consortium (W3C) published a set of guidelines (the 'Web Content Accessibility Guidelines', version 1.0) to assist developers; these are available on the web at www.w3.org/TR/WAI-WEBCONTENT. A working draft of the second version of the guidelines was made available for public review in June 2003; at the time of writing no approved version is available. The draft can be found at www.w3.org/TR/2003/WD-WCAG20-20030624. Several pieces of software are available to test whether a web page complies with the W3C guidelines.

W3C also produces accessibility guidelines for authoring tools. As stated in version 1.0 of these guidelines, they are intended to ensure 'that the authoring tool be accessible to authors regardless of disability, that it produce accessible content by default, and that it support and encourage the author in creating accessible content'. Because most of the content on the web is created using authoring tools, they play a critical role in ensuring the accessibility of the web. Since the web is both a means of receiving information and communicating information, it is important that both the web content produced and the authoring tool itself be accessible.

The Disability Rights Commission commissioned a study of web accessibility for the disabled, which resulted in a report entitled The Web: Access and Inclusion for Disabled People. This report is available at www.drc-gb.org/publicationsandreports/2.pdf. The study included a survey of 1,000 home pages and found that 81 per cent, including many government sites, failed to comply with even the lowest level of the W3C guidelines. Among the commonest reasons why disabled users experienced difficulty were:

- page layout was unclear and confusing;
- the navigation mechanisms were confusing and disorienting;

- there was poor contrast between the text and the background and colours were used inappropriately;

- graphics and text were too small;

- links and images were poorly labelled;

- the web pages were incompatible with the software designed to assist disabled users (screen readers, magnification software).

It is striking that the first four of these, and possibly the fifth, are a source of difficulty for all web users. Eliminating these faults would not only improve the accessibility of the web to disabled users, but would also enhance its usability for everyone.

It is clear from the report that a great deal needs to be done before there is widespread compliance with the requirements of the Disability Discrimination Act as it applies to access to the web. The most urgent requirement is one of education.

DISCRIMINATION ON GROUNDS OF RELIGION OR BELIEF, OR SEXUAL ORIENTATION

In 2000, the EU's Equal Treatment Framework Directive (No.2000/78) was issued. It required member states to legislate to make discrimination in employment matters on grounds of disability, religion, sexual orientation or age unlawful.

As regards discrimination on grounds of sexual orientation and religious belief, the EU directive is implemented in the UK by the Employment Equality (Sexual Orientation) Regulations 2003 and the Employment Equality (Religion or Belief) Regulations 2003, both of which came into effect in December 2003. These regulations follow the pattern established by the Sexual Discrimination Act 1975 and the Race Relations Act 1976. They differ in certain important respects, however:

- They are limited to discrimination in employment, education, and related matters, and do not refer to discrimination in the provision of services or accommodation, for example.

- They explicitly make harassment unlawful, defining it as 'unwanted conduct which has the purpose or effect of violating a person's dignity or creating an intimidating, hostile, degrading, humiliating or offensive environment. Although the courts and industrial tribunals had accepted that racial or sexual harassment constituted discrimination, this was not explicitly covered by previous anti-discrimination legislation.

- They do not make any body, such as the Commission for Racial Equality, responsible for promoting the implementation of the legislation nor do they create any new body for this purpose. However, in October 2003, the government announced its plans for a single equality body for the UK to take over the responsibilities of the Equal

Opportunities Commission, the Commission for Racial Equality, and the Disability Rights Commission. This proposed body was given the working title of the Commission for Equality and Human Rights (CEHR). Under the proposals, the CEHR will also take responsibility for the new regulations on religion and belief, and sexual orientation (and age, when these come into effect). Support for human rights will also be included within the CEHR's remit. It is not yet clear when the CEHR will come into operation, but it is likely that the current equality bodies will continue their work until at least the latter part of 2006.

This legislation raises many difficult questions that are well beyond the scope of this book and it will be some years before a sufficient body of case law has been accumulated to provide reliable answers.

DISCRIMINATION ON GROUNDS OF AGE

Regulations making it unlawful to discriminate on grounds of age, the Equal Treatment Directive, will not become law in the UK until 2006. However, their effect will be very widespread, more so than that of any other anti-discrimination legislation except for sex discrimination. They could, for example, mean the end of compulsory retirement ages. They could mean that it is unlawful for employers to seek specifically to recruit new graduates. (This would be indirect age discrimination because a much smaller proportion of over-50s fall into the category of 'new graduates' than of the under-25s.)

The Equal Treatment Directive is, however, careful to be quite explicit in allowing for discrimination on the grounds of age in a number of important cases. It allows, for example:

- special treatment of different age groups in order to protect them (e.g. not allowing children under a certain age to be employed);
- different premiums for life insurance policies, depending on the age of the person at the time the policy is taken out, and different pension rates depending on the age of retirement (but these must not amount to sex discrimination);
- fixing a maximum age for recruitment based on the need for a reasonable period of employment after training and before retirement;
- fixing a minimum age, a minimum amount of professional experience or a minimum number of years with the company before a person will be regarded as eligible for a given post or eligible for certain employment benefits (e.g. additional annual leave).

The regulations to implement the directive as it applies to age discrimination in the UK have not yet been published, but it is a reasonable assumption that the exceptions allowed by the directive will be reflected in the UK regulations.

The software industry has traditionally been a youthful one and many companies have discriminated against older job applicants, albeit unconsciously or unintentionally, As the industry itself has grown older, the average age of its employees has been increasing, so this phenomenon has become less marked. Legislation against age discrimination will probably have little direct effect on the industry beyond accelerating this tendency.

AVOIDING DISCRIMINATION

It is not enough for an employer to support anti-discrimination legislation and resolve to comply with it. In an organization of any size, it is necessary to ensure that all members of the organization share the employer's resolve. Even if this is achieved, the organization may have to deal with such problems as unlawful harassment from its customers or unjustified accusations of discrimination.

Effective compliance with anti-discrimination legislation in the workplace requires three things:

- a suitable written policy, well publicized, and freely and easily available;
- a training programme for new and existing staff, to ensure that they are all aware of the policy and its importance;
- effective procedures for implementing the policy.

It is a sad fact that an employer's ability to rebut an accusation of unlawful discrimination will often depend as much on their ability to demonstrate that proper procedures have been followed as on whether any discrimination took place.

The three bodies charged with responsibility for tackling discrimination (the Commission for Racial Equality, the Equal Opportunities Commission, and the Disability Rights Commission) all provide extensive guidance to employers. The Commission for Racial Equality, for example, publishes a sample equal opportunities policy and a code of practice on eliminating discrimination.

FURTHER READING

The URLs of the websites of the three bodies responsible for tackling discrimination are:

- Equal Opportunities Commission: www.eoc.org.uk
- Commission for Racial Equality: www.cre.gov.uk
- Disability Rights Commission: www.drc-gb.org

These sites are extremely helpful in providing summaries of the law, links to the legislation itself, guidance to employers and employees, and sample documents such as equal opportunities policies.

The BCS has published its own guide to the Disability Discrimination Act: British Computer Society (2000) *Disability Discrimination Act – Access for All: A Practical Guide for Professionals & Business Managers*. BCS, Swindon.

12 Software Contracts and Liability

After studying this chapter, you should:

- *understand the purpose of contracts in the computer industry and the different types of contractual arrangement that are commonly used;*
- *be familiar with the main issues that such contracts address;*
- *understand the different types of liability for defective software that can arise and the factors that affect these.*

INTRODUCTION

A contract is simply an agreement between two or more persons (the *parties* to the contract) that can be enforced in a court of law. The parties involved may be legal persons or natural persons. There is no specific form for a contract; in particular, in England and Wales a contract need not be written down. What is essential is:

- all the parties must intend to make a contract;
- all the parties must be competent to make a contract, that is, they must be old enough and of sufficiently sound mind to understand what they are doing;
- there must be a 'consideration', that is, each party must be receiving something and providing something.

Contract law is largely based on common law. It has a long history and is well adapted to handling the disputes that arise in fulfilling commercial agreements.

The existing contract law showed itself perfectly adequate to handle contracts for the supply of computers, software and associated services. However, the coming of the internet and e-commerce has created a need for new provisions to deal with such matters as electronic signatures and which country's laws should govern transactions made over the internet when the parties to the transaction are in different countries.

In this chapter we are not very much concerned with the law relating to contracts. We are much more concerned with what should go into contracts for providing software and services in different circumstances and with issues of liability when software fails.

FIXED PRICE CONTRACTS FOR BESPOKE SYSTEMS

The first type of contract we shall consider is the type that is used when an organization is buying a system configured specifically to meet its needs. Such systems are known as *tailor-made* or *bespoke* systems. A bespoke system may consist of a single PC equipped with a word processor, a spreadsheet, and a set of macros adapted to the customer's needs or it may consist of several thousand PCs spread across 50 offices in different parts of the world, connected by a wide-area network, with large database servers and a million lines of specially written software.

Typically, the contract for the supply of a bespoke system consists of three parts:

- A short *agreement*, which is signed by the parties to the contract: This states who the parties are and, very importantly, says that anything that may have been said or written before does not form part of the contract. An example of such an agreement is given in Appendix B.

- The *standard terms and conditions*, which are normally those under which the supplier does business; and

- A set of *schedules* or *annexes*, which specify the particular requirements of this contract, including what is to be supplied, when it is to be supplied, what payments are to be made and when, and so on.

An example of the standard terms and conditions will be found in Appendix C. You should realize that these are the sort of terms and conditions that are used on fairly large contracts. Many small-scale development projects are carried out perfectly satisfactorily using much simpler contracts, often no more than an exchange of letters.

We shall look at the standard terms and conditions for the provision of large bespoke systems for a fixed price in some detail, not because such contracts occur very frequently but because they illustrate many of the issues that can arise in IT contracts.

What is to be produced

It is clearly necessary that the contract states what is to be produced. There are usually two levels of reference here: the standard terms and conditions refer to an annex and the annex then refers to a separate document that constitutes the requirements specification. It is important that the reference to the requirements specification identifies that document uniquely; normally this will mean quoting a date and issue number.

Information systems engineers will be familiar with the problems of producing requirements specifications. A specification sets out the detailed requirements of the client. Ideally, the specification should be complete, consistent and accurate and set out all that the client wants to be done in the performance of the contract. Unfortunately, we know that it is very difficult to achieve this ideal standard and, even if we succeed, the requirements of the client may evolve as the contract proceeds, and sometimes the changes may be substantial. How are these changes to be accommodated by a contract which, in a sense, freezes the requirements of the parties to those at one particular time by incorporating the original specification into the contract? The answer is that the contract should provide a procedure for making variations to the specification or job description, then follow this through by providing a method of calculating payment for work done to facilitate the changes, and also perhaps provide for a variation of the level of anticipated performance, and maybe also vary the method of acceptance testing. In other words, the contract should anticipate events and provide an agreed formula for modification.

What is to be delivered

Producing software for a client is not, usually, a matter of simply handing over the text of a program which does what is required. It is important, therefore, that the contract states (usually in an annex) what precisely is to be provided. The following is a non-exhaustive list of possibilities:

- source code;
- command files for building the executable code from the source and for installing it;
- documentation of the design and of the code;
- reference manuals, training manuals and operations manuals;
- software tools to help maintain the code;
- user training;
- training for the client's maintenance staff;
- test data and test results.

Ownership of rights

It is important that the contract should also state just what legal rights are being passed by the software house to the client under the contract. Ownership in physical items such as books, documents or disks will usually pass from the software house to the client, but other intangible rights, known as intellectual property rights, present more problems. Intellectual property law forms the subject matter of Chapter 13. As we shall see there, software is potentially protectable by a number of intellectual property rights, such as copyright, design rights, confidentiality and trademarks. It is important for the contract to state precisely who is to own these rights but we shall leave discussion of this to Chapter 13.

Confidentiality

It is almost inevitable that, when a major bespoke software system is being developed, the two parties will acquire confidential information about each other. The commissioning client may well have to pass confidential information about its business operations to the software house. On the other side of the coin, the software house may not want the client to divulge to others details of the program content or other information gleaned about its operations by the client. It is usual in these circumstances for each party to promise to maintain the confidentiality of the other's secrets, and for express terms to that effect to be included in the contract. The law relating to confidential information is part of intellectual property law and is discussed in Chapter 13.

Payment terms

The standard terms and conditions will specify the payment conditions, that is something along the lines of:

> Payment shall become due within thirty days of the date of issue of an invoice. If payment is delayed by more than thirty days from the due date, the Company shall have the right, at its discretion, to terminate the contract, or to apply a surcharge at an interest rate of 2 per cent above the bank base lending rate.

In practice, such clauses are only brought into effect in extreme cases, since using them is likely to destroy the goodwill between supplier and client on which the success of the project depends.

It would be unusual, in a project of any significant length, for all payment to be delayed until the work is complete and accepted. An annex will usually specify a pattern of payments such as the following:

- an initial payment of, say, 15 per cent of the contract value becomes due on signature of the contract;
- further stage payments become due at various points during the development, bringing the total up to, say, 65 per cent;
- a further 25 per cent becomes due on acceptance of the software;
- the final 10 per cent becomes due at the end of the warranty period.

Such a pattern has advantages for the supplier in that it reduces the financial risk arising from possible insolvency of the client or from default for other reasons and it reduces possible cash flow difficulties. If the client is not prepared to accept a payment pattern of this type, the supplier is likely to demand a premium to cover the increased risk and the costs of financing the development. In negotiating the payment pattern, the supplier will usually seek to have the stage payments becoming due on fixed calendar dates, while the client will try to have them tied to the achievement of specific project milestones, for example, approval of the design specification.

Calculating payments for delays and changes

It happens not infrequently that progress on the development of a piece of software is delayed by the failure of the client to meet obligations on time.

While the supplier will be expected to use its best endeavours to rearrange activities so as to avoid wasting effort, this is not always possible. The contract should therefore make provision for payments to compensate for the wasted effort, incurred, for example, when the client fails to provide information on a due date or when changes are requested that result in extra work.

The contract must specify the process by which these extra payments are to be calculated. Typically, an annex will include daily charging rates for each grade of staff employed on the contract and the amount of extra effort to be paid for will be agreed at progress meetings.

Delay payments and payments for variations to the original requirements are, perhaps, the commonest cause of contractual disputes, not only in software engineering but in most other contracting industries – the construction industry is a notorious example. One reason for this is that competitive bidding for fixed price contracts often means that the profit margin on the original contract is very low so that companies seek to make their profit on these additional payments.

Penalty clauses

The previous subsection dealt with compensation for delays caused by the client; delays caused by the supplier are handled differently.

The normal mechanism used is to include a penalty clause that provides that the sum payable to the supplier is reduced by a specified amount for each week that acceptance of the product is delayed, up to a certain maximum. Thus, on a contract of value £1 million, the penalty might be specified as £5,000 per week up to a maximum of £100,000.

Delays in delivering working software are notoriously common; it might therefore be expected that contracts for the supply of software would normally include such a penalty clause. Paradoxically, such provision is comparatively rare. There are three reasons for this:

- Suppliers are very reluctant to accept penalty clauses and anything stronger than the example quoted above is likely to lead to reputable suppliers refusing to bid.

- If the contract is to include penalty clauses, the bid price is likely to be increased by at least half the maximum value of the penalty.

- If the software is seriously late and penalties approach their maximum, there is little incentive for the supplier to complete the work since they will already have received in stage payments as much as they are going to get.

It should be realized that the cost of delays on fixed price contracts is very high, regardless of penalty payments. Every delay eats into the supplier's profit margin. As a result, suppliers are strongly motivated to produce the software on time and delay is usually the result of genuine technical difficulties (or incompetence!) rather than lack of motivation.

Obligations of the client

In almost all cases where work is being carried out for a specific client, the client will have to fulfil certain obligations if the contract is to be completed successfully. The following is a (non-exhaustive) list of possibilities:

- provide documentation on aspects of the client's activities or the environment in which the system will run;
- provide access to appropriate members of staff;
- provide machine facilities for development and testing;
- provide accommodation, telephone and secretarial facilities for the company's staff when working on the client's premises;
- provide data communications facilities to the site.

The general terms and conditions will normally state that a list of specific obligations and the dates at which they will be required is given in an annex. It will also state that failure to meet these obligations may render the client liable for delay payments.

Standards and methods of working

The supplier is likely to have company standards, methods of working, quality assurance procedures, and so on, and will normally prefer to use these. More sophisticated clients will have their own procedures and may require that these be adhered to. In some cases, the supplier may be required to allow the client to apply quality control procedures to the project. The contract must specify which is to apply.

Progress meetings

Regular progress meetings are essential to the successful completion of a fixed price contract and it is advisable that standard terms and conditions require them to be held. The minutes of progress meetings, duly approved and signed, should have contractual significance in that they constitute evidence that milestones have been reached (so that stage payments become due) and that delay payments have been agreed.

Project managers

Each party needs to know who, of the other party's staff, has day-to-day responsibility for the work and what the limits of that person's authority are. The standard terms and conditions should therefore require each party to nominate, in writing, a project manager. The project managers must have at least the authority necessary to fulfil the obligations that the contract places on them. It is particularly important that the limits of their financial authority are explicitly stated, that is, the extent to which they can authorize changes to the cost of the contract.

Acceptance procedure

Acceptance procedures are a critical part of any fixed price contract for they provide the criteria by which successful completion of the contract is judged. The essence of the acceptance procedure is that the client should provide a fixed set of acceptance tests and expected results and that successful performance of these tests shall constitute acceptance of the system. The tests must be provided at or before the start of the acceptance procedure; within reason, there may be as many tests as the client wishes, but extra tests cannot be added once the test set has been handed over. The purpose of this restriction is to ensure that the acceptance procedure can be completed in reasonable time.

Other points to be addressed under this heading include who shall be present when the tests are carried out and what happens if the tests are not completed successfully.

Warranty and maintenance

Once the product has been accepted, it is common practice to offer a warranty period of, typically, 90 days. Any errors found in the software and reported within this period will be corrected free of charge. This clause is, of course, subject to negotiation; reducing or eliminating the warranty period will reduce the overall cost of the contract and prolonging the period will increase it.

Once the warranty period is over, the supplier may offer, or the client demand, that maintenance will continue to be available on request. Since such maintenance is likely to involve enhancement of the software rather than simply correction of faults, the resources required are unpredictable – the client almost certainly does not know what enhancements will be required in two years' time. For this reason, a fixed price for the maintenance will not be appropriate. Maintenance will therefore usually be charged on a time and materials basis; the client may possibly be required to commit to taking a fixed number of days of effort each year in order to compensate the supplier for the need to retain knowledge of the system.

Inflation

In lengthy projects or projects where there is a commitment to long-term maintenance, the supplier will wish to ensure protection against the effects of unpredictable inflation. To handle this problem, it is customary to include a clause which allows charges to be increased in accordance with the rise in costs.

The clause should state how often (once a year, twice a year) charges can be increased and how the effect on the overall price is to be calculated.

Indemnity

It could happen that, as a result of the client's instructions, the supplier is led unwittingly to infringe the intellectual property rights of a third party or that, through carelessness or dishonesty, the supplier provides a system which infringes such rights – perhaps through using proprietary software as a component of the system delivered. For this reason, it is advisable to include a clause under which each party indemnifies the other (that is, guarantees to cover any costs the other party becomes subject to) for liability arising from its own faults in this respect.

Termination of the contract

There are many reasons why it may become necessary to terminate a contract before it has been completed. It is not uncommon, for example, for the client to be taken over by another company that already has a system of the type being developed, or for a change in policy on the part of the client to mean that the system is no longer relevant to its needs. It is essential, therefore, that the contract make provision for terminating the work in an amicable manner. This usually means that the supplier is to be paid for all the work carried out up to the point where the contract is terminated, together with some compensation for the time needed to redeploy staff on other revenue earning work. The question of ownership of the work so far carried out must also be addressed.

Arbitration

Litigation (court action) is always expensive and the people who benefit most from it are usually lawyers. Contracts often therefore contain a clause saying that, in the event of a dispute that they cannot solve themselves, the parties agree to accept the decision of an independent arbitrator. In the case of computer-related contracts, it is usually stated that the arbitrator is to be appointed either by the President of the BCS or by the President of the IEE. Both bodies maintain lists of qualified arbitrators who have the necessary technical understanding.

An arbitration clause will usually state that, if arbitration is required, it will take place in accordance with the Arbitration Act 1996. This Act of Parliament lays down a set of rules for arbitration that cover many eventualities, and reference to it avoids the need to spell these out in detail; most of the provisions of the Act are optional, in the sense that they come into effect only if the contract contains no alternative provision.

Applicable law

Where the supplier and the client have their registered offices in different legal jurisdictions or performance of the contract involves more than one jurisdiction, it is necessary to state under which laws the contract is to be interpreted.

CONSULTANCY AND CONTRACT HIRE

Contract hire is an arrangement in which the supplier agrees to supply the customer with the services of a certain number of staff at agreed daily or hourly charge rates. The customer takes responsibility for managing the staff concerned. Either party can terminate the arrangement at fairly short notice, typically one week, either in respect of a particular person or as a whole. The supplier's responsibility is limited to providing suitably competent people and replacing them if they become unavailable or are adjudged unsuitable by the client.

The contract for such an arrangement is usually fairly simple. Payment is on the basis of a fixed rate for each day worked; the rate depends on the experience and qualifications of the staff.

Contract hire agreements are very much simpler than fixed price contracts because the supplier's involvement and responsibility are so much less. Issues such as delay payments, acceptance tests and many others simply do not arise; however, as mentioned earlier, ownership of intellectual property rights generated in the course of the work must be addressed.

Contract hire is sometimes referred to disparagingly as 'body shopping'. Closely related are the freelance agreements under which individuals sell their own services to clients on a basis similar to contract hire.

Consultancy is essentially an up-market version of contract hire. Consultants are experts who are called in by an organization to assess some aspect of its operations or its strategy and to make proposals for improvements. This means that the end product of a consultancy project is usually a report or other document.

Consultancy projects are usually undertaken for a fixed price but the form of contract is very much simpler than the fixed price contracts so far described. There are two reasons for this. First, the sums of money are comparatively small and neither side stands to lose a great deal. Secondly, while it is possible to demonstrate beyond doubt that a piece of software does not work correctly and thus that the supplier has failed to fulfil the contract, it is not usually possible to demonstrate unequivocally that a report fails to fulfil a contract. The client has to rely on the desire of the supplier to maintain a professional reputation and in practice this usually proves sufficient to ensure that the work is of an acceptable standard.

There are four important aspects of a consultancy contract:

- Confidentiality: Consultants are often in a position to learn a lot about the companies for which they carry out assignments and may well be in a position to misuse this information for their own profit.

- Terms of reference: It is important that the contract refers explicitly to the terms of reference of the consultancy team and, in practice, these are perhaps the commonest source of disagreements in consultancy projects. As a result of their initial investigations, the consultants may discover that they need to consider matters that were outside their original terms of reference but the client may be unwilling to let this happen, for any one of a number of possible reasons;

- Liability: Most consultants will wish to limit their liability for any loss that the customer suffers as a result of following their advice. Customers may not be happy to accept this and, in some cases, may insist on verifying that the consultant has adequate professional liability insurance.

- Who has control over the final version of the report: It is common practice for the contract to require that a draft version of the final report be presented to the client. The client is given a fixed period to review the report and, possibly, ask for changes. The revised version that is then submitted by the consultant should be the final version.

TIME AND MATERIALS

A time and materials contract (often referred to as a 'cost plus' contract) is somewhere between a contract hire agreement and a fixed price contract. The supplier agrees to undertake the development of the software in much the same way as in a fixed price contract, but payment is made on the basis of the costs incurred, with labour charged in the same way as for contract hire. The supplier is not committed to completing the work for a fixed price, although a maximum payment may be fixed beyond which the project may be reviewed. Many of the complications of fixed price contracts still occur with time and materials contracts – ownership of rights, facilities to be provided by the client, progress monitoring arrangements, for instance – but others, such as delay payments and acceptance testing, do not; this is not to say that no acceptance testing is done, only that it has no contractual significance since nothing contractual depends on its outcome.

It may be wondered why any client should prefer a time and materials contract to a fixed price contract – surely it is better to have a contract which guarantees performance for a fixed price rather than one in which the price is indeterminate and there is no guarantee of completion? In the first place, it often happens that the work to be carried out is not sufficiently well specified for any supplier to be prepared to offer a fixed price; part of the supplier's task will be to discover what is required and to specify it in detail. Secondly, a supplier always loads a fixed price contract with a contingency allowance, to allow for the risk that unexpected factors will cause the project to require more resources than originally estimated. If all goes well, the supplier makes an extra profit; this is the reward for risk taken. By accepting a time and materials contract, this risk and the possibility of extra profit (in the form of a lower cost) are effectively transferred to the client, who also avoids the dangers of having to pay excessive sums to have minor changes incorporated into the specification. All this having been said, it remains the case that there has been a strong movement away from time and materials towards fixed price, noticeably in the defence field.

OUTSOURCING

Outsourcing, sometimes known as facilities management, is the commercial arrangement under which a company or organization (the customer) hands over the planning, management and operation of certain functions to another organization (the supplier). This definition covers many common situations – most of us, for example, choose to give the responsibility for supplying our home with electricity to a company that specializes in this, rather than buying our own generator and doing it ourselves; in other words, we outsource the supply of electricity.

The past 25 years have seen a rapid increase in outsourcing in the UK. This was led by the Civil Service. Civil Service salaries were low in comparison with salaries in the IT industry so that the Civil Service had great difficulty in retaining competent IT staff. This difficulty was reflected in the poor quality of government information systems. Outsourcing IT provision to specialist companies provided a means of overcoming this problem while, at the same time, allowing the government to reduce the number of civil servants, a political objective to which it was committed.

The logic behind outsourcing is that a company that specializes in a particular area, be it IT or office cleaning, is likely to be able to make a better job of running services than an organization whose main area of expertise is elsewhere. Twenty-five years ago, companies would employ their own staff to develop software, run the staff canteen, clean the offices, carry out market research, and so on. Nowadays, they are likely to outsource all these operations to specialist companies so that they can concentrate on their core business, that is, the business that is the main source of their revenue.

IT outsourcing contracts are inherently complex and depend very much on individual circumstances. It is not appropriate to go into detail here about such contracts but the following is a list of just some of the points that need to be addressed:

- how is performance to be monitored and managed;
- what happens if performance is unsatisfactory;
- which assets are being transferred;
- staff transfers;
- audit rights;
- contingency planning and disaster recovery;
- intellectual property rights in software developed during the contract;
- duration of the agreement and termination provisions.

The first two items above are key element in IT outsourcing and are often treated as a separate agreement known as a service level agreement.

LICENCE AGREEMENTS

When customers buy some software, they are buying a copy of the software together with the right to use it in certain ways. There are many different types of restrictions that a licence agreement may place on the extent to which a customer can use the software. Here are some examples:

- A licence may allow the licensee to use one copy of the software on his computer. This is the type of licence commonly granted when software such as a computer game is purchased from a retail outlet.

- A licence may allow the licensee to run the software on a server on his local area network and for it to be used by any number of users simultaneously, up to some agreed maximum number. This type of licence is used, for example, for large multi-user database management systems and for applications such as accounting packages intended for the corporate market.

- A licence may allow the licensee to run as many copies of the software as he wishes on computers at specified premises. This often known as a *site licence.*

There are several things that a software vendor may be concerned about when providing a customer with a licence to use one of its products:

- making sure that it is not giving away any of its own rights in the software;

- limiting the extent to which the customer can use the software, so that if the customer wants to use it more extensively he must pay an additional licence fee;

- ensuring a regular income from support activities, possibly an annual maintenance charge, possibly fees for consultancy services;

- ensuring that, as far as is possible, it will not be liable for any defects in the software.

We shall return to licensing in Chapter 13.

LIABILITY FOR DEFECTIVE SOFTWARE

Suppliers of software and hardware are very reluctant to give a contractual commitment that it is fit for any purpose whatsoever. Standard terms and conditions will invariably contain a clause that tries to limit the supplier's liability if it turns out that the software or hardware is defective. The law, however, limits how far such clauses can be effective.

Most contracts will limit the extent of any liability either to the purchase price of the product or to some fixed maximum figure. This means that, if the product completely fails to work, the supplier agrees to refund the purchase price or possibly a bit more if some other maximum is specified.

The Unfair Contract Terms Act 1977 restricts the extent to which clauses in standard terms and conditions limiting liability can be effective. In particular, it is not possible to limit the damages payable if a defect in the product causes death or personal injury. This applies as much to software as it does to motor vehicles, say. Thus if a company supplies software to control a light railway link and a defect in the software leads to an accident in which people are killed or injured, then any clause in the contract for the supply of that software that claims to restrict liability will not be enforceable in respect of the claims for damages for the deaths and injuries.

This restriction is an important one for companies that produce safety-critical software and it also led at least one hardware supplier to refuse to sell its products to the nuclear industry. However, although this is very relevant when buying, say, a motor car, it is not very relevant to most individuals or companies when dealing with software, because the software that they use or develop is very unlikely to cause death or personal industry. They are much more likely to be concerned about software that doesn't do what it was claimed to do or that has too many bugs to be usable.

At this point we need to distinguish between consumer sales and non-consumer sales. For a sale to be treated as a consumer sale: the buyer must be a private person; the buyer must buy from a seller who is acting in the course of a business; and the goods must be of a type ordinarily supplied for private use or consumption. In a consumer sale, the requirements of the Sale of Goods Act 1979 and the Supply of Goods and Services Act 1982 cannot be excluded. The most important requirement of the Sale of Goods Act in the context of software is that goods sold must be fit for the purpose for which such goods are commonly supplied. This means, for example, that if you buy a printer for use on your computer at home, it must be capable of printing reliably and clearly, at a usable speed.

There is, unfortunately, a problem about software. Because software is intangible, it has never been satisfactorily decided whether or not it comes under the definition of 'goods' and hence it is not clear whether the Sale of Goods Act 1979 applies to the sale of software. It is generally thought that it does apply to the sale of retail software or software sold under a shrink-wrapped licences, but that it would not apply to bespoke software, which would therefore come under the Supply of Goods and Services Act 1982. This only requires that 'reasonable skill and care' has been used. This is a very difficult test to apply and, in practice, would provide little protection.

The Unfair Contract Terms Act 1977 again comes to the rescue. Whether or not the sale is a consumer sale, it allows liability to be limited or excluded only to the extent that it is reasonable to do so.

The view that a court will take depends very much on the circumstances of a particular case but a particularly illuminating example is the 1996 case of *St Albans City and District Council v International Computers Ltd.* The facts were that the council had ordered a computer system from ICL to enable it to compute the Community Charge (a system of local taxation that is no longer in use) for the forthcoming year. ICL insisted on using its standard terms and conditions which stated that its liability 'will not exceed the price or charge payable for the item of Equipment, Program or Service in respect of which liability arises or £100,000 (whichever is the lesser) …'. Errors in the software and incorrect advice from ICL's project manager meant that the population of the area was overestimated, so the residents were undercharged and the council lost £1.3 million.

The judge at the initial hearing found that the software was not fit for the purpose for which it was provided and that ICL's project manager had been negligent. ICL was therefore in breach of contract. The clause limiting liability had to be measured against the requirement of reasonableness. The judge noted that ICL was a substantial organization with worldwide product liability insurance of £50 million; that all potential suppliers of the system dealt on similar standard terms; that the council was under pressure to install the system before the Community Charge was introduced; that, although the council was a business and not a consumer, it did not usually operate in the same commercial field as a normal business and that it would be impractical for it to insure against commercial risks. On balance, the judge found that the clause limiting liability to £100,000 was not reasonable and was therefore ineffective. ICL appealed, but the Court of Appeal confirmed the judgement. However, the value of this case as a precedent will be limited, for each case turns on its facts.

HEALTH AND SAFETY

The Health and Safety at Work Act (1974) completely changed the approach to safety in Britain. European thinking was also affected by the Act and there has been fruitful exchange of ideas.

It is not appropriate to go into detail about the provisions of the Act here, but it is important to understand the implications that the Act has for information systems engineers. The Act states: 'It shall be the duty of every employer to ensure, so far as is reasonably practicable, the health, safety and welfare at work of all his employees.' It breaks this duty up into a number of more specific duties. The ones that are of particular concern to software engineers are:

- provision and maintenance of safe plant;
- provision and maintenance of safe systems of work;
- provision of such information, instruction, training, and supervision as necessary;
- ensuring the workplace is maintained in a safe condition;
- provision and maintenance of a safe working environment and adequate welfare arrangements.

The Act also requires employers to ensure that their activities do not expose the general public to risks to their health and safety. Manufacturers of equipment to be used at work also have a responsibility to ensure that it is safe.

Failure to comply with the Health and Safety at Work Act is a criminal offence and, in serious cases, can lead to criminal proceedings being taken against individuals.

Trains, ships and aeroplanes are all places where people work and where the general public are present. The safety obligations listed above therefore apply to them. Furthermore, they all involve equipment that is controlled by software and accidents may occur as a result of defects in that software.

Modern manufacturing plants are usually software controlled and can be dangerous; robots in particular can be dangerous for people working with them. Modern chemical plants, oil refineries, and power stations, especially nuclear ones, are all software controlled and software failures can result in accidents that affect not only the workforce but also the general public.

This book is not the appropriate place to discuss how software is or should be written in order to meet the high levels of reliability required for safety-related applications. You should understand clearly, however, that there is an extensive literature on the subject and that there are national and international standards relating to it. An organization that undertakes to develop safety-related software without employing staff who are familiar with the appropriate development techniques is likely to be in breach of the Health and Safety at Work Act. The clause in the BCS Code of Conduct (and similar clauses in other codes) regarding claims of competence are also relevant.

FURTHER READING

The following book, from the BCS/Springer Practitioner series, covers IT outsourcing in depth and is written specifically for information systems professionals. It contains one chapter dedicated to contractual matters:

Sparrow, E. (2003) *Successful IT Outsourcing*. Springer Verlag, London.

Fuller coverage of the material in this chapter, including health and safety issues, will be found in Chapters 5, 9 and 10 of:

Bott, M.F., Coleman, J.A., Eaton, J., and Rowland, D. (2001) *Professional Issues in Software Engineering*, 3rd Edition. Taylor and Francis, London.

13 Intellectual Property Rights

After studying this chapter, you should:

- *be familiar with the main types of intellectual property right;*
- *understand how these rights can be used to protect software;*
- *be aware of the limitations of this protection;*
- *understand the main issues in the continuing debate about software patents.*

INTRODUCTION

If someone steals your bicycle, you no longer have it. If someone takes away a computer belonging to a company, the company no longer has it.

This seems very obvious. In fact, it hides an important and subtle point. If you invent a drug that will cure all known illnesses and leave the formula on your desk, someone can come along, read the formula, remember it, and go away and make a fortune out of manufacturing the drug. But you still have the formula even though the other person now has it as well. This shows that the formula – more generally, any piece of information – is not property in the same way that a bicycle is.

The legal definition of theft involves taking away a piece of someone's property with the intention permanently to deprive them of it. As we have just seen, this cannot apply to a piece of information.

Property such as bicycles or computers is called tangible property, that is, property that can be touched. It is protected by laws relating to theft and damage. Property that is intangible is known as *intellectual property*. It is governed by a different set of laws, concerned with *intellectual property rights*, that is, rights to use, copy, or reveal information about intellectual property.

Intellectual property crosses national borders much more readily than tangible property and the international nature of intellectual property rights has long been recognized. The international law relating to trade marks and patents is based on the Paris Convention, which was signed in 1883. The Berne Convention, which lies at the basis of international copyright law, was signed in 1886.

Rapid changes in technology and the commercial developments that follow them present the law with new problems. The law relating to intellectual property rights is evolving very rapidly and most of this evolution is taking place in a global or regional context. For the UK, European Union law regarding intellectual property rights is critically important, but this law is itself much influenced by developments elsewhere, particularly in the USA.

Software can be very valuable, as the balance sheets of companies such as Oracle, IBM or Microsoft show. But software is intangible property. The industry can only therefore protect its assets by using intellectual property rights. Hence the importance of the topic for information systems engineers and hence the length of this chapter.

DIFFERENT TYPES OF INTELLECTUAL PROPERTY RIGHTS

There are several different rights that relate to intellectual property. In this book, we shall only be concerned with those that are relevant to software and the information systems industry. These rights should be looked on as a package; different rights may be used to protect different aspects of a piece of software.

Copyright is, as the name suggests, concerned with the right to copy something. It may be a written document, a picture or photograph, a piece of music, a recording, or many other things, including a computer program.

Patents are primarily intended to protect inventions, by giving inventors a monopoly on exploiting their inventions for a certain period.

Confidential information is information that a person receives in circumstances that make it clear they must not pass it on.

Trade marks identify the product of a particular manufacturer or supplier.

Any or all of these rights can be used to protect a piece of software. Suppose, for example, that a company has developed an innovative computer game called 'Spookcatcher'. The game is marketed in packaging that features the name superimposed on the image of a ghost. It comes with an add-on device that the company has invented called a wailer. This attaches to the computer and emits very convincing ghostly wails at suitable points in the action. The software uses some very clever data structures developed within the company that make it possible to achieve very high performance.

The law of copyright automatically protects the source code and all documentation of the package from copying. The company might be able to patent the wailer, in which case no one else would be able to produce a similar product. The law relating to confidential information could be used to prevent any employee who left to join a competitor from passing on details of the clever data structure. And the name and the logo could be registered as a trade mark to prevent other companies from using it on their products.

In the next four sections we shall discuss each of these rights separately and explain the conditions under which they come into existence and what their effects are. The use of internet domain names can conflict with trade marks and, arguably, domain names are themselves a special type of intellectual property right. We therefore devote a separate section to domain names below.

COPYRIGHT

As the name suggests, copyright is associated primarily with the right to copy something. The 'something' is known as the work. Only certain types of work are protected by copyright law. The types that concern us here are 'original literary, dramatic, musical or artistic' works. The 1988 Copyright Design and Patents Act states that the term 'literary work' includes a table or compilation, a computer program, preparatory design material for a computer program and certain databases.

Copyright comes into existence when the work is written down or recorded in some other way. It is not necessary to register it in any way.

The rights of the copyright owner

Copyright law gives the owner of the copyright certain exclusive rights. The rights that are relevant to software and, more generally, to written documents, are the following:

- The right to make copies of the work: Making a copy of a work includes copying code from a disc into RAM (random access memory) in order to execute the code. It also includes downloading a page from the web to view on your computer, whether or not you then store the page on your local disk.

- The right to issue copies of the work to the public, whether or not they are charged for it.

- The right to adapt the work: This includes translating it – whether from English to Chinese or from C to Java.

In other words, no one can do any of these things without the copyright owner's permission. In some cases, the permission may be implied rather than explicit. The act of making a document available on the web implies that people are allowed to view it over the internet, which involves copying it into the memory of their own computer; however, it does not necessarily extend to allowing people to store copies on their local disc or to print it.

In general, these rights last for 70 years after the death of the author; there are, however, many exceptions and special cases. This is far longer than is likely to be commercially relevant for software, although there is software still in use that was written well over 30 years ago.

It is very important to realize that copyright law does not give the owner of the copyright any power to prevent someone else using or publishing identical material, provided they can show that they did not produce it by copying the copyright work. (This is in marked contrast to patent law.) This means that programmers do not need to worry that they will be breaching copyright if they inadvertently produce code that is identical to that produced by another programmer somewhere else – something that can easily happen.

What you can do to a copyright work

The law specifically permits certain actions in relation to a copyright work and some of these are of particular relevance to software.

First, it is explicitly stated that it is not an infringement of copyright to make a backup of a program that you are authorized to use. However, only one such copy is allowed. If the program is stored in a filing system with a sophisticated backup system, multiple backup copies are likely to come into existence.

Secondly, you can 'decompile' a program in order to correct errors in it. You can also decompile a program in order to obtain the information you need to write a program that will 'interoperate' with it, provided this information is not available to you in any other way.

Thirdly, you can sell your right to use a program in much the same way that you can sell a book you own. However, when you do this, you sell all your rights. In particular, you must not retain a copy of the program.

Databases

Copyright subsists in a database if 'its contents constitute the author's own intellectual creation'. There are many databases that do not satisfy this criterion but which, nonetheless, require a lot of effort and a lot of money to prepare. Examples might include databases of hotels, pop songs, or geographic data. In order to encourage the production of such modest but useful databases, regulations were introduced in 1997 to create a special intellectual property right called the database right. The database right subsists in a database 'if there has been substantial investment in obtaining, verifying or presenting the contents of the database'. It lasts for 15 years and prevents anyone from extracting or reusing all, or a substantial part of, the database without the owner's permission. Fifteen years is much less than the protection given by copyright but is, in practice, likely to be longer than the commercially valuable life of the database, unless it is updated. If it is updated, however, a new 15-year period will start.

Copyright infringement

Anyone who, without permission, does one of the things that are the exclusive right of the copyright owner is said to infringe the copyright. There are two sorts of infringement. Primary infringement takes place whenever any of the exclusive rights of the copyright owner is breached. It is a matter for the civil courts and the usual remedies are available: a claim for damages or an injunction to refrain from the infringement are the most likely. Secondary infringement occurs when primary infringement occurs in a business or commercial context. In the case of software, this could involve trading in pirated software or it could involve using pirated software within a business. This is a much more serious matter and may result in criminal proceedings leading to a substantial fine or imprisonment and the confiscation of the copying equipment, as well as civil damages.

Software and other material distributed in digital form is now often protected against copying by some sort of technical device. Inevitably, information about how to circumvent this protection has appeared on the web and ready-made devices to do it are available from certain sources. The 1988 Act provides that anyone who publishes such information or makes, imports or sells such devices will be treated in the same way as if they were infringing the copyright in a protected work.

There are some cases in which it may be difficult to demonstrate that copying has taken place. Books of mathematical tables fall into this category, because the numbers in them have an objective existence – the square root of 2 correct to four decimal places is 1.4142, regardless of who calculated it. In order to protect their copyright, the compilers of mathematical tables commonly insert a few small, random errors (one unit in the last decimal place) in their tables. Anyone who copies the tables rather than recalculating them will reproduce the errors and this can be adduced as evidence to show that copying has taken place. A similar technique could be used to help demonstrate that copying of source code had taken place. In this case, the writer could insert the occasional statement that had no functional effect. If the code were copied, the presence of such statements would be convincing evidence of the fact.

Ownership and licensing

As a general rule, the copyright in a work belongs initially to its author. If the work is jointly written by several authors, they jointly own the copyright. There is one important exception to this. If the author is an employee and has written the work as part of his or her job, then the copyright belongs to the employer, unless there is an explicit, written agreement to the contrary. Note that the copyright nevertheless extends to 70 years after the author (or the last of the joint authors) dies, even though it is very improbable that it will be possible to trace their names!

The employer owns the copyright only if the author is legally an employee. If the author is an independent contractor, he or she will own the copyright unless there is an agreement to the contrary. For this reason, if a company commissions an independent contractor (freelance programmer) to write software, it is important to have a formal agreement regarding ownership of the copyright in the resulting software.

It is very common for the owner of the copyright in a piece of software to license other people or organizations to carry out some of the activities that are otherwise the exclusive right of the copyright owner. The copyright remains the property of the owner, but the *licensees* (the people to whom the software is licensed) acquire certain rights. There are many different types of licence in use. We have already seen examples of licences for different types of usage but there are other types of licences, for example, the licensee may itself be a marketing company that is granted the right to license other people to use the software. Companies that produce software packages frequently do not have the expertise to market the software outside their own countries and they therefore license agents to sell it for them in other countries. Computer games are usually produced by fairly small companies that have no capacity to market their games. Instead, they license large international companies to market them.

Licences themselves may be granted i*n perpetuity* (that is, for ever), or for some fixed period. Licences for retail software are usually granted in perpetuity. Licences for corporate software are typically granted on an annual basis; the initial fee may be larger than the fee for the annual renewal. Marketing licences are normally for a fixed period.

The owner of the copyright can transfer ownership to someone else. This is known as assignment of the copyright and must be done in writing. In this case, the new owner of the copyright has all the rights that the previous owner had.

When an organization commissions bespoke (that is, tailor-made) software from another company, it is important that both sides think carefully about the licensing and ownership of the copyright in the software produced. There was a time when the customer would expect to take ownership of the copyright in all the software supplied. This is no longer realistic. Parts of the software supplied are likely to be proprietary products that the supplier has developed to enable them to construct such systems quickly and efficiently; they are part of the supplier's fixed assets and it would be absurd to transfer ownership of them to a customer. Other parts of the software may be products acquired from other sources (possibly open source software) and the supplier will not have the right to assign copyright in them. The customer's needs can almost certainly be satisfied by a suitable licence. However, the customer must take into account the long-term need for maintenance and ensure that they have the right, for example, to give another contractor access to the source code and documentation for maintenance purposes.

Where does copyright law come from?

The primary source of law relating to copyright in the UK is the Copyright, Design and Patents Act 1988; important amendments to the Act were made by the Copyright (Computer Programs) Regulations 1992, the Copyright and Rights in Databases Regulations 1997, and the Copyright and Related Rights Regulations 2003. Many of these amendments were made in order to comply with EU legislation and the description of copyright given here is broadly valid throughout the EU. A much larger number of countries (121) have signed the Berne Convention, last revised in 1979. Countries that sign the Berne Convention agree to establish national laws protecting copyright along the lines described above. In practice, details such as the length of time for which protection is provided may vary, as may the enthusiasm with which countries pursue cases of copyright infringement.

PATENTS

What is a Patent?

A patent is a temporary right, granted by the state, enabling an inventor to prevent other people from exploiting his invention without his permission. Unlike copyright, it does not come into existence automatically; the inventor must apply for the patent to be granted. However, the protection it gives is much stronger than copyright, because the grant of a patent allows the person owning it (the *patentee*) to prevent anyone else from exploiting the invention, even if they have discovered it for themselves.

Patents were originally intended to encourage new inventions, and in particular to encourage the disclosure of those new inventions. Inventors are often hesitant to reveal the details of their invention, for fear that someone else might copy it. A government-granted temporary monopoly on the commercial use of their invention provides a remedy for this fear, and so acts as an incentive to disclose the details of the invention. After the monopoly period expires, everyone else is free to practice the invention. And because of the disclosure made by the inventor, it is very easy to do so.

The temporary monopoly also gives the inventor a chance to recoup investments made during the development of his invention. They could, for instance, use the patent to monopolize the market, excluding possible competitors by enforcing their patent. They could then set a high price and make a nice profit. They could also request money from others in return for a license to practice the invention. The licensing income then provides extra income. Licensing a patent can be a very lucrative business.

What can be patented?

In Europe, the law relating to patents is based on the European Patent Convention. This was signed in 1973 by 27 European countries, and came into force in 1978. The UK's obligations under the Convention were implemented in the Patents Act 1977, although there have been some subsequent modifications. The 1977 Act states that an invention can only be patented if it:

- is new;
- involves an inventive step;
- is capable of industrial application;
- is not in an area specifically excluded.

Similar criteria apply in all the countries that are signatories to the Convention.

The requirement that the invention must be new means that it must not have been disclosed or used publicly before the date on which the patent application was made. This applies as much to publication or use by the inventor as by anyone else. Thus if Alexander Graham Bell had demonstrated the telephone or written an article about it before he applied for his patent, the patent would not have been granted.

When a patent application is filed, officials at the Patent Office will search existing patents as well as the literature in the area to see whether the invention has been described before. The searches will not be limited to the literature published in the country where the application is made and they may go back many years. Provided it is publicly available (even if only with great difficulty) any publication describing the invention, no matter how obscure the source, will lead to the rejection of the application.

The requirement for an 'inventive step' means essentially that the invention should not be obvious. In other words, it must not be something that anyone reasonably competent in the field would have produced if faced with the same requirements. Thus, leaving aside any other considerations, a program to print invoices for a company is unlikely to satisfy the requirement for an inventive step, even if no one has ever written precisely the same program before, because any competent programmer would have written very much the same program.

The requirement that the invention is capable of industrial application is simply a requirement that the invention must have a practical application (sometimes referred to as a 'technical effect').

Following the European Patent Convention, the Patents Act 1977 excludes the following:

- Scientific theories: The theory of gravity cannot be patented although a machine that uses it in a novel way could be.

- Mathematical methods: This means, for example, that the methods used for carrying out floating point arithmetic cannot be patented. A machine that uses the ideas can however be patented.

- A literary, dramatic, musical or artistic work or any other aesthetic creation: As we have already seen, these are protected by copyright.

- The presentation of information: Again this is covered by the law of copyright.

- A scheme, rule or method for performing a mental act, playing a game or doing business, or a program for a computer.

The last of these exclusions is the one that is by far the most important for the readers of this book and we shall discuss it at length later in this section.

Obtaining a patent

Unlike copyright, which comes into existence automatically when the protected work is recorded, whether in writing or otherwise, a patent must be explicitly applied for. Applying for a patent can be an expensive and time-consuming business.

Patents are granted by national patent offices. Inventors who want protection in several different countries must, in principle, apply separately to the patent offices of each country. In practice, there are schemes run by the European Patent Office and the World Intellectual Property Organization

(WIPO) that provide some assistance by simplifying the process of applying for patents in several countries simultaneously and by reducing its cost.

The requirement that an invention must be new if a patent is to be granted means that the date at which the patent application is first filed is critical, because it is at this date that the invention must be new. If someone else filed a similar application the day before, then that one will have priority. An initial application to one national patent office is enough to establish priority, provided it is followed within 12 months by the submission of a full patent specification to the national patent offices of all the countries in which a patent is sought, possibly through the European Patent Office or through WIPO.

The full patent specification needs to be prepared by a specialist patent attorney and it can take up to four years for the process of obtaining patents to be completed.

Because computing is a global industry, any patents relating to computing need to be taken out in enough countries to make sure that the market in which the invention is not protected is too small to attract a competitor.

Enforcing a patent

The grant of a patent is not a guarantee that it can be effectively enforced. If you own a patent and you find that someone is infringing the patent, you may have to go to the courts to enforce your rights. In the court hearing, the offender can challenge your patent on the grounds that it does not satisfy the criteria listed above. The commonest challenge is on grounds of 'prior art', that is, that the invention is not new. The other likely challenge is that it does not involve an inventive step, in other words, that anyone of reasonable competence in the field could have produced the invention simply by following established practice.

The problem is that enforcing a patent that you own or challenging a patent held by someone else is a time-consuming and expensive process. This means that if a large company finds that a small competitor is producing something that can be claimed to infringe the large company's patent, even though that patent might be impossible to defend, the small company may have to give in because it cannot afford the legal costs involved. It also means that if an individual or a small company owns a patent, a large company can challenge that patent or even blatantly infringe it, knowing that the holder of the patent cannot afford to contest the challenge effectively.

Software patents

For many years, the US Patent and Trade Mark Office (PTO) refused to grant patents for any invention that involved a computer program. In 1981, however, it was ordered by the Supreme Court to grant a patent on a method for 'curing rubber', the novel element of which was a computer program to calculate the optimal way of heating the rubber.

Very roughly, the position in the USA is now that software can be patented if:

- it is part of a product that is itself eligible to be patented;
- it controls a process that has some physical effect (e.g. curing rubber);
- it processes data that arises from the physical world.

As we have seen, the European Patent Convention and the Copyright, Designs and Patents Act 1988 both state unequivocally that a patent cannot be granted for a computer program. Despite these provisions, the European Patent Office has been granting patents for software since 1998, as has the UK Patent Office. Patent offices in the different European countries have adopted different policies towards the patenting of software, with the result that there is much confusion about what is and what is not patentable. The result is that there is a conflict between the law and practice, a very undesirable situation.

In order to clarify the situation, the European Commission produced a draft directive. When this was submitted to the European Parliament, it was extensively modified. The resulting version has been heavily criticized and is unlikely to be accepted. The confusion therefore looks set to continue.

The question of software patents has proved to be extremely controversial. There are very many websites and many organizations dedicated to opposing the idea of software patents. The arguments for and against the patenting of software can be summed up as below.

On the one hand, it is illogical and unfair that something that would be clearly patentable if implemented completely in hardware should not be patentable if implemented in software. Furthermore, patents encourage investment because:

- a patent is a well-defined asset that allows shareholders and, in particular, venture capitalists to be confident that their investment is producing something of value;
- patents ensure that the benefit of research and development accrues to the people who financed it.

On the other hand, the software industry has been immensely productive and successful. Much of its success is due to the efforts of small companies. Patents are not helpful to small companies. Even if they can afford to file for patents, they cannot afford to defend their patents or defend themselves against invalid claims for patent infringement coming from large companies. Anyway, the industry has done well enough without patent protection.

Many of the patents granted are 'bad' patents because they are not new or because there is no inventive step. A very great deal of software was written before software patents were thought possible. This means the records of prior art are very patchy. Although such patents could not be successfully defended in court, the threat of patent litigation, which is always likely to be both expensive and protracted, could restrict the activities of many smaller companies or even force them out of business.

CONFIDENTIAL INFORMATION

As we have already explained, information cannot be 'stolen'. Nevertheless, it is possible to take action in a civil court to prevent someone from using or revealing information that they have received in confidence. The critical point is that the information must have been given to that person in circumstances that give rise to what is known as an *obligation of confidence*.

It is common for an obligation of confidence to come into existence as a result of a specific clause in a contract. Contracts for consultancy services or the provision of bespoke software will invariably include specific clauses binding each party to keep confidential any information it obtains about the operations or products of the other. Non-disclosure agreements are agreements that are specifically intended to set up obligations of confidence. It is common, for example, when two companies are discussing possible collaboration, for each side to sign such a non-disclosure agreement to protect the information that they exchange.

Where there is no specific contractual term that creates an obligation of confidence, such an obligation may still exist under equity, that part of the law that reflects general notions of fair dealing. Under equity, an obligation of confidence exists whenever a reasonable person, placed in the position of the recipient of the information, would reasonably understand that the information was being given to them in confidence.

One important aspect of confidential information relates to ideas that are likely to be the subject of a patent application. Because the application may be rejected if it can be shown that the ideas had already been made public, it is important that the inventor only discusses them in conditions where an obligation of confidence exists, whether this is through the signing of a non-disclosure agreement or otherwise.

Another important example of confidential information is information about current sales prospects. In practice, not many software companies have the type of trade secrets the disclosure of which would cause them serious damage. However, at any time, nearly all of them will be engaged in sales negotiations with a range of prospective customers and a knowledge of the content of these negotiations could certainly enable a competitor to gain a considerable advantage. If a member of the sales staff of company X gives notice of the intention to leave and join a competitor Y, it would be unwise to rely purely on the obligation of confidence, however clearly this is spelt out in the contract of employment. The difficulty is that it might be very difficult to prove that they had revealed crucial information that subsequently enabled Y to win a contract that X was expecting to win. For this reason, it is common for sales staff, and other staff who are likely to have sensitive knowledge about sales negotiations, to be employed on contracts of employment that specify comparatively long periods of notice – typically three or six months. When such employees give notice, they are immediately removed from the sensitive work and assigned to such important and worthy tasks as reorganizing the company's technical library.

Confidential information is not at all the same thing as professional skill and expertise. If, as part of your employment, you learn to programme in Perl or to design using UML (Unified Modeling Language) you take these skills with you and you are entitled to use them in your new employment.

An obligation of confidentiality is not absolute. A court may rule that it is in the public interest that certain confidential information is disclosed. While this rules out an action for breach of confidence, it does not prevent an employee who discloses such information from being dismissed. Over the years, there have been a number of well-publicized instances in which employees have disclosed confidential information about malpractice on the part of their employer; they have done this because they felt strongly that the malpractice – be it illegal price fixing or serious environmental damage – should be stopped. For a long time there was nothing to protect such employees, who are often known as 'whistle blowers' (see Chapter 10), from being fired by their employers, often in such circumstances that it was difficult or impossible for them to get another job. There are, however, many more instances in which employees have been victimized for drawing their employer's attention to matters that the employer would rather not be told about. The author knows of one instance in which an employee was effectively dismissed for drawing his employer's attention to a systematic fraud going on in the organization.

In 1998, Parliament passed the Public Interest Disclosure Act, which provides some protection for employees in these circumstances. First, the Act defines what sort of disclosure of information is covered. A 'qualifying disclosure', that is a disclosure to which the Act applies, means any disclosure of information which the person making the disclosure reasonably believes shows that one or more of the following has occurred or is about to occur:

- a criminal offence;
- failure to comply with a legal obligation;
- a miscarriage of justice;
- danger to health and safety;
- environmental damage;
- information showing that any of these has been concealed.

A worker making a qualifying disclosure will only be protected against victimization if the disclosure is made in the right circumstances. In this case, the disclosure is known as a protected disclosure. The rules defining the circumstances in which a disclosure become protected are complicated but they encourage the worker first of all to raise the matter internally – many employers have produced codes of practice on Public Interest Disclosure, which specify who the worker should make the disclosure to and the procedures for handling it. In more serious cases, or if the internal route has proved ineffective, it may be appropriate to disclose the information to a professional body or to a public official. Only in the most serious of cases will disclosure to the media be protected.

TRADE MARKS AND PASSING OFF

The law regarding trade marks in the UK is based on the Trade Marks Act 1994, which consolidated and updated existing legislation. The Act defines a trade mark as:

> ... any sign capable of being represented graphically which is capable of distinguishing goods or services of one undertaking from those of other undertakings. A trade mark may, in particular, consist of words (including personal names), designs, letters, numerals or the shape of goods or their packaging.

Some of the best known examples of trade marks include the name Coca Cola, the characteristic shape of the Coca Cola bottle, and the large M that serves to advertise McDonalds hamburger outlets. Microsoft is a trade mark, as are the names of many Microsoft products such as Outlook.

Provision is made for registering trade marks and most trade marks are now registered. In the UK this is done through the UK Patent Office. The Patent Office maintains a database of registered trade marks and their owners that can be searched over the internet. Trade marks are associated with particular classes of products so that it is quite possible for the same trade mark to belong to several different owners because each has registered it for a different class of product. There are comprehensive rules limiting what can be registered as a trade mark. Place names and the names of people, for example, will not generally be accepted for registration.

The 1994 Act makes it an offence to:

- apply a unauthorized registered trade mark (that is, a registered trade mark that you do not own or do not have the owner's permission to use) to goods;

- sell or offer for sale (or hire), goods or packaging that bear an unauthorized trade mark;

- import or export goods that bear an unauthorized trade mark;

- have in the course of business, goods for sale or hire goods (or packaging) that bear an unauthorized trade mark.

In most circumstances, the offence will be criminal and punishable by a fine or up to two years' imprisonment. However, the trade mark owner can also bring civil proceedings to claim for the financial damage he may have suffered.

Under the General Agreement on Tariffs and Trade (GATT), to which most countries are signatories, countries that do not have suitable laws to protect trade marks (or intellectual property rights more generally) or where such laws are not effectively enforced will face trade sanctions. It is hoped that this will stamp out the flagrant piracy that exists at present.

Even where a trade mark is not registered, action can be taken in the civil courts against products that imitate the appearance or 'get up' of an existing product. This is known as the tort of 'passing off'. It is, however, usually better to register the trade mark than to rely on protection under civil law, because the legal action involved in defending it will be much more straight-forward.

Trade marks are an effective way of protecting retail package software from piracy. Given that pirated software can be distributed over the internet with no physical packaging, it is desirable to display the trade mark prominently when the software is loaded, as well as displaying it on the packaging.

DOMAIN NAMES

Internet domain names are ultimately managed by the Internet Corporation for Assigned Names and Numbers (ICANN). ICANN is an internationally organized, non-profit making corporation. Its main responsibility is ensuring the 'universal resolvability' of internet addresses; that is, ensuring that the same domain name will always lead to the same internet location wherever it is used from and whatever the circumstances. In practice, ICANN delegates the responsibility for assigning individual domain names to other bodies, subject to strict rules.

Domain names were originally meant to be used just as a means of simplifying the process of connecting one computer to another over the internet. However, because they are easy to remember, they have come to be used as a way of identifying businesses. Indeed, they are frequently used in advertising. Conversely, it is not surprising that companies should want to use their trade marks or their company names as their internet domain names.

The potential for conflict between trade marks and domain names is inherent in the two systems. Trade marks are registered with public authorities on a national or regional basis. The owner of the trade mark acquires rights over the use of the trade mark in a specific country or region. Identical trade marks may be owned by different persons in respect of different categories of product. Domain names are usually allocated by a non-governmental organization and are globally unique; they are normally allocated on a first come, first served basis. This means that if different companies own identical trade marks for different categories of product or for different geographical areas, only one of them can have the trade mark as domain name, and that will be the first to apply.

The inconsistencies between the two different systems of registration has made it possible for people to register, as their own domain names, trade marks belonging to other companies. This is sometimes known as cyber squatting. They then offer to sell these domain names to the owner of the trade mark at an inflated price. It is usually cheaper and quicker for the trade mark owner to pay up than to pursue legal remedies, even when these are available.

In 1999, the WIPO published a report entitled 'The management of internet names and addresses: Intellectual property issues'. WIPO is an international organization with 177 states as members. The report recommended that ICANN adopt a policy called the Uniform Domain Name Dispute Resolution Policy (UDRP), which includes specific provisions against cyber squatting. This policy has proved reasonably effective. Within two years, over 3,000 complaints had been dealt with by one of the arbitration centres alone, with 80 per cent being resolved.

In 2001, WIPO published a second report, 'The recognition of rights and the use of names in the internet domain system'. This addresses conflicts between domain names and identifiers other than trade marks. Examples of such conflicts are the use of personal names in domain names or the use of the names of particular peoples or geographic areas by organizations that have no connection with them. These conflicts are more difficult to deal with than conflicts between trade marks and domain names because the international framework that underlies trade marks is missing in these other cases.

EXAMINATION QUESTIONS

The following examination question is taken from a special paper set in 2003. It illustrates well how candidates are expected to be able to apply their knowledge to specific scenarios.

Discuss the issues that the following scenarios raise:

a) Parsley is a company that produces accounting software. It is successful and its software is widely used. Nevertheless, it has a major weakness in that it doesn't detect file overflow; if file overflow occurs, transactions are lost without warning. Customers are told that they must check the size of certain files weekly. Peter was, until recently, head of quality control at Parsley and repeatedly drew attention to this problem. Nevertheless, management refused to allocate the fairly substantial resources necessary to rectify it.

Peter has now moved to Juniper, one of Parsley's competitors. Since then, Parsley's sales staff have noticed that, in sales situations where they are competing directly with Juniper, potential customers have been asking them how their software handles file overflow conditions. Under determined questioning, the sales staff have had to admit to the problem. As a result, they have lost a large number of sales to Juniper. Parsley now wishes to take action against Peter for breach of confidentiality.

[10 marks]

b) Talybont Games Ltd is a small games developer, employing about 20 staff. It has developed a very successful game that is marketed by the games publisher MegaPastimes under the trade mark Boglehunter. (Bogle is a Scots word for a ghost.)

A few months ago, Alice and Brian, two of the senior games designers at Talybont Games left the company to join Borth Simulators Ltd, a company specializing in the development of simulation games. Borth recently produced a game very similar to Boglehunter, which is marketed by another large games publisher Goldengames. It is sold under the name Boglecatcher at a price some 30 per cent less than Boglehunter. Its packaging resembles that of Boglehunter to the extent that the colour schemes and type styles are similar.

Both Talybont Games and MegaPastimes wish to take legal action against what they regard as piracy.

[15 marks]

Part (a) is clearly about confidential information (see 'Confidential information' on page 163). In order for the action to succeed, Parsley will need to demonstrate that:

- potential customers are being led to ask about the handling of file overflow conditions as a result of prompting by Juniper's sales staff; and
- that Juniper's sales staff are doing this as a result of information they have received from Peter; and
- that this information was the subject of an obligation of confidence.

The first two of these are likely to prove difficult because information about the deficiency in the software might easily have come from other users of Parsley's products – it is common practice when purchasing software to consult colleagues in other companies about their experiences with the packages under consideration – or from articles in the trade press. Peter is certainly under an obligation of confidence deriving from his position as a senior employee in Parsley, whether or not there is an express term in his contract of employment. However, Juniper might be able to argue that the problem was common knowledge in the industry and not therefore the subject of an obligation of confidence. All in all, it seems that Parsley will have difficulty in taking effective legal action. Peter would not be able to avail himself of the protection offered by the Public Interest Disclosure Act, even if he needed it, because the information would not constitute a qualifying disclosure.

In part (b), action could be taken under the law of confidential information, copyright law, or trade mark law.

Talybont could take action against Alice and Brian for breach of confidentiality. They are clearly under an obligation of confidence so far as specific pieces of information acquired during their employment by Talybont are concerned. However, it is not at all clear that they have used any information during their employment by Borth that could not have been acquired simply by purchasing a copy of Boglehunter. Their knowledge of how to develop games programs is part of their professional expertise and is not subject to the law regarding confidential information. Finally, they are probably not rich enough to be worth suing.

A second course of action might be to take action against either or both of Borth or Goldengames for breach of copyright. This action would only succeed if it could be shown that a substantial part of the software for Boglecatcher had been copied from Boglehunter. If this is the case, fine, but it is unlikely.

The most promising line is for MegaPastimes to take action against Goldengames for infringement of its trade mark. This could be done under the tort of passing off or under the Trade Marks Act 1994. The latter is likely to be simpler. In either case it will be necessary to persuade the court that the name Boglecatcher is sufficiently similar to Boglehunter to cause confusion on the part of the public.

April 2000 question 3

NewSoft develop bespoke software for other organizations. Each project involves the production of a new computerized information system to the requirements of the client. Judith is a self-employed contractor and has recently been asked to produce a web-based electronic commerce system for a client of NewSoft, a furniture retailer called Sofas & Co. The e-commerce system allows the client organization to take orders and manage its customers electronically. Given the potential demand for similar systems, NewSoft has decided to reuse the software developed for the client and create a packaged solution.

Discuss the intellectual property rights involved in this situation.

[17 marks]

What action could have been taken either by Sofas & Co or by Judith?

[8 marks]

April 2002 question 1

a) The following are established ways of protecting intellectual property rights in software. Describe the purpose of each of these approaches and explain how each of them can be used to protect property rights in software.

i) **Copyright** [6 marks]

ii) **Patent** [6 marks]

iii) **Trade mark** [6 marks]

b) In a court case of North Software plc versus South Systems Ltd, it was established that North produced a market leading global positioning system. The systems director of North left the company and established a new company, South, to develop a competitive product. The new product was produced quickly and bore a strong resemblance to the North product. North is considering taking South to court.

Discuss the case between North and South, showing what North has to show to prove that its intellectual property rights have been infringed.

[7 marks]

APRIL 2003 QUESTION 6(a)

AMOS Ltd, a computer game developer, accessed ZULU Ltd's intranet to discover the design for a prototype game being developed by this competitor. Discuss how each of the following statutes relates to this situation:

i) **the UK Computer Misuse Act 1990**

ii) **the UK Copyright, Designs and Patents Act 1988.**

[10 marks]

FURTHER READING

The material in this chapter is covered in a great deal more detail in Chapter 6 of:

Bott, M. F., Coleman, J.A., Eaton, J. and Rowland, D. (2001) *Professional Issues in Software Engineering* (3rd edition). Taylor and Francis, London.

Software patents and the patenting of business methods are highly controversial topics that generate a great deal of material on the web and elsewhere. In particular, much space is devoted to trying to prevent the EU from following in the steps of the USA and allowing a wide range of software and business methods to be patented.

The UK government's position on the patenting of software and of business methods can be found in a report produced by the UK Patent Office in March 2001. This is available on the web at:

www.patent.gov.uk/about/consultations/conclusions.htm

A clear statement of the position in the USA can be found at:

www.bitlaw.com/software-patent/index.html

The two reports relating to domain names produced by the WIPO, 'The management of internet names and addresses: Intellectual property issues' (1999) and 'The recognition of rights and the use of names in the internet domain system' (2001), can be found in the WIPO website at:

wipo.int

14 Data Protection, Privacy and Freedom of Information

After studying this chapter, you should:

- *understand the concerns that led to the passing of legislation regarding data protection, freedom of information and privacy of communications;*
- *be familiar with the data protection principles enshrined in UK law;*
- *understand the main obligations that legislation in these areas imposes on the information systems professional.*

BACKGROUND

Public concern about data protection was first aroused when it was realized that a very large amount of data about individuals was being collected and stored in computers and then used for purposes that were not only different from those intended when the data was collected, but also unacceptable. There were also concerns that unauthorized people could access such data and that the data might be out of date, incomplete or just plain wrong. These concerns surfaced in the 1970s. They were particularly strong in the UK and the rest of Europe and led to a Council of Europe Convention on the subject. The first UK Data Protection Act, passed in 1984, was designed to implement the provisions of the Convention. It was designed to protect individuals from:

- the use of inaccurate personal information or information that is incomplete or irrelevant;
- the use of personal information by unauthorized persons;
- the use of personal information for purposes other than that for which it was collected.

It was meant primarily to protect individuals against the misuse of personal data by large organizations, public or private. Such misuse might occur, for example, if data-matching techniques are used on credit card records to build up a picture of a person's movements over an extended period. Further, errors can often creep into data that has been collected or data may be interpreted in a misleading way, and it was difficult to persuade the holders of the data to correct these. For example, credit rating agencies might advise against giving a person a loan because someone who previously lived at the same address defaulted on a loan.

By the mid-1990s, a different danger had become apparent. As individuals began to use the internet for an ever wider range of purposes, it became possible to capture information about the way individuals use the internet and to build profiles of their habits that can be used for marketing purposes and also, perhaps, for more sinister purposes such as blackmail. What is more, this can be done by much smaller and much shadowier organizations than those that were the object of the 1984 Act. These and other concerns led in 1995 to the European Directive on Data Protection which, in turn, led to the 1998 Data Protection Act.

A related but more general concern is that of individual privacy. Most people feel that they are entitled to keep personal information, such as their bank balance, their medical history or how they vote in elections, private. This extends to other things that don't obviously fall under the heading of information – personal correspondence, phone calls, or photographs taken on private occasions, for example. UK law does not recognize any general right to privacy but the European Convention on Human Rights, which forms part of UK law, states, in section 8(1): 'Everyone has the right to respect for his private and family life, his home and his correspondence.' Concern over telephone tapping and e-mail monitoring, by employers as much as by the security services, led to the Regulation of Investigatory Powers Act (2000).

While most people will accept that individuals have a right to privacy, they do not feel that this should extend to governments. Governments are traditionally reluctant to release information to their citizens, even when no question of security arises. There have been many cases where governments appear to have kept information secret in order to avoid acknowledging their responsibilities or compensating individuals for government mistakes. As a result, there has been pressure for more open government and for legislation that will guarantee freedom of information. Australia, Canada, the USA, and a few other countries enacted such legislation in the 1979s and 1980s. The UK had to wait for the passing of the Freedom of Information Act 2000. Many countries still have no legislation in this area.

(You should notice that the terms *data* and *information* are used in a very confused way in UK legislation and you should not read any significance into the use of one rather than the other!)

DATA PROTECTION

As we have seen, the first UK legislation on data protection was the 1984 Data Protection Act. However, this was superseded by the 1998 Act and it is on this that we shall base our discussion.

Terminology

The Act defines a number of terms that are widely used in discussions of data protection issues. In some cases these are different from the terms used in the 1984 Act.

Data means information that is being processed automatically or is collected with that intention or is recorded as part of a relevant filing system (see below).

Data controller means a person who determines why or how personal data is processed. This may be a legal person or a natural person.

Data processor, in this context, means anyone who processes personal data on behalf of the data controller and who is not an employee of the data controller. This might include an application service provider, such as a company that provides online hotel booking services.

Personal data means data which relates to a living person who can be identified from data, possibly taken together with other information the data controller is likely to have (but see 'Scope of the Act' on page 187). It includes expressions of opinion about the person and indications of the intentions of the data controller or any other person towards the individual (for example, whether their manager is planning to promote them).

Data subject means the individual who is the subject of personal data.

Sensitive personal data means personal data relating to the racial or ethnic origin of data subjects, their political opinions, their religious beliefs, whether they are members of trade unions, their physical or mental health, their sexual life, or whether they have committed or are alleged to have committed any criminal offence. The rules regarding the processing of sensitive personal data are stricter than for other personal data.

Processing means obtaining, recording or holding the information or data or carrying out any operations on it,

including:

(a) organization, adaptation or alteration of the information or data,

(b) retrieval, consultation or use of the information or data,

(c) disclosure of the information or data by transmission, dissemination or otherwise making available, or

(d) alignment, combination, blocking, erasure or destruction of the information or data.

This is an extremely comprehensive list and it is difficult to imagine anything that one might do to personal data that is not included within it.

The Act provides for the appointment of a Data Protection Commissioner and the establishment of a Data Protection Tribunal.

Data protection principles

The 1998 Act lays down eight data protection principles, which apply to the collection and processing of personal data of any sort. Data controllers are responsible for ensuring that these principles are complied with in respect of all the personal data for which they are responsible.

First data protection principle

> Personal data shall be processed fairly and lawfully and in particular shall not be processed unless (a) at least one of the conditions in Schedule 2 is met and (b) in the case of sensitive personal data, at least one of the conditions in Schedule 3 is also met.

The most significant condition in Schedule 2 of the Act is that the data subject has given their consent. If this is not the case, then the data can only be processed if the data controller is under a legal or statutory obligation for which the processing is necessary.

For processing sensitive personal information, Schedule 3 requires that the data subject has given explicit consent. The difference between 'consent' and 'explicit consent' is not spelt out in the Act. In either case, existing case law suggests that something more positive than, for example, failing to tick an opt-out box when ordering a product is required. 'Explicit consent' almost certainly requires the nature of the likely processing and any likely disclosure to be made explicit to the data subject before they give consent.

The requirement for consent was first introduced in the 1998 Act; it was not required by the earlier Act. One consequence of the change is that, because cookies may be used to gather personal data, it is now necessary to inform users of a website explicitly if it uses cookies and to give them the opportunity of refusing to accept them.

This principle requires that the processing of personal data is fair. The courts have ruled that establishing a person's credit rating only on the basis of their address constitutes unfair processing.

Second data protection principle

> Personal data shall be obtained only for one or more specified and lawful purposes, and shall not be further processed in any manner incompatible with that purpose or those purposes.

Data controllers must notify the Information Commissioner of the personal data they are collecting and the purposes for which it is being collected.

Third data protection principle

> Personal data shall be adequate, relevant and not excessive in relation to the purpose or purposes for which they are processed.

Many violations of this principle are due to ignorance rather than to intent to behave in a way contrary to the Act. Local government has a bad record of compliance with this principle, for example requiring people wanting to join a public library to state their marital status. Shops that demand to know customers' addresses when goods are not being delivered are also likely to be in breach of this principle.

Fourth data protection principle

Personal data shall be accurate and, where necessary, kept up to date.

While this principle is admirable, it can be extremely difficult comply with. In the UK, doctors have great difficulty in maintaining up-to-date data about their patients' addresses, particularly patients who are students, because students change their addresses frequently and rarely remember to tell their doctor. Universities have similar difficulties.

Fifth data protection principle

Personal data processed for any purpose or purposes shall not be kept for longer than is necessary for that purpose or those purposes.

This principle raises more difficulties than might be expected:

- It is necessary to establish how long each item of personal data needs to be kept. Auditors will require that financial data is kept for seven years. Action in the civil courts can be initiated up to six years after the events complained of took place so that it may be prudent to hold data for this length of time. It is appropriate to keep some personal data indefinitely (e.g. university records of graduating students). In all cases, the purpose for which the data is kept must be included in the purposes for which it was collected.
- Procedures to ensure that all data is erased at the appropriate time are needed, and this must include erasure from backup copies.

Sixth data protection principle

Personal data shall be processed in accordance with the rights of data subjects under this Act.

The rights of data subjects are discussed in the next subsection.

Seventh data protection principle

Appropriate technical and organizational measures shall be taken against unauthorized or unlawful processing of personal data and against accidental loss or destruction of, or damage to, personal data.

Of the eight principles this is the one that has the most substantial operational impact. It implies the need for access control (through passwords or other means), backup procedures, integrity checks on the data, vetting of personnel who have access to the data, and so on.

Eighth data protection principle

> Personal data shall not be transferred to a country or territory outside the European Economic Area unless that country or territory ensures an adequate level of protection for the rights and freedoms of data subjects in relation to the processing of personal data.

This principle can be viewed in two ways. It can be seen as protecting data subjects from having their personal data transferred to countries where there are no limitations on how it might be used. It can also be seen as specifically allowing businesses to transmit personal data across national borders provided there is adequate legislation in the destination country. In practice, of course, if a website is physically located in a country that does not have adequate data protection legislation, a visitor to that website from a country that does have such legislation has no protection.

Rights of Data Subjects

The 1984 Act gave data subjects the right to know whether a data controller held data relating to them, the right to see the data, and the right to have the data erased or corrected if it is inaccurate.

The 1998 Act extends this right of access so that data subjects have the right to receive:

- a description of the personal data being held;
- an explanation of the purpose for which it is being held and processed;
- a description of the people or organizations to which it may be disclosed;
- an intelligible statement of the specific data held about them;
- a description of the source of the data.

All these rights apply to data that is held electronically and, in some cases, to data that is held in manual filing systems. If, however, the data is processed automatically and is likely to be used as the sole basis for taking a decision relating to data subjects – for example, deciding whether to grant them a loan – they have the right to be informed by the data controller of the logic involved in taking that decision. They can also demand that a decision relating to them that has been taken on a purely automatically basis be reconsidered on some other basis.

The 1998 Act also gives data subjects the right:

- to prevent processing likely to cause damage and distress;
- to prevent processing for the purposes of direct marketing;

- to compensation in the case of damage caused by processing of personal data in violation of the principles of the Act.

Scope of the Act

The directive applies not only to data processed automatically, but also to manual data provided it is contained in a 'relevant filing system' or 'accessible record'. A relevant filing system means any information relating to individuals which, although not processed automatically, is structured either by reference to individuals or by reference to criteria relating to individuals, in such a way that specific information relating to a particular individual is readily accessible. This includes, for example, a set of paper files relating to individuals and organized in any sort of systematic way. This is in contrast to the earlier, 1984, Act, which referred only to data held on a computer. Following a recent judgement by the Court of Appeal, however, very few manual filing systems are likely to fall into the category of 'relevant filing systems' (see the 'Further reading' section).

The same case also clarified the question of what constitutes personal data. It ruled that, in order to constitute personal data, the information must, among other things, have the individual 'as its focus rather than some other person with whom he may have been involved or some transaction or event in which he may have figured or have had an interest'. This means, for example, that a list, in the minutes of a meeting, of the names of those attending does not constitute personal data about them.

The Act provided for the appointment of a Data Protection Commissioner and the establishment of Data Protection Tribunals. Their powers were subsequently extended to cover freedom of information and they were renamed Information Commissioner and Information Tribunals respectively. (See 'Freedom of information' on page 189.) Data controllers are required to notify the Information Commissioner of any processing of personal data that they carry out, including the purposes for which it is held and processed. However, the Act applies to the processing of personal data, whether or not there has been a notification. (This closes a loophole in the 1984 Act under which if a data controller had not registered the processing of personal data, the remainder of the Act was not applicable.)

There are two classes of personal data that are exempt from all the provisions of the Act. These are data related to national security and data used for domestic or household purposes (including recreation).

There are a number of important exceptions or limitations to the right of subject access, for example:

- where disclosing the information may result in infringing someone else's rights;
- where the data consists of a reference given by the data controller;
- examination candidates do not have the right of access to their marks until after the results of the examinations have been published;

- personal data consisting of information recorded by candidates during an academic, professional or other examination are exempt from the right of access.

In addition to these (and many other) specific cases included in the Act, the Secretary of State is given the power to make further exemptions in other areas.

PRIVACY

The general issue of privacy and the law is far too large and complex to be considered here. We shall therefore consider only those specific issues that relate to the use of information systems and the internet. The starting point is the Regulation of Investigatory Powers Act 2000, which sets up a framework for controlling the lawful interception of computer, telephone and postal communications. The Act allows government security services and law enforcement authorities to intercept, monitor and investigate electronic data only in certain specified situations such as when preventing and detecting crime. Powers include being able to demand the disclosure of data encryption keys.

Under the Act and the associated regulations, organizations that provide computer and telephone services (this includes not only ISPs (internet service providers) and other telecommunications service providers but also most employers) can monitor and record communications without the consent of the users of the service, provided this is done for one of the following purposes:

- to establish facts, for example, on what date a specific order was placed;
- to ensure that the organization's regulations and procedures are being complied with;
- to ascertain or demonstrate standards which are or ought be to be achieved;
- to prevent or detect crime (whether computer-related or not);
- to investigate or detect unauthorized use of telecommunication systems;
- to ensure the effective operation of the system, for example, by detecting viruses or denial of service attacks;
- to find out whether a communication is a business communication or a private one (e.g. monitoring the emails of employees who are on holiday, in order to deal with any that relate to the business);
- to monitor (but not record) calls to confidential, counselling helplines run free of charge by the business, provided that users are able to remain anonymous if they so choose.

Organizations intercepting communications in this way are under an obligation to make all reasonable efforts to inform users that such interception may take place.

The Act itself granted certain government agencies – police and intelligence services, the Inland Revenue, and Customs and Excise – the right to ask for interception warrants to allow them to monitor communications traffic to or from specific persons or organizations. Subsequent regulations have, however, extended the right to a ragbag of bodies (including, for example, fire authorities and local councils) that have little obvious reason for needing such information and no track record of being able to handle it. This extension has caused particular concern to civil liberties groups.

The Act and the regulations issued under it have also been heavily criticized by security experts and by some sectors of the telecommunications industry. Security experts argue that:

- there are many ways in which the Act can be rendered ineffective;

- the provisions that allow for the seizure of keys will undermine the security of public key systems.

FREEDOM OF INFORMATION

The primary purpose of the Freedom of Information Act is to provide clear rights of access to information held by bodies in the public sector. Under the terms of the Act, any member of the public can apply for access to such information. The Act also provides an enforcement mechanism if the information is not made available.

The legislation applies to Parliament, government departments, local authorities, health trusts, doctors' surgeries, universities, schools and many other organizations.

The main features of the Act are:

- There is a general right of access to information held by public authorities in the course of carrying out their public functions, subject to certain conditions and exemptions.

- In most cases where information is exempted from disclosure, there is a duty on public authorities to disclose where, in the view of the public authority, the public interest in disclosure outweighs the public interest in maintaining the exemption in question.

- There is a new office of the Information Commissioner (see the 'Further reading' section for the website) and a new Information Tribunal, with wide powers to enforce the rights, was created.

- A duty was imposed on public authorities to adopt a scheme for the publication of information. The schemes, which must be approved by the Information Commissioner, specify the classes of information the authority intends to publish, the manner of publication and whether the information is available to the public free of charge or on payment of a fee.

'Information' in this context has a rather wider meaning than in normal usage so that it includes the text of documents such as minutes of meetings.

The Act does not apply to personal information: the Data Protection Act already gives individuals access to information held about themselves and prevents a member of the public having access to personal information held about anyone else. There is, however, a possible conflict with the Data Protection Act in cases where documents include personal information, because the information that has to be released under the Freedom of Information Act may include personal data that must be kept confidential under the Data Protection Act.

The USA also has a Freedom of Information Act. It was passed in 1967 and is thus much older than the UK Act. It is fundamentally different from the UK Act. In particular, since 1975, the US Act has applied to personal data, including that held by the law enforcement agencies and has, notoriously, been used by criminals to force them to reveal the information they hold about the applicant's criminal activities. It has created a very substantial administrative burden for US government agencies; the FBI, for example, claims to have handled over 300,000 requests under the Act.

Unlike the other legislation discussed in this chapter, the Freedom of Information Act creates a requirement for new information systems and for packages that can be used to develop them. Such systems are commonly known as record management systems and document management systems.

EXAMINATION QUESTIONS

The Regulation of Investigatory Powers Act and the Freedom of Information Act are pieces of recent legislation and have thus only recently been included in the BCS syllabus. There are therefore no past questions on the topics. The following examination questions relate to the data protection issues.

APRIL 2000 QUESTION 2

Explain the main purposes of the Data Protection Act 1984.

[15 marks]

Describe the main differences between this original Act and the new Data Protection Act 1998.

[6 marks]

Discuss why these changes were considered necessary.

[4 marks]

APRIL 2002 QUESTION 3(b)

Explain whom the Data Protection Act 1998 is meant to protect, and what it is meant to protect against.

[7 marks]

APRIL 2003 QUESTION 2(c)

A medical centre has six PCs for use by doctors, and one PC for use by administrative staff for producing repeat prescriptions. Due to an error in the software used, the medication for two different patients attending the medical centre is mixed up, and the patients are given the wrong prescriptions. One evening the medical centre is broken into and one of the PCs containing patient details is stolen.

Explain how the Data Protection Act 1998 relates to this scenario.

[8 marks]

OCTOBER 2003 QUESTIONS 4(a), 4(b) AND 4(c)

a) You have set up your own small e-commerce business and hold the personal details of all the customers who have used your website on a database. You use this data to e-mail your customers regarding forthcoming special offers. Someone manages to gain access to your website and alters the prices displayed and some of the customers' details.

Discuss how the UK Data Protection Act 1998 and the UK Computer Misuse Act 1990 relate to this scenario.

[13 marks]

The Data Protection Act 1998 requires that the data is collected fairly and lawfully and that data subjects have given their consent to the processing. You should therefore tell all your customers that you are going to collect their personal details in order to email them about special offers and you must give them the chance to withdraw if they do not want it. In any case, data subjects have the right to prevent the data being used for direct marketing. It is advisable to provide a special box for them to tick to give their consent to it being used in this way.

The 1998 Act also requires you to take appropriate security precautions to protect the data held. If reasonable precautions were in place but were breached by a very sophisticated attack there is probably no problem. If, however, as is likely, the precautions were inadequate and could not prevent a relatively simple attack from succeeding, then a breach of the Act has occurred.

Under the Computer Misuse Act (see Chapter 16), the intruder is almost certainly guilty of the basic offence of unauthorized access to a computer system and of the Section 3 offence of unauthorized modification of the contents of a computer. Depending on the purpose of the intrusion, they may also be guilty of the Section 2 offence of unauthorized access with the intent to commit a serious crime.

191

b) Explain why it is necessary to display terms and conditions of purchase on an e-commerce website.

[4 marks]

Unless the terms and conditions of purchase are made explicit, the purchaser cannot be bound by them. The vendor can then only rely on common law or statute, neither of which will necessarily give the vendor the protection needed.

c) Explain why it is necessary to have a disclaimer on a website to inform users of the website when cookies are being used.

[4 marks]

Cookies can gather personal information about the user without users being aware of it and therefore without their agreement. This is inherently unfair and in breach of the first data protection principle. Announcing that a site uses cookies allows users to decline to access the site. If they continue, they can be assumed to have given their consent.

FURTHER READING

The website of the Information Commissioner:

www.informationcommissioner.gov.uk/

contains much useful information relating both to data protection and freedom of information. In particular, it contains guidance, based on the case of *Durant v FSA* (referred to in 'Scope of the Act', page 187), regarding what constitutes personal data and what is meant by a relevant filing system.

The following book contains a good, practically-oriented discussion of data protection:

Holt, J. and Newton, J. (eds) (2004) *A Manager's Guide to IT Law*. BCS, Swindon.

In contrast, the following book describes the development of data protection legislation and the thinking behind it, starting from the Younger Committee's report of 1972:

Bott, M.F., Coleman, J.A., Eaton, J. and Rowland, D. (2001) *Professional Issues in Software Engineering* (3rd edition). Taylor and Francis, 2001.

15 Internet Issues

After reading this chapter, you should understand:

- *the reasons why misuse of the internet gives cause for concern;*
- *the scope and limitations of the legislation that governs the use of the internet at present;*
- *why it is difficult to enact legislation that will effectively regulate the use of the internet.*

INTRODUCTION

The benefits that the internet has brought are almost universally recognized. It has made access to all sorts of information much easier. It has made it much easier for people to communicate with each other, on both an individual and a group basis. It has simplified and speeded up many types of commercial transaction. And, most importantly, these benefits have been made available to very many people, not just to a small and privileged group – although, of course, the internet is still far from being universally available, even in developed countries.

Inevitably, a development on this scale creates its own problems. In this chapter we shall be looking at three topics – pornography, defamation and spam – that are a matter of concern to everyone professionally involved in the internet, as well as to many other people. These are topics that cannot sensibly be discussed in technical terms alone. There are social, cultural and legal issues that must all be considered. Different countries approach these issues in very different ways but the internet itself knows no boundaries.

Every country has laws governing what can be published or publicly displayed. Typically, such laws address defamation, that is, material that makes unwelcome allegations about people or organizations, and pornography, that is, material with sexual content. They may also cover other areas such as political and religious comment, incitement to racial hatred, or the depiction of violence.

Although every country has such laws, they are very different from each other. Some countries, for example, consider that pictures of scantily clad women are indecent and have laws that prevent them from appearing in publications and advertisements. In other countries, such pictures are perfectly acceptable. In some countries, publication of material criticizing the government or the established religion is effectively forbidden, while in others it is a right guaranteed by the constitution and vigorously defended by the courts.

The coming of the internet (and satellite television) has made these differences much more apparent and much more important than they used to be. Since material flows across borders so easily, it is both much likelier that material that violates publication laws will come into a country and more difficult for the country to enforce its own laws.

The roles and responsibilities of ISPs are a central element in the way these issues are addressed and we therefore start by discussing the legal framework under which ISPs operate. Then we shall look at the problems of different legal systems. Only then can we address the specific issues of defamation, pornography and spam.

INTERNET SERVICE PROVIDERS

The central issue we need to consider is how far an ISP can be held responsible for material generated by its customers.

In Europe, the position is governed by the European Directive 2000/31/EC. In the UK this directive is implemented through the Electronic Commerce (EC Directive) Regulations 2002. These regulations follow the EC Directive in distinguishing three roles that an ISP may play: *mere conduit*, *caching*, and *hosting*.

The role of mere conduit is that in which the ISP does no more than transmit data; in particular, the ISP does not initiate transmissions, does not select the receivers of the transmissions, and does not select or modify the data transmitted. It is compatible with the role of mere conduit for an ISP to store information temporarily, provided this is only done as part of the transmission process. Provided it is acting as a mere conduit, the regulations provide that an ISP is not liable for damages or for any criminal sanction as a result of a transmission.

The caching role arises when the information is the subject of automatic, intermediate and temporary storage, for the sole purpose of increasing the efficiency of the transmission of the information to other recipients of the service upon their request. An ISP acting in the caching role is not liable for damages or for any criminal sanction as a result of a transmission, provided that it:

1. does not modify the information;
2. complies with conditions on access to the information;
3. complies with any rules regarding the updating of the information, specified in a manner widely recognized and used by industry;
4. does not interfere with the lawful use of technology, widely recognized and used by industry, to obtain data on the use of the information; and
5. acts expeditiously to remove or to disable access to the information he has stored upon obtaining actual knowledge of the fact that the information at the initial source of the transmission has been removed from the network, or access to it has been disabled, or that a court or an administrative authority has ordered such removal or disablement.

These apparently complicated conditions are simply designed to ensure that an ISP that claims to be playing a caching role is behaving in accordance with industry practice.

Where an ISP stores information provided by its customers, it is acting in a hosting role. In this case, it is not liable for damage or criminal sanctions provided that:

- it did not know that anything unlawful was going on;
- where a claim for damages is made, it did not know anything that should have led it to think that something unlawful might be going on; or
- when it found out that that something unlawful was going on, it acted expeditiously to remove the information or to prevent access to it, and
- the customer was not acting under the authority or the control of the service provider.

In the USA, ISPs enjoy much broader immunity than in Europe. In effect, even when they are hosting, they enjoy the immunity that in Europe is only granted to ISPs acting as mere conduits.

A further issue regarding ISPs is the question of anonymous and pseudonymous postings. It is common for contributors to bulletin boards and newsgroups to use pseudonyms for their postings. Their ISP will be aware of their true identity. Is the ISP allowed to release, and can it be compelled to release, this information to someone wishing to take legal action against the contributor? In the UK, the ISP is allowed to release the information and can be compelled to do so by a court. In the USA, ISPs cannot in general be required to release the information, although they may be required to do so in the case of serious crimes.

LAW ACROSS NATIONAL BOUNDARIES

How law operates across national boundaries is a difficult and intensely technical topic. We can only give the most superficial description here.

Criminal law

Suppose a person, X, commits a criminal offence in country A and then moves to country B. Can country A ask that X be arrested in country B and sent back to A so that he can be put on trial? Or can X be prosecuted in country B for the offence commited in country A?

The answer to the first of these questions is that, provided there exists an agreement (usually called an *extradition treaty*) between the two countries, then in principle X can be extradited, that is, arrested and sent back to face trial in A. However, this can only be done under the very important proviso that the offence that X is alleged to have committed in A would also be an offence in B. What is more, extradition procedures are usually extremely complex, so that attempts at extradition often fail because of procedural weaknesses. Within the EU, the recent proposals for a European arrest warrant are intended to obviate the need for extradition procedures.

In general, the answer to the second question is that X cannot be prosecuted in B for an offence committed in A. However, in certain cases some countries, including the UK and the USA, claim *extraterritorial jurisdiction*, that is the right to try citizens and other residents for crimes committed in other countries; in particular, this right is used to allow the prosecution of people who commit sexual offences involving children while they are abroad. However, the issue of extraterritoriality is much wider than this and attempts to claim extraterritorial jurisdiction make countries very unpopular.

What does this mean in the context of the internet? Suppose that you live in country A and on your website there you publish material that is perfectly legal and acceptable in country A, but which it is a criminal offence to publish in country B. Then you can't be prosecuted in country A and it is very unlikely that you would be extradited to country B. You might, however, be unwise to visit country B voluntarily.

The International Convention on Cybercrime

In 2001, the Council of Europe approved a draft convention on 'cybercrime'. It deals with child pornography on the internet, criminal copyright infringement, computer-related fraud and hacking. There is an additional protocol relating to incitement to religious or racial hatred, to which signatories to the protocol may also sign up.

The Council of Europe is quite separate from the EU. It has 43 members; four countries outside Europe (the USA, Canada, Japan and South Africa) are associated with it. Of these 47 countries, 37 have signed the treaty but only five have ratified it. The USA has explicitly indicated that it will not sign up to the protocol relating to hate material because this would be contrary to the First Amendment (see 'The regulation of pornography in the USA' on page 202).

International conventions inevitably are slow to take effect. Governments sign the treaty showing that they approve of it. However, in many cases they will have to persuade their legislature to approve it and the laws necessary to implement it. This process, known as *ratification*, can take a long time and is often not at the top of a government's priorities. Governments may be replaced and the incoming government may not feel committed to ratification.

All this means that the convention is unlikely to have much effect until, say, 2015 at the earliest.

Civil law

There are some parts of the civil law where the position is reasonably clear cut. Any contract that involves parties from more than one country should, and usually will, state explicitly under which jurisdiction (that is, which country's laws) it is to be interpreted. Where intellectual property law is concerned, there are international agreements to which most countries are signatories so that there is a common framework, even if it can be very difficult to enforce the rights in certain countries.

In many cases, the plaintiff will have some choice about where to take action. Very often the decision will be taken on practical grounds – there is little point in taking action in a country in which defendant has no legal presence or few assets and it is probably unwise to take action in a country where the legal process is well known to be lengthy and expensive.

Consider the case of an ISP based in the USA, with a European office in London. One of its customers is an Italian, resident in Italy, who posts on his website, which is hosted by the ISP, an allegation about a French politician. The French politician complains but the ISP does nothing to remove the allegation. If the French politician wishes to take action, he can, in theory, take action in any of the four countries involved – England, France, Italy or the USA. His best hope of winning a court action may well be in France but there is little point in bringing an action in France unless the ISP has some sort of legal presence there. The same applies to Italy, a country where, in any case, the law is not renowned for bringing cases to a rapid conclusion. The politician will probably opt for action in England, on the grounds that, in such cases, English law is much more sympathetic to the person claiming to be wronged than is American law. It may still be necessary to persuade the English court that this is a matter that it can properly consider.

One concrete example is that a court in New Zealand recently ruled that an organization based in New Zealand could take action in a New Zealand court against an Australian newspaper that, it was claimed, had published defamatory statements about it on its website in Australia.

DEFAMATION

Consider the following scenario. A university provides internet services for its students and allows them to mount personal web pages. One student, who is a passionate fan of Llanbadarn United football club, believes the referee in their last game made a bad decision that caused them to lose the match. He believes that the decision was so obviously wrong that the referee must have been bribed. He puts a statement on his web page saying that the referee is corrupt. Someone draws the referee's attention to this allegation. The referee believes that his reputation has been badly damaged by this and he wants compensation.

This situation is covered by the law of defamation. Defamation means making statements that will damage someone's reputation, bring them into contempt, make them disliked, and so on. In England and Wales, a distinction is made between slander, which is spoken, and libel, which is written or recorded in some other way (including email).

There can be little doubt that, on the face of it, the statement in question constitutes libel. The first issue to consider, however, is who should the referee take action against. He could sue the student, but the student probably doesn't have enough money to pay any damages that might be awarded. Can the referee also sue the university, which presumably could pay damages?

The Defamation Act 1996 states that a person has a defence if they can prove that:

> (a) he was not the author, editor or publisher of the statement complained of,
>
> (b) he took reasonable care in relation to its publication, and
>
> (c) he did not know, and had no reason to believe, that what he did caused or contributed to the publication of a defamatory statement.

(Presumably, this is intended to read $a \lor (b \land c)$.)

The author, the editor and the publisher of the libel can all be held responsible. If the allegation had been published in a traditional student newspaper, printed on paper and sold to students and others through newsagents or the Students' Union, the referee would have been able to sue the publisher of the newspaper – probably the Students' Union if it had a separate legal existence, if not, the university – and the editor. This is reasonable because everything published in the newspaper is directly under the control of the editor, who is the agent of the publisher.

When the libel is published on a web page, on the university site, the university can reasonably argue that it cannot possibly vet everything that every one of its 10,000 students puts on their personal web page. It is not, in fact, publishing the pages, it is only providing an infrastructure that allows students to publish their own web pages. In the terminology used in the 2002 Regulations it is acting in a hosting role. Provided, therefore, that it removed the offending material as soon as it had reason to suspect its presence and that the student was not acting under its authority or control, the university cannot be subject to an action for damages.

ISPs receive a significant number of complaints, many apparently from companies. Given the cost and management time involved in defending a libel action, it is not surprising that in these circumstances ISPs make no attempt to assess whether a complaint is justified. Instead, they immediately remove or block access to the offending material, with the result that they can avail themselves of the defence that the 2002 Regulations provide. This may not always be in the public interest. There may well be occasions when allegations of corruption, for example, are justified and that it is in the public interest for this to be publicized. In such circumstances, in suppressing the allegations, the ISP is carrying out a function that more properly belongs to the courts.

Despite the provisions of the 2002 Regulations, there are many areas of uncertainty regarding the position of ISPs and also many practical problems with complying with the law. We have given a very simplified picture here. The reader who wishes to pursue the matter further is referred to the Law

Commission report referenced in the 'Further reading' section at the end of this chapter.

Because so much material on the internet originates in the USA, it is appropriate here to say a little about the position there. US law relating to defamation is much more favourable towards authors and publishers than is the law in the UK. The First Amendment to the United States Constitution guarantees a right to free speech that the US courts have always been eager to defend. The result is that many statements that might be considered defamatory in the UK would be protected as an exercise of the right of free speech in the USA. This is particularly the case where the defamatory statement refers to a public figure. In this case, to succeed in a libel action, the public figure needs to show not only that the statement was factually incorrect but also that it was made maliciously or recklessly.

Suppose that an internet site in the USA, hosted by an American ISP, contains a statement about someone living in the UK that would be considered defamatory in the UK but not in the USA (a statement accusing a British politician of corruption, for example). The person who is the subject of the statement can reasonably say: 'I am British. I live in the UK. This statement can be read by anyone in the UK. Surely, I am entitled to the protection offered by British law.' The author of the statement and the ISP can both say: 'We live in the United States and we are governed by its laws. We understand those laws and we comply with them. We cannot be expected to know the law as it exists in all the other countries of the world and we cannot be expected to comply with those laws.' The complainant may be able to take action in the UK against the ISP, provided the ISP has a legal presence in the UK, but only in respect of the circulation of the defamatory statement in the UK. A court in the USA will not enforce British law over such matters.

This is a case in which the global nature of the internet magnifies an issue. American newspapers and magazines do not contain much material about British politics nor do they have a very wide circulation in the UK. If the statement had appeared in an American newspaper or magazine, it would not have achieved a wide circulation in the UK. But it is more likely that such a statement will be made on the internet and it is more likely that it will then be read in the UK.

PORNOGRAPHY

More or less every country has laws concerned with pornography. Beyond this simple statement it is almost impossible to generalize. What is considered pornographic varies widely from country to country. What is accepted as normal by everyone in one country may be considered pornographic in another country. In some countries the possession of pornography may be a criminal offence, in others possession is not an offence but distribution and/or publication are. We are not concerned here with what should or should not be considered pornographic or what should or should not be prohibited. We are concerned simply with a country's ability to enforce the laws that it has chosen to enact.

Until the late 1980s, a country could expect to enforce its laws regarding pornography reasonably effectively. It was a comparatively simple matter for the police to stop the sale of material that was regarded as pornographic. It was easy to prevent cinemas showing films considered pornographic; again this could be done by the police. And, apart from a few areas near its borders, the only television broadcasts that could be received in the country would be ones that were broadcast from within the country and could therefore be controlled.

Two developments changed this. It became possible to broadcast television programmes via satellite, which meant that programmes could be broadcast from one country to be received in another. And the advent of the worldwide web meant that individuals could receive pornographic material, in the form of images or text, in a way that was extremely difficult for the authorities to detect. In other words, pornography became available in an intangible form.

There is a second aspect to the problem of pornography. This is the problem of unsolicited pornography sent to people who find it offensive. This, however, is part of the wider problem of spam, which we deal with in the next section. In this section, we are concerned with the problems that a country faces in enforcing its laws against pornography, in the face of internet users who are willing receivers of it.

There is one important difference between laws regarding defamation and laws regarding pornography. In most instances of defamation, any legal action will be under the civil law and will be initiated by the person or organization who is the target of the defamation. In most cases concerning the publication of pornography, action will be under the criminal law and will be initiated by state prosecution services on the basis of information provided by the police.

The law in the UK

In England and Wales, the law relating to pornography is based on the Obscene Publications Act 1959. This Act states that:

> an article shall be deemed to be obscene if its effect or the effect of any one of its items is, if taken as a whole, such as to tend to deprave and corrupt persons who are likely, having regard to all relevant circumstances, to read, see or hear the matter contained or embodied in it.

Two important features of this definition are that the effect is to be 'taken as a whole' and that it is the effect on 'persons who are likely . . . to read, see or hear' the material that matters. Although the Act has been modified by subsequent legislation, some intended to bring its provisions into line with the world of computers and the internet, the definition of obscenity has not been changed. However, its interpretation has changed considerably; much material that would almost certainly have been found by a court to be obscene at the time that the Act was passed would now be regarded as quite acceptable. The 1959 Act does not make it an offence simply to possess obscene material. It is, however, an offence to publish obscene material or to possess it with a view to publication for profit; publication in this case includes distribution electronically. Possible defences are that the material has artistic merit or that its publication is for the public good.

The position regarding child pornography is very different. The Protection of Children Act 1978 and subsequent legislation make the simple possession of indecent, that is, sexually explicit, material involving children a serious criminal offence. Since there is also wide international agreement that child pornography should be banned, it has proved possible to take effective action. Publishers of child pornography on the internet rely on credit card payments. If such a site is raided, credit card numbers of its customers can be collected and passed on to the police in the countries where they live. The result has been a number of widely reported cases in which large numbers of customers of sites publishing pornography have been successfully prosecuted. While it is too soon to claim that the problem of child pornography has been overcome, the necessary mechanisms are available.

The effectiveness of the campaign against child pornography is the result of several factors:

- Mere possession is an offence. It is not necessary to prove that the possessor is publishing, or intends to publish, the material for commercial gain.
- The material does not have to be obscene. It is not necessary to prove that it will 'tend to deprave and corrupt', only that it is indecent.
- There is general international agreement that this sort of material should be suppressed.
- Sites that supply the material want to make a profit from it, so that customers have to provide credit card numbers, making it possible to trace them.

These conditions do not apply in relation to other types of pornographic material and there is little likelihood of effective action being taken against them in the same way. The wide differences in attitudes from country to country towards sexually explicit material and different sexual practices make it unlikely that wider international agreement can be reached. In some countries, for example, representation of the naked body is regarded as pornographic and is forbidden by law; in other countries, paintings and sculptures by great artists, depicting the naked body, are considered to be among the countries' greatest artistic treasures. Novels that are enjoyed as great literature in some countries are banned as pornographic in others. In some countries, homosexuality is illegal and so is the depiction in text or images of homosexual relationships; in other countries, the rights of homosexuals are guaranteed by law and any discrimination is illegal. Furthermore, constitutional provisions guaranteeing freedom of speech and expression will often lead to a country tolerating pornographic material that most of its population would find extremely offensive, and more general considerations of individual freedom make it unlikely that many countries would want to make simple possession of pornography illegal.

The regulation of pornography in the USA

The First Amendment to the US Constitution famously states that:

> **Congress shall make no law respecting an establishment of religion, or prohibiting the free exercise thereof; or abridging the freedom of speech, or of the press; or the right of the people peaceably to assemble, and to petition the government for a redress of grievances.**

The clauses about freedom of speech and of the press have been enthusiastically defended by the courts since the 1950s. In particular, attempts by individual states to enact provisions against pornography have been struck down as unconstitutional by the Supreme Courts of the states themselves and an act of Congress that would have made the internet subject to much stricter control than other media was struck down by the Federal Supreme Court.

There is a slight difference of emphasis between the USA and Europe in the concerns felt about pornography on the internet. The main (or, at least, the most vociferously expressed) concern in the USA is the concern that parents have regarding the material that their children may look at on the internet. It is not the presence of such material that worries the parents so much as its accessibility.

In the UK (and to a considerable extent elsewhere in Europe) the main concerns are, first, that the availability of certain types of illegal pornography encourages violent sexual crime, and, secondly, that the very presence of child pornography implies that children have been abused to produce it. The emphasis is therefore much more on eliminating the material at source.

These differences are reflected in two different organizations, one based in the UK and one based in the USA that were both set up to combat pornography on the internet. The two bodies co-operate closely but they have fundamentally different approaches.

The Internet Watch Foundation

In the UK, the Internet Watch Foundation (IWF) was set up in 1996 to monitor and, where desirable and possible, take action against illegal and offensive content on the UK internet. It has the support of the UK government, the police and the ISPs. It can act against websites, newsgroups and online groups that:

- contain images of child abuse, originating anywhere in the world.
- contain adult material that potentially breaches the Obscene Publications Act in the UK.
- contain criminally racist material in the UK.

The IWF operates a 'hot-line', through which members of the public can report any internet content that they believe may be illegal. The IWF will locate and assess the material. If the material is considered illegal and falls within the IWF remit, the IWF will pass the information to the police and inform the ISP that is hosting it. If images of children originating in other countries are involved, it will also inform Interpol and the police in the countries concerned.

The IWF receives around 20,000 complaints per year, of which about a third relate to material that is assessed as being potentially illegal. In the first full year of IWF operation, 18 per cent of the illegal material was traced to sources within the UK. By 2003, this had been reduced to 1 per cent.

In the UK, the provisions of the Electronic Commerce (EC Directive) Regulations 2002, discussed in 'Internet service providers' (page 194), apply to pornography as well as to defamatory material. This means that ISPs will not be subject to criminal action in respect of pornographic material on sites that they host provided that they did not know of its presence; they removed it when they became aware of its presence; and those responsible for publishing it were not under the ISP's authority or control. If ISPs are left to deal directly with complaints from the public, they will inevitably feel they have to remove all the material complained about, regardless of whether it is potentially illegal, in order to keep their immunity from prosecution. If the complaints are routed through the IWF, an ISP only receives those that the specialized staff at the IWF believe relate to potentially illegal material. Complaints about material that is offensive to the complainant but not potentially illegal never reach the ISP.

The Internet Content Rating Association

The Internet Content Rating Association (ICRA) is an international, independent organization whose mission, it claims, is: 'to help parents to protect their children from potentially harmful material on the internet, whilst respecting the content providers' freedom of expression.' Its board includes representatives from the major players in the internet and communications markets, including AOL, BT, Cable and Wireless, IBM, Microsoft and Novell.

The ICRA provides a framework that enables content providers to label their sites or individual pages systematically with labels that describe the nature of the content under such categories as nudity and sexual content, bad language, violence, use of drugs and alcohol, and so on. The content provider fills in a questionnaire. This is submitted to the ICRA site, which generates the label and sends it back so that the provider can paste it on to his site. The technology used is the Platform for Internet Content Selection (PICS) developed by W3C. This is a specification for a standard way of labelling the content of web pages.

The ICRA provides filter software, which can be used to control which sites and pages can be accessed. A user can download and install this software and then configure it to allow access only to web pages and sites that satisfy particular labelling criteria. This allows parents discretion about how they control their children's use of the internet. Some parents may be quite unconcerned about their children viewing material involving nudity but may feel that they want to protect them from violent images, a common view in Sweden, for example. Others may take the opposite approach.

In addition to developing its own filter software, the ICRA is in discussion with suppliers of browsers in an effort to persuade them to make their browsers read and act on the ICRA labels.

The ICRA approach will only be successful if enough content providers can be persuaded to label their sites or pages and to label them accurately. It is argued that it is very much in the interests of content providers to label their sites, since many users will set the filter so that unlabelled content is inaccessible. Furthermore, there is little point in labelling the content misleadingly because the content providers have no interest in attracting to their sites people who are not going to be interested in the material available. In any case, users who feel that a site is misleadingly labelled can complain to ICRA who will investigate.

Future developments

There is a fundamental difference between the approach of the IWF, which seems likely to be adopted elsewhere in Europe, and that of the ICRA, which is largely American driven. The IWF concentrates on attacking the sources of illegal material by enforcing existing laws; its approach to child protection concentrates on trying to eliminate pornography involving children. It supports content labelling but sees this as very much a secondary issue.

The ICRA is concerned with the provision of mechanisms to allow people to identify and avoid pornographic material and, in particular, to make it possible for parents to prevent their children from gaining access to pornographic sites, whether deliberately or accidentally. This reflects the American concern with freedom of speech, as guaranteed by the First Amendment.

It seems likely that the IWF and similar organizations in other countries of the EU will be successful in eradicating child pornography from websites within the EU. Because of the differences in standards between countries, even within the EU, it is very unlikely that it will be possible to go beyond this.

SPAM

Spam is best defined as 'unsolicited email sent without the consent of the addressee and without any attempt at targeting recipients who are likely to be interested in its contents'. Any regular user of email will be familiar with spam. We find our mailboxes filled with emails offering Viagra, penis enlargement treatments, incitements to visit pornographic sites, advertisements for dubious financial investments, and so on. It is estimated that around half of the traffic on the internet is spam. Internet users find it irritating and often offensive. If they respond to any of these invitations, they may also find themselves defrauded and their bank accounts raided. It is easy to miss important emails in the welter of spam. Some spam carries viruses. The effectiveness of the internet is much reduced by the load of spam that it carries. Not surprisingly, there is considerable pressure on governments to legislate to eliminate or at least alleviate the problem and a number of organizations have been set up specifically to fight spam.

There are some technical means of fighting spam, for example:

- closing loopholes that enable spammers to use other people's computers to relay bulk messages;

- the use of machine learning and other techniques to identify suspicious features of message headers;

- the use of virus detection software to reject emails carrying viruses;

- keeping 'stop lists' of sites that are known to send spam.

Most of these methods require constant vigilance, however, and are more suitable for use by organizations than by individual users. Furthermore, they carry a real risk that genuine email will be mistaken for spam and rejected.

The problem of spam is perceived as being of the utmost importance by the industry and substantial efforts are being made to develop technical solutions but these need to be backed up by effective legislation.

European legislation

The European Community Directive on Privacy and Electronic Communications (2002/58/EC) was issued in 2002 and required member nations to introduce regulations to implement it by December 2003. In the UK, the directive was implemented by the Privacy and Electronic Communications (EC Directive) Regulations 2003.

The directive addresses many issues that are not relevant here, but its essential features relating to unsolicited email are:

- Unsolicited email can only be sent to individuals (as opposed to companies) if they have previously given their consent.

- Sending unsolicited email that conceals the address of the sender or does not provide a valid address to which the recipient can send a request for such mailings to cease is unlawful.

- If an email address has been obtained in the course of the sale of goods or services, the seller may use the address for direct mailings, provided that the recipient is given the opportunity, easily and free of charge, with every message, to request that such mailings cease.

In the UK, the enforcement of the regulations is in the hands of the Information Commissioner. The maximum penalty is a fine of £5,000 in a magistrate's court but the matter can be taken to a higher court, where an unlimited fine can be imposed.

The directive is widely seen as a step in the right direction. Its main weakness, however, is that it can only be effective in relation to spam sent from within the EU; it is estimated that some 90 per cent of the spam received in the UK originates in the USA. It has also been criticized because it does not prohibit the sending of spam to companies and because the penalties are felt to be too light.

Legislation in the USA

A superficially similar Act came into force in the USA at the start of 2004. This is the Controlling the Assault of Non-Solicited Pornography and Marketing Act 2003, otherwise known as the CAN SPAM Act. Unfortunately, the Act has fundamental weaknesses, of which the main one is that it is legal to send spam provided that:

- the person sending the spam has not been informed by the receiver that they do not wish to receive spam from that source; and

- the spam contains an address that the receiver can use to ask that no more spam be sent.

These provisions mean that email users will have to respond to every piece of spam they receive, asking for no more to be sent. Dishonest spammers will be able to use these messages to confirm the validity of the email addresses. In Europe, it is the responsibility of the spammer to get the recipient's permission before sending the spam; in the USA it is the responsibility of the recipient to inform the spammer that he doesn't want to receive the spam.

The law actually has some very good provisions, mostly the technical ones that require valid return addresses and make it illegal to forge other routing information that accompanies each message. Coupled with some changes in the architecture of internet mail handling and increased anti-spam vigilance by ISPs and network operators, these could, over time, have real impact on spam's volume.

At the time of writing, there is little sign that the CAN SPAM Act is having any effect. There has been no detectable reduction in the amount of spam and very little of it complies with the provisions of the Act. However, it would be unrealistic to expect enforcement to be immediately effective. The Act allows ISPs to sue for damages in certain cases and several ISPs have initiated court action against spammers.

Registration

Both the USA and the UK operate successful schemes that allow individuals to register their telephone numbers as ones to which unsolicited direct marketing calls must not be made. On the face of it this should act as a model for preventing spam; indeed, the CAN SPAM Act specifically requires the Federal Trade Commission to produce plans for such a register within six months. Unfortunately, the technical differences between the internet and the telephone network mean that this model is unlikely to work with spam. In order to enforce the law, it is necessary to be able to identify reliably the source of the communication. Telephone operators keep records of calls showing the originator and the destination of the call; such records are needed for billing purposes. It is therefore easy, in most cases, to identify the source of any direct marketing call about which a consumer complains and then take the action necessary to enforce the law.

In most cases, use of the internet is not charged on the basis of individual communications but on the basis of connect time, so there is no recording of individual emails and it costs no more to send an email from Australia to the UK than it does to send an email to one's colleague in the next office. Furthermore, 'spoofing' (forging the sender's address on an email) and relaying (using other people's mail servers to send your spam) are easily achieved. This means there are no reliable records that can be used to identify where the spam really came from and the use of relaying may mean that it is impossible even to determine in which country it originated. In these circumstances, there is little possibility that a prohibition on sending unsolicited email to addresses on a register could be enforced effectively.

FURTHER READING

The issues discussed in this chapter change rapidly. The best sources of information are therefore usually to be found on the web, but it is important to make sure that you know the date of any article you look at. An article on spamming dated 1997, for example, cannot reflect the current situation. You should also realize that many websites are maintained by small groups of people who have very strong views. You should not assume that what you read is necessarily balanced or even factually correct.

In December 2002, the Law Commission (an official UK body responsible for reviewing UK law) produced a report entitled 'Defamation and the Internet'. The report is clearly written and (comparatively) easy for a non-lawyer to understand. If you want to know more about this topic it is strongly recommended. It can be found on the internet at

www.lawcom.gov.uk/files/defamation2.pdf

Although it dates from 1997, the following reference is a valuable and comprehensive source of information:

Akdeniz, Y. (1997) Governance of pornography and child pornography on the global internet: A multi-layered approach. In Edwards, L. and Waelde, C. (eds), *Law and the Internet: Regulating Cyberspace,* Hart Publishing.

It is available on the internet at

www.cyber-rights.org/reports/governan.htm

More up to date but much less comprehensive is the following page:

www.cultsock.ndirect.co.uk/MUHome/cshtml/index.html

The Internet Watch Foundation can be found at:

www.iwf.org.uk

And the Internet Content Rating Association can be found at:

www.icra.org

16 Computer Misuse

After reading this short chapter, you should:

- *understand the Computer Misuse Act and how it applies to common offences;*
- *appreciate the way in which computer fraud is handled at present and the proposals for changes in the law.*

INTRODUCTION

In recent years, the public (or, at least, the media) has been much more concerned about the misuse of the internet than about the more general misuse of computers. Nevertheless, crimes committed using computers form a significant proportion of so-called white collar crime and it has been necessary to introduce legislation specifically aimed at such activities. Until 1990, when the UK's Computer Misuse Act was passed, hacking, that is, gaining unauthorized access or attempting to gain unauthorized access to a computer, was not in itself an offence. Attempts were made to convict hackers of stealing electricity but the quantity of electricity involved was minute and impossible to measure. Courts were reluctant to convict and, even if a conviction was obtained, the penalty was trivial.

As a result of the UK Court of Appeal decision in 1988 to uphold the appeal of two people who had hacked into private mailboxes, legislation to tackle computer crime was brought forward remarkably quickly, resulting in the Computer Misuse Act 1990.

It is a good general principle that legislation should not be introduced to deal with special situations that already fall within the purview of more general laws. For this reason, the Computer Misuse Act does not address some topics, in particular computer fraud, which are better dealt with by more general legislation.

THE COMPUTER MISUSE ACT 1990

The Computer Misuse Act creates three new offences that can briefly be described as:

- unauthorized access to a computer;
- unauthorized access to a computer with intention to commit a serious crime; and
- unauthorized modification of the contents of a computer.

We shall look at each of these in more detail below. It is important to note that the offences are committed if either the computer in question or the offender (or both) are in the UK at the time of the offence. This means that someone who hacks into a computer in the UK or infects it with a virus from anywhere in the world is guilty of a criminal offence and can, in principle, be prosecuted in the UK.

Section 1 of the Computer Misuse Act 1990 states that

a person is guilty of an offence if

1. he causes a computer to perform any function with intent to secure access to any program or data held in any computer;

2. the access he intends to secure is unauthorized; and

3. he knows at the time when he causes the computer to perform the function that that is the case.

This is called the unauthorized access offence. It is punishable by a fine of up to £5,000 or up to six months' imprisonment.

There are several points that need to be emphasized. First, a person can only be guilty of the offence if they intend to gain unauthorized access and know, or should know, that the access is unauthorized. In other words, you cannot be guilty of the offence by accident.

Secondly, the wording of the Act makes it clear that a person who is authorized to access some programs or data on a computer is guilty of the offence if they attempt to gain access to other programs or data to which they are not authorized to have access.

Finally, it is no defence to claim that no harm was done. The attempt to gain unauthorized access itself constitutes the offence.

Section 2 of the Act is concerned with gaining unauthorized access to a computer with the intention of committing a more serious offence. A blackmailer might attempt to gain unauthorized access to medical records, for example, in order to identify people in prominent positions who had been treated for sexually transmitted diseases, with a view to blackmailing them. A terrorist might try to get access to a computer system for air traffic control with a view to issuing false instructions to pilots in order to cause accidents to happen.

The need for this offence arises because, if a criminal is apprehended as a result of unauthorized access, before committing the more serious offence, they cannot be prosecuted for the serious offence, even though there may be ample evidence to show what they intended to do. This offence carries a penalty of up to five years' imprisonment or an unlimited fine.

Section 3 of the Act states that:

> a person is guilty of an offence if
>
> 1. he does any act which causes an unauthorized modification of the contents of any computer; and
>
> 2. at the time when he does the act he has the requisite intent and the requisite knowledge.

The Act then goes on to explain that:

> the requisite intent is an intent to cause a modification of the contents of any computer and by so doing
>
> 1. to impair the operation of any computer;
>
> 2. to prevent or hinder access to any program or data held in any computer; or
>
> 3. to impair the operation of any such program or the reliability of any such data.

Furthermore, the Act goes on to make clear that it is not necessary to have any particular computer or any particular program or data in mind. Like the offence under Section 2, this offence carries a maximum penalty of five years' imprisonment or an unlimited fine.

It is the offence created by Section 3 that gives the Act its power. For example, it makes each of the following a criminal offence:

- intentionally spreading a virus, worm, or other pest;
- encrypting a company's data files and demanding a ransom for revealing the key required to decrypt it;
- concealed redirection of browser home pages;
- implanting premium rate diallers (that is, programs that replace the normal dial-up code for the computer with the code for a premium rate service).

THE 2004 REVIEW OF THE COMPUTER MISUSE ACT

In 2004, the All-Party Parliamentary Internet Group (APIG), a group of British MPs and Members of the House of Lords, carried out a review of the workings of the Computer Misuse Act. They took evidence from a large number of individuals and organizations, including the BCS and the IEE, many of whom urged the need to extend the Act to include many more specific offences.

APIG concluded that the Act needed comparatively little modification. It recommended an additional offence of 'impairing access to data', which could be used to prosecute the perpetrators of denial of service attacks, which cannot always be prosecuted under Section 3 of the Act. (A denial of service attack is an attack on a website in which it is flooded with so many requests for service that either the links to the site or the site itself are no longer able to respond to legitimate requests. Such attacks have become extremely common.)

APIG also recommended an increase from six months to two years in the maximum prison sentence for the unauthorized access offence. The main purpose of the change is to make it apparent that Parliament regards the offence as a serious one. The change would also have the side-effect of making the offence an extraditable one; that is, a British court could order that a person in Britain who was accused of committing the offence in another country could be sent to that country to stand trial.

The number of cases brought under the Computer Misuse Act is comparatively small. In 1999 and 2000 together, proceedings under the Act were brought against a total of 32 persons, of whom 26 were found guilty. Seven of these received immediate custodial sentences and seven were fined. Five received community sentences, one received a suspended sentence, and six were absolutely or conditionally discharged (i.e. found guilty but given no further punishment; in the case of a conditional discharge, if the offender offends again within a specified time limit, they can then be punished for both offences).

Given the extent of hacking and the number of viruses and other pests in circulation, these figures are extraordinarily low. APIG felt that this was not due to any weakness in the Act. Rather, it was due partly to the fact that many people did not understand how wide the scope of the Act was and partly because of lack of police resources available for following up reports of offences. They made recommendations for alleviating these difficulties.

COMPUTER FRAUD

Computer fraud involves manipulating a computer dishonestly in order to obtain money, property, or services, or to cause loss. Most of the techniques that are used are much older than computers. Such tricks as placing fictitious employees on the payroll or setting up false supplier accounts and creating spurious invoices are still the commonest type of fraud as they were before computers appeared. The introduction of computers has made it possible to carry out more spectacular frauds and, because of the reluctance that many people have to question computer output, has perhaps made it less likely that these will be uncovered. Nevertheless, the offences are the same as before.

The UK law regarding fraud is very untidy and there is no criminal offence of fraud as such. There is a common law criminal offence of conspiracy to defraud, which has the unexpected and undesirable result that, by agreeing to do something, two people may be guilty of a criminal offence even though it would not be an offence if either of them did it in the absence of the agreement. There are eight statutory offences of 'deception', including, for example, obtaining services dishonestly and by deception. One problem with this approach is that new technology may generate new opportunities for criminal activity that are not covered by the legislation. There is also the rather legalistic objection that only a person can be the subject of deception, not a machine.

There are also statutory offences relating to so-called specialist fraud, such as forgery, false accounting and benefit fraud (that is, dishonestly obtaining state benefits) but these are, on the whole, satisfactorily addressed by the existing legislation.

Apart from the issue of deceiving a machine, none of the problems of the law relating to fraud is specific to computer fraud and it would not be sensible to make provisions to tackle computer fraud specifically.

In 2002, the Law Commission published a report on the law relating to fraud. This report recommended that a criminal offence of fraud should be introduced covering

- false representation (i.e. lying);

- wrongfully failing to disclose information;

- abuse of office that is, using the authority of one's position dishonestly.

In each case, the behaviour must be dishonest and must aim at securing a gain for the defendant or a loss for someone else. There would be a second offence of obtaining services dishonestly. The term 'deception' has been avoided.

In May 2004, the UK Home Office issued a consultation document based on the Law Commission's report and it seems probable that the recommendation will adopted but it is unlikely that any legislation will become operative before 2006.

EXAMINATION QUESTIONS

The examination questions below relate to the material covered in this chapter.

APRIL 2000 QUESTION 5(d)

Write short notes on FIVE of the following:

. . .

d) the Computer Misuse Act 1990;

. . .

[5 marks]

APRIL 2000 QUESTION 3(b)

What are the main provisions of the Computer Misuse Act 1990 and why was the Act thought to be necessary?

[10 marks]

The Computer Misuse Act 1990 created three new criminal offences. The basic offence was deliberately gaining unauthorized access, or attempting to gain unauthorized access, to a computer system, or to parts of a system. This offence carries a penalty of a maximum of six months' imprisonment or a fine of up to £5,000.

The second offence is committed when the basic offence is committed with the intent to commit a serious crime. It carries a penalty of up to five years' imprisonment or an unlimited fine.

The third offence is committed if a person deliberately does anything that causes the unauthorized modification of the contents of any computer and could impair the operation of any computer, prevent or hinder access to any program or data held in any computer, or impair the operation of any such program or the reliability of any such data. The penalties are the same as for the second offence.

The Act was necessary because, before its passage, it was almost impossible to take effective criminal action against hackers, and civil action was usually ineffective or inappropriate.

APRIL 2002 QUESTION 3(a)

Briefly describe the three criminal offences created by the Computer Misuse Act 1990, giving an example of each.

[8 marks]

APRIL 2003 QUESTIONS 2(a) AND (b)

a) Many organizations have IT security packages installed that control the security profiles of IT users within the organization. This typically includes access limitations on data and computer programs in terms of read, update and execute capabilities. In addition many organizations have procedures for checking that software originating outside the organization is not contaminated by viruses. Explain how these practices relate to the UK Computer Misuse Act 1990.

[9 marks]

b) Compare and contrast the protection offered to citizens and organizations respectively by the UK Data Protection Act 1998 and the UK Computer Misuse Act 1990.

[8 marks]

APRIL 2003 QUESTION 4(a)

You have set up your own small e-commerce business and hold the personal details of all the customers who have used your website

on a database. You use this data to e-mail your customers regarding forthcoming special offers. Someone manages to gain access to your website and alters the prices displayed and some of the customers' details.

Discuss how the UK Data Protection Act 1998 and the UK Computer Misuse Act 1990 relate to this scenario.

[13 marks]

FURTHER READING

The Computer Misuse Act is available from the website

www.hmso.gov.uk/acts.htm#acts

The first three sections are fairly easy to read but the succeeding sections, while necessary, are highly technical (in the legal sense) and relate to questions of jurisdiction and mechanisms for enforcing the Act.

The APIG report is comparatively easy to read. It is well worth reading for its explanation of the background to the recommendations. It can be found at

www.apig.org.uk/CMAReportFinalVersion1.pdf

Appendix A: The BCS Code of Conduct

What follows is a verbatim copy of the BCS Code of Conduct taken from the Society's website on 7 April 2004. Some typographical changes have been made in order to fit in with the design of this book.

INTRODUCTION

This Code sets out the professional standards required by the Society as a condition of membership. It applies to members of all grades, including students, and affiliates, and also non-members who offer their expertise as part of the Society's Professional Advice Register.

Within this document, the term 'relevant authority' is used to identify the person or organisation which has authority over your activity as an individual. If you are a practising professional, this is normally an employer or client. If you are a student, this is normally an academic institution.

The Code governs your personal conduct as an individual member of the BCS and not the nature of business or ethics of the relevant authority. It will, therefore, be a matter of your exercising your personal judgement in meeting the Code's requirements.

Any breach of the Code of Conduct brought to the attention of the Society will be considered under the Society's disciplinary procedures. You should also ensure that you notify the Society of any significant violation of this Code by another BCS member.

THE PUBLIC INTEREST

1. You shall carry out work or study with due care and diligence in accordance with the relevant authority's requirements, and the interests of system users. If your professional judgement is overruled, you shall indicate the likely risks and consequences.

   The crux of the issue here, familiar to all professionals in whatever field, is the potential conflict between full and committed compliance with the relevant authority's wishes, and the independent and considered exercise of your judgement. If your judgement is overruled, you are encouraged to seek advice and guidance from a peer or colleague on how best to respond.

2. In your professional role you shall have regard for the public health, safety and environment.

   This is a general responsibility, which may be governed by legislation, convention or protocol. If in doubt over the appropriate course of action to take in particular circumstances you should seek the counsel of a peer or colleague.

3. You shall have regard to the legitimate rights of third parties.

   The term 'third party' includes professional colleagues, or possibly competitors, or members of 'the public' who might be affected by an information systems project without their being directly aware of its existence.

4. You shall ensure that within your professional field/s you have knowledge and understanding of relevant legislation, regulations and standards, and that you comply with such requirements.

   As examples, relevant legislation could, in the UK, include The UK Public Disclosure Act, Data Protection or Privacy legislation, Computer Misuse law, legislation concerned with the export or import of technology, possibly for national security reasons, or law relating to intellectual property. This list is not exhaustive, and you should ensure that you are aware of any legislation relevant to your professional responsibilities.

   In the international context, you should be aware of, and understand, the requirements of law specific to the jurisdiction within which you are working, and, where relevant, to supranational legislation such as EU law and regulation. You should seek specialist advice when necessary.

5. You shall conduct your professional activities without discrimination against clients or colleagues

   Grounds of discrimination include race, colour, ethnic origin, sexual orientation. All colleagues have a right to be treated with dignity and respect.

   You should adhere to relevant law within the jurisdiction where you are working and, if appropriate, the European Convention on Human Rights.

   You are encouraged to promote equal access to the benefits of information systems by all groups in society, and to avoid and reduce 'social exclusion' from information systems wherever opportunities arise.

6. You shall reject any offer of bribery or inducement.

DUTY TO RELEVANT AUTHORITY

7. You shall avoid any situation that may give rise to a conflict of interest between you and your relevant authority. You shall make full and immediate disclosure to them if any conflict is likely to occur or be seen by a third party as likely to occur.

8. You shall not disclose or authorise to be disclosed, or use for personal gain

or to benefit a third party, confidential information except with the permission of your relevant authority, or at the direction of a court of law.

9. You shall not misrepresent or withhold information on the performance of products, systems or services, or take advantage of the lack of relevant knowledge or inexperience of others.

DUTY TO THE PROFESSION

10. You shall uphold the reputation and good standing of the BCS in particular, and the profession in general, and shall seek to improve professional standards through participation in their development, use and enforcement.

   As a Member of the BCS you also have a wider responsibility to promote public understanding of information systems – its benefits and pitfalls – and, whenever practical, to counter misinformation that brings or could bring the profession into disrepute.

   You should encourage and support fellow members in their professional development and, where possible, provide opportunities for the professional development of new members, particularly student members. Enlightened mutual assistance between information systems professionals furthers the reputation of the profession, and assists individual members.

11. You shall act with integrity in your relationships with all members of the BCS and with members of other professions with whom you work in a professional capacity.

12. You shall have due regard for the possible consequences of your statements on others. You shall not make any public statement in your professional capacity unless you are properly qualified and, where appropriate, authorised to do so. You shall not purport to represent the BCS unless authorised to do so.

   The offering of an opinion in public, holding oneself out to be an expert in the subject in question, is a major personal responsibility and should not be undertaken lightly.

   To give an opinion that subsequently proves ill founded is a disservice to the profession, and to the BCS.

13. You shall notify the Society if convicted of a criminal offence or upon becoming bankrupt or disqualified as Company Director.

PROFESSIONAL COMPETENCE AND INTEGRITY

14. You shall seek to upgrade your professional knowledge and skill, and shall maintain awareness of technological developments, procedures and standards which are relevant to your field, and encourage your subordinates to do likewise.

15. You shall not claim any level of competence that you do not possess. You shall only offer to do work or provide a service that is within your professional competence.

    You can self-assess your professional competence for undertaking a particular job or role by asking, for example:

    a. *am I familiar with the technology involved, or have I worked with similar technology before?*

    b. *have I successfully completed similar assignments or roles in the past?*

    c. *can I demonstrate adequate knowledge of the specific business application and requirements successfully to undertake the work?*

16. You shall observe the relevant BCS Codes of Practice and all other standards which, in your judgement, are relevant, and you shall encourage your colleagues to do likewise.

17. You shall accept professional responsibility for your work and for the work of colleagues who are defined in a given context as working under your supervision.

Appendix B: Sample Agreement

CAMBRIAN CONSULTANTS LIMITED

AGREEMENT

This agreement is made between Cambrian Consultants Limited ('the Company'), whose registered office is at . . . ., and
. . . . ('the Client'), whose registered office is at . . . .

Unless otherwise agreed by the Company in writing, this agreement, together with the terms and conditions attached as schedule A and schedule B, constitute the entire agreement between the Company and the Client and shall apply in place of, and prevail over,

a)   any other terms or conditions contained, or referred to, in correspondence or other documents, or

b)   any terms or conditions implied by trade custom and practice, or

c)   any other purported provisions or oral representations.

This agreement is made on the . . . . . day of . . . . , 200 . .

Signed, for and on behalf of   Signed, for and on behalf of,

Cambrian Consultants Limited, ... ,

Name:. . . . .   Name: . . . .
Director   Position: . . . .

Appendix C: Sample Terms and Conditions for a Fixed Price Contract

CAMBRIAN CONSULTANTS LIMITED

TERMS AND CONDITIONS FOR FIXED PRICE CONTRACTS

1 Scope

These terms and conditions shall apply to the supply of a system meeting the requirements specified in the Requirements Specification identified in Schedule B (the 'System'), to be provided by the Company to the Client.

Contract management

2.1 The Company and the Client shall each appoint a project manager for the contract and shall inform the other of his identity immediately the contract is signed.

2.2 If it becomes necessary for either party to change the identity of its project manager, this shall be done in writing immediately it is known.

2.3 Progress meetings shall be held at least every four weeks and shall be attended by both parties' project managers and such other employees or subcontractors of either party as may be appropriate.

2.4 The Company's project manager shall chair the progress meetings and the Company shall minute the meetings. Minutes shall be signed by both project managers before they become effective.

2.5 The Company's project manager shall have the authority to negotiate changes to the System and to the contract price, up to a maximum value of 10% of the original contract value. Any such change shall become operative only after it has been recorded in the minutes of a progress meeting and the minutes have been signed by both parties. The Client acknowledges that the Company's project manager shall not have the authority to agree to any other change or waiver of the terms and conditions of this Agreement.

3 Price

3.1 The Company shall supply the System for the fixed sum stated in Schedule B. This price does not include Value Added Tax or any other tax that may from time to time be levied. To the extent that the supply of the System is subject to such taxes, the price will be increased by the amount of such taxes and the Company reserves the right to issue invoices in respect of such taxes at any time as they fall due.

3.2 The fixed sum may be increased only as expressly provided in this Agreement or as otherwise agreed between the parties.

4 Payment conditions

4.1 Invoices shall become issuable as specified in Schedule B. Payment is due within 30 days of the date of the issue of an invoice. Unless otherwise agreed by the Company in writing, all payments shall be made in pounds sterling either by cheque or by direct transfer to the company's bank account. No deductions from any payment due may be made by the Client without the prior written consent of the Company.

4.2 If payment is delayed beyond 30 days from the date of issue of the invoice, the Company shall have the right to charge interest on the sum due in respect of the period from the due to date to the date of the actual payment, at a rate no more than 3% above the Lloyds Bank plc base rate from time to time in force.

4.3 If the Client shall fail to pay any sum due, the Company may, after giving the Client 14 days' notice of its intention and without prejudice to any other remedy, cease all work in progress in respect of the System, or any part thereof, until the payment be made. In such a case, the Client shall grant to the Company an appropriate extension of the period of supply and the Company shall be entitled to invoice the Client for all work in progress then remaining to be charged and for its reasonable expenses occasioned by such cessation and any subsequent resumption of work.

5 Delivery and acceptance

5.1 The Company shall deliver the System to the Client in the form and with the documentation described in Schedule B.

5.2 The Company and the Client shall agree the nature of the acceptance tests; the nature of the acceptance tests may be modified by mutual agreement and the Client shall not unreasonably withhold agreement to such modifications.

5.3 The Client shall prepare test data and results within the framework agreed under 5.2 and shall provide the Company with this data by the date shown in Schedule B.

5.4   The Client shall conduct the acceptance tests within the period shown in Schedule B, subject to pro-rata extension should any faults occur that render further testing impossible. The Company's employees shall be entitled to attend any or all stages of testing.

5.5   The Client shall advise the Company promptly of any fault occurring during acceptance testing and supply detailed supporting documentation and evidence. The Company shall correct any such faults with urgency or supply a workaround to avoid delaying the acceptance testing.

5.6   The Company reserves the right to charge at its standard daily fee rates for all time spent by its employees on investigating results that are submitted as faults but are established to be the result of correct functioning according to the System Requirement as defined in Schedule B.

5.7   The System shall be deemed to be accepted by the Client when:

a. the System passes the agreed acceptance tests; *or*

b. the System is used by the Client otherwise than for acceptance testing purposes; *or*

c. faults notified during the acceptance testing period specified in Schedule B have been corrected,

whichever of these occurs first.

6 Intellectual Property Rights

6.1   The copyright, patent and other intellectual property rights (the 'IPR') in the System shall be the property of the Company.

6.2   Immediately all payments due under this agreement have been made, the Company shall grant to the Client a non-exclusive licence to copy, modify and use the System for such time as the IPR in the System subsists, except that

a. if the Client breaches the terms of use granted under this Agreement, either before or after completion of the System, the licence to use shall terminate forthwith; or

b. if the Company terminates the Agreement in accordance with clause 14, the licence to use shall end upon such termination and not be deemed to continue after the termination unless otherwise agreed in writing by the Company.

6.3   The System and any copies shall be used for the Client's own internal purposes only, unless otherwise agreed in writing by the Company.

7 Information, facilities and materials to be provided by the client

7.1   The Client recognises that the Company is dependent on the Client for certain information and materials in order to meet its obligations under this agreement. Schedule B shows this list of information and materials and the date by which such information must be delivered to the Company in order that it may meet its obligations.

7.2 The Client agrees to provide the Company with certain facilities in order that the Company may fulfil its obligations under this agreement. These facilities and the periods for which they are required are shown in Schedule B.

7.3 In the event that extra costs are incurred as a result either of the Client's failure to meet his obligations under clauses 7.1 and 7.2 or of faults, errors or omissions in what is supplied, the Company reserves the right to charge on a time and materials basis, at its standard fee rates and on its standard conditions for time and materials work, for the extra work and other costs.

7.4 The Company shall not be liable for any delay or fault in the supply of the System arising directly or indirectly from any failure by the Client to meet his obligations under clauses 7.1 and 7.2 or from any faults, errors or omissions in what is supplied.

7.5 If at any time during the supply of the System either party shall notice or suspect that any wrong assumptions have been made or wrong directions taken by either party they shall forthwith inform the other party in writing.

8 Conditions relating to staff

8.1 Each party undertakes that its staff engaged in the supply of the System or in related work shall possess the skills and experience appropriate for the tasks assigned to them and shall be available at such times as may be agreed between the parties. Such staff shall, so far as practicable, be fully acquainted with the contents of this agreement.

8.2 Both parties have the right to replace any of their staff engaged in the supply of the System or in related work at any time.

8.3 The staff of the Company engaged in the supply of the System shall at all times remain under the direction and control of the Company.

8.4 Each party undertakes that, when its staff are working on the premises of the other party, they shall comply with such rules and regulations as are notified to them for the conduct of staff on those premises.

8.5 Each party undertakes not to make any claim whatsoever against the staff of the other party (whether in respect of the supply of the System or otherwise) without the prior written consent of the other party.

8.6 Each party shall have the right to employ sub-contractors in order to meet its obligations under this agreement and agrees that the provisions of this agreement with regard to its staff or employees shall apply to its sub-contractors.

9 Change Control

9.1 Either party may request at any time before the start of the acceptance test period, as specified in Schedule B, that some change be made to the system.

9.2 The Company will advise the Client of the likely impact of any recommended or requested change, including any effect on the Company's charges to the Client and/or on the timescales for the Supply of the System, subject to clause 9.5 below.

9.3 Any requested or recommended change shall become operative only after it has been formally approved in writing by authorised representatives of both parties, until which time the Company shall continue with the Supply of the System as if such change had not been requested.

9.4 All changes requested, recommended or approved shall be reported to the next Progress Meeting following the request, recommendation or approval. All outstanding change requests or recommendations that have neither been approved nor rejected shall be reviewed at each Progress Meeting.

9.5 Neither party shall be obliged to agree to any change request or recommendation, provided that the System in the unchanged form remains feasible.

9.6 Both parties recognise that the process of responding to change requests, whether ultimately accepted or not, may lengthen the timescale of the supply due to the necessary use of staff on the critical path of the supply of the System.

9.7 The Company reserves the right to charge on a time and materials basis, at its standard fee rates and on its standard conditions for time and materials work for all work on change requests.

10 Warranty

The Company shall, at its own expense, correct any defect in a deliverable reported to it by the Client within 90 days of the date of acceptance of the deliverable.

11 Liability for Loss or Damage

11.1 The company shall use all reasonable care in the provision of the System.

11.2 The Company's liability to the Client for death or personal injury resulting from its own negligence or that of its employees shall not be limited.

11.3 The Company shall not be liable to the Client for loss of profits or good-will or for any type of special, indirect, incidental or consequential loss (including, but not limited to, loss or damage suffered by the Client as a result of an action brought by a third party) even if such loss were reasonably foreseeable or the Company had been advised of the possibility of the Client incurring such loss.

11.4 The Company shall have no liability in respect of any product or services to be supplied by the Client or any third party.

11.5 Save as expressly provided herein, all other terms and conditions, warranties or representations, whether expressed or implied (by statute or otherwise), relating to the System and its supply or imposing liability on the Company, are hereby excluded.

11.6 Subject to the limit set out in 11.7 below, the Company shall accept liability in respect of damage to the tangible property of the Client resulting directly from the negligence of the Company or its employees or subcontractors.

11.7 Except in relation to liability that is by law incapable of exclusion, the Company's liability hereunder or otherwise arising from the provision of the System shall not exceed in aggregate £50,000 or the full value of the charges due from the Client under this Agreement, whichever is the lesser.

12 Confidentiality

12.1 Each party agrees not to publish or reveal to any third party any confidential information relating to the other party and its operations, except with prior consent in writing of the other party.

12.2 The provisions of 12.1 shall not apply to information that is, or becomes, public knowledge otherwise than through the default of the party concerned, or is already in the receiving party's possession, or is legally acquired from a third party, or is required by law to be disclosed.

12.3 Either party may seek the consent of the other to publicise the supply of the System, which consent shall not be unreasonably withheld.

12.4 Both parties shall take reasonable steps to ensure that their staff and sub-contractors are bound by the provisions of this clause.

12.5 The provisions of this clause shall continue in force for five years after the termination of the other provisions of this Agreement.

13 Indemnity

13.1 The Client shall indemnify the Company against any action by a third party for breach of copyright, patent rights, or other intellectual property right arising from the Company's following instructions given by the Client.

13.2   The Company shall indemnify the Client against any action by a third party for breach of copyright, patent rights, or other intellectual property right arising from the use of the deliverables of the contract, provided such use does not violate any provisions of the contract.

14 Termination

14.1   Either party may terminate the Agreement forthwith by written notice to the other party if:

a.   the other party shall be in in substantial breach (including, but not limited to, late payment) of any of its obligations under this Agreement and shall not have remedied the breach within four weeks of receiving written notice of the breach; or

b.   the other party shall become bankrupt or have a receiver appointed otherwise than for the purpose of an amalgamation or reconstruction in which the emergent company assumes all the obligations of the party in liquidation or receivership.

14.2   The Client may terminate the Agreement by giving 28 days notice of termination. The Client thereby becomes liable to pay for all work carried out up to that date, to be charged at the Company's standard rates as shown in Schedule B.

15 Force Majeure

15.1   Neither party shall be liable for any delay in meeting, or failure to meet, any of its obligations due to any cause outside its reasonable control, including (without limitation) Acts of God, war, riot, malicious damage, fire, acts of any government or public body, failure of the public electricity supply, failure or delay on the part of any sub-contractors beyond its reasonable control, or the unavailability of materials.

15.2   The Company shall not be liable for any delay or failure resulting from a request by the Client for any change to be made to the System.

15.3   If the Company is prevented from meeting its obligations by any of the causes listed in sections 15.1 and 15.2, it shall notify the Client of the circumstances and the Client shall grant a reasonable extension for the performance of the Agreement.

16 Notices

Any formal notice, consent or communication required to be given or served under this Agreement shall be given or served by sending it by first class mail to the registered office of the party concerned or to such other address as the party may advise in writing from time to time.

17 Arbitration

In the event of a dispute concerning the interpretation of this contract, which cannot be resolved by the parties themselves, both parties agree to refer the matter to an arbitrator nominated by the President of the British Computer Society, under the terms of the Arbitration Act 1996.

18 Applicable law

This construction, validity and performance of this Agreement shall be governed by the laws of England and Wales and the parties hereby submit to the jurisdiction of the courts of England and Wales.

Appendix D: Sample Contract of Employment

CAMBRIAN CONSULTANTS LIMITED

Contract of Employment for Permanent Professional Employees below the Rank of Director

This contract of employment is made between <*employee name*> ('the employee') and Cambrian Consultants Limited ('the company').

1. This contract shall become effective on <*start date of the employment*> and shall subsist until either it is terminated by either side in accordance with section 8 or until the employee reaches the retiring age as specified in section 9.

2. This contract supersedes all other contracts or agreements between the parties, whether oral or written.

   [As usual, the contract needs to make sure that things that may have been said during negotiations have no legal weight.]

3. The employee shall be employed as a <*job title*> (grade <*A to F*>) at an initial salary of <*starting salary*> pounds per annum, which shall be paid monthly in arrears, no later than the last day of the month. This grade and salary will be reviewed after the first six months of employment and annually thereafter.

4. The employee's normal place of work shall be the company's premises located at <*full address of place of work*>. The employee may be required from time to time to work elsewhere; in such cases travel and subsistence expenses shall be payable in accordance with the company's usual rates and procedures.

5. Normal office hours shall be from 9.00 am to 5.30 pm, Mondays to Fridays, with an hour's break for lunch. The employee shall normally work these hours, or such other hours as may be agreed with the company, and may from time to time be required to work longer hours.

6. The employee shall be entitled to 24 days' annual holiday per calendar year, in addition to statutory holidays. Holiday entitlement can only be carried over from one calendar year to the next with the written

permission of a director or authorised manager. For employees starting or terminating their employment during the year, holiday entitlement is accrued at the rate of two days per complete calendar month; employees who have holiday entitlement outstanding when their employment terminates shall be entitled to a payment in lieu of one 1/240th of their annual salary for each complete day of holiday outstanding.

7. The duties of the employee shall be such as are from time to time assigned to him or her by the Board of Directors or by authorised management.

8. After the employee's first month of completed service, the contract of employment may be terminated by either party giving one week's notice in writing to the other for each year of the employee's completed years of service, subject to a minimum of four weeks and a maximum of twelve weeks.

   [There are lots of other ways that notice conditions may be specified. It is quite common for all employees above a certain grade or with more than one year's service to be on three months' notice.]

9. An employee shall retire at the age of 65 or on the date at which he or she becomes eligible to receive the state retirement pension, whichever is earlier, unless otherwise agreed in writing by the company. The company does not operate any pension scheme and a contracting out certificate issued by the Occupational Pensions Board is not in force for this employment. After the employee has completed one year of service with the company, the company will contribute to an approved private pension scheme held by the employee; the amount of this contribution shall be the same as that contributed by the employee, up to a maximum of 6% of the employee's salary.

   [Clauses such as this one could well become unenforceable when legislation outlawing discrimination on grounds of age comes into effect in 2006.]

10. In the event of the employee being unable to work due to sickness or injury, the company will pay the employee's full basic salary for a period of eight weeks. Thereafter the employee will be entitled to statutory sick pay up to the expiry of 28 weeks from the first notification of the incapacity.

    [Statutory sick pay is payable at the rate of £66.15 (2004 rate), for up to 28 weeks, to employees who are unable to work because of sickness or ill health. It is paid by the employer. In practice, professional staff are usually treated much more generously than this, as this clause shows.]

11. All intellectual property developed by the employee as part of his or her employment shall be the property of the company and the employee shall, at the request of the company and at its expense, undertake any

actions necessary to confirm such ownership, including but not limited to the filing of patent applications.

[This clause and the next are included to emphasize and confirm conditions arising from other legislation and from common law.]

12. Unless otherwise agreed by the company, the employee shall treat as confidential all information he or she acquires as a result of the employment, unless and until that information enters the public domain. In particular, the employee shall obtain the permission of the company before publishing any material arising from the employment, such permission not to be unreasonably withheld. The obligation of confidentiality shall continue for a period of five years following the termination of the employment.

13. The employee shall at all times act in good faith and in such a way as to promote the best interests of the company.

14. The employee shall abide by all the rules and procedures promulgated within the company.

15. The employee shall not make any financial commitment on behalf of the company except as duly authorised.

16. The employee shall not, for a period of twelve months following the termination of the employment, solicit business from, or otherwise approach, any client of the company, except with the prior agreement in writing of the company.

    [This clause and the next attempt to limit the way in which an employee who leaves the company can compete with it or damage it by enticing away its staff. Such clauses are not always enforceable, because they can be considered a 'restraint of trade', but limiting the period covered to 12 months makes it more likely that a court would be prepared to enforce the clauses.]

17. The employee shall not, for a period of twelve months following the termination of the employment, entice or seek to entice any employee of the company to leave its employment, except with the prior agreement in writing of the company.

18. The employee shall abide by any additional conditions that may from time to time be imposed as a result of the company's contracts with its clients.

19. At the request of the company, the employee shall apply for, and maintain, professional registration and corporate membership of an appropriate professional body.

    [Consultancy companies in particular often require their senior staff to hold and maintain chartered status or other appropriate professional qualifications.]

20. The employee shall ensure that his or her dress and personal appearance are appropriate to the environment in which he or she is working.

    [Consultancy companies have a very wide range of clients. It makes no sense to impose a single dress code. What is required is that employees fit into the environment in which they are working.]

21. The employee accepts that he or she has a responsibility for the health and safety of all employees and shall abide by all health and safety regulations promulgated by the company and its clients.

    [Again, as for clauses 11 and 12. this is simply to emphasize a statutory obligation.]

22. An employee who believes that he or she has a grievance against the company shall, in the first instance, raise the matter in writing with the Managing Director, who will endeavour to settle the matter to the employee's and the company's satisfaction. If the matter cannot be satisfactorily resolved in this way, the employee and the Managing Director shall each submit to the Chairman of the Board of Directors a written statement of the grievance and the efforts made to resolve it. The decision of the Chairman shall be final.

    [This is an example of a grievance procedure. See the section 'Constructive dismissal' within 'Contracts of employment', Chapter 10.]

Signed . . . .(Director)
for and on behalf of Cambrian Consultants Limited
Date . . . .

Signed . . . .(the employee)
Date . . . .

Further Reading

Akdeniz, Y. (1997) Governance of pornography and child pornography on the global internet: A multi-layered approach. In Edwards, L. and Waelde, C. (eds), *Law and the Internet: Regulating Cyberspace*, Hart Publishing, Oxford. Available from www.cyber-rights.org/reports/governan.htm.

Atrill, Peter and McLaney, Eddie (2004) *Accounting and Finance for Non-Specialists, 4th Edition*. Pearson Education, Harlow.

Bagert, Donald J. (2002) Texas licensing of software engineers: All's quiet, for now. *Communications of the ACM* 45(11), 92–94.

Blackstaff, M. (1998) *Finance for IT Decision Makers*. Springer Verlag, London.

Bott, M.F., Coleman, J.A., Eaton, J., and Rowland, D. (2001) *Professional Issues in Software Engineering*, 3rd Edition. Taylor and Francis, London.

British Computer Society (2000) *Disability Discrimination Act – Access for All: A Practical Guide for Professionals & Business Managers*. BCS, Swindon.

Department of Trade and Industry (2003) *Transfer of Undertakings: A Guide to the Regulations* (PL699 rev 6). Department of Trade and Industry, London.

Handy, C. (1993) *Understanding Organizations*. Penguin, London.

Handy, C. (1995) *Gods of Management*. Penguin, London.

Holt, J. and Newton, J. (eds) (2004) *A Manager's Guide to IT Law*. BCS, Swindon.

Leveson, Nancy, and Turner, Clark S. (1993) An investigation of the Therac-25 accidents. *IEEE Computer,* 25(7), 18-41. An updated version of the paper is available from http://sunnyday.mit.edu/therac-25.html.

Lickert, R. (1961) *New Patterns of Management*. McGraw Hill, New York.

Lickert, R. (1967) *The Human Organization*. McGraw Hill, New York.

Sparrow, E. (2003) *Successful IT Outsourcing*. Springer Verlag, London.

Thames Regional Health Authority (1993) *Report of the Inquiry Into The London Ambulance Service*. Communications Directorate, South West Thames Regional Health Authority. Available from www.cs.ucl.ac.uk/staff/A.Finkelstein/las.html.

Index

BCS Products and Services

Other products and services from the British Computer Society, which might be of interest to you include:

Publishing

BCS publications, including books, magazine and peer-review journals, provide readers with informed content on business, management, legal, and emerging technological issues, supporting the professional, academic and practical needs of the IT community. Subjects covered include Business Process Management, IT law for managers and transition management. **www.bcs.org/publications**

BCS Professional Products and Services

The BCS promotes the use of the SFIA*plus* IT skills framework which forms the basis of a range of professional development products and services for both individual practitioners and employers. This includes BCS Skills *Manager* and BCS Career *Developer*. **www.bcs.org/products**

Qualifications

Information Systems Examination Board (ISEB) qualifications are the industry standard both here and abroad, and with over 100,000 practitioners now qualified, it is proof of their popularity. They ensure that IT professionals develop the skills, knowledge and confidence to perform to their full potential. There is a huge range on offer covering all major areas of IT. In essence, ISEB qualifications are for forward looking individuals and companies who want to stay ahead – who are serious about driving business forward. **www.iseb.org.uk**

The BCS Professional Examination is examined to the academic level of a UK honours degree and is the essential qualification for a career in computing and IT. Whether you seek greater job recognition, promotion or a new career direction, you will find that the BCS Professional Examination is internationally recognised, flexible and suited to the needs of the IT industry. **www.bcs.org/exam**

European Certification of IT Professionals (EUCIP) is aimed at IT Professionals and Practitioners wishing to gain professional certification and competency development. **www.bcs.org/eucip**

European Computer Driving Licence ™ (ECDL) is the internationally recognised computer skills qualification which enables people to demonstrate their competence on computer skills. ECDL is managed in the UK by the BCS. ECDL Advanced has been introduced to take computer skills certification to the next level and teaches extensive knowledge of particular computing tools. **www.ecdl.co.uk**

Networking and Events

The BCS's national network of branches and specialist groups enables members to exchange ideas and keep abreast of latest developments. **www.bcs.org/sg**

The Society's programme of social events, lectures, awards schemes, and competitions provides more opportunities to network. **www.bcs.org/events**

Further Information

This information was correct at the time of publication, but could change in the future. For the latest information, please contact:
The British Computer Society,
1 Sanford Street,
Swindon, Wiltshire,
SN1 1HJ.
Telephone: +44 (0) 1793 417 424
E-mail: bcs@hq.bcs.org.uk
Web: **www.bcs.org**

Lightning Source UK Ltd.
Milton Keynes UK
UKOW020010170812

197630UK00004B/6/P